KT-386-006

THE POPE FROM POLAND

John Whale was born in Oxford in 1931, and read classical history and philosophy there. He has been leader-writer on *The Sunday Times* since 1969, and religious affairs correspondent since 1979.

Peter Hebblethwaite was born near Manchester in 1930. He read (and later taught) languages at Oxford. A former Jesuit, now based in Rome, he has written books and articles on Roman Catholic affairs, contributing to *The Sunday Times* since 1977.

Muriel Bowen was born in Clonea Castle, County Waterford in 1926. She has worked for *The Irish Independent, The Daily Express, The Washington Post* and – since 1966 – *The Sunday Times*.

Nicholas Carroll was born in London in 1916. He joined the staff of Kemsley Newspapers (then owners of *The Sunday Times*) in 1934, was the paper's Warsaw correspondent 1946/7 and has been its diplomatic correspondent since 1949.

Tana de Zulueta was born in Colombia in 1951, of Spanish/English parentage. Since 1976 she has been a journalist based in Rome, contributing chiefly to *The Sunday Times* and *The New Statesman*.

Other books available

by Peter Hebblethwaite

THE NEW INQUISITION? – Schillebeeckx and Küng
(*Fount Paperbacks, April 1980*)

THE RUNAWAY CHURCH (*Collins*)

THE YEAR OF THREE POPES (*Fount*)

by Hans Küng

INFALLIBLE? (*Fount*)

ON BEING A CHRISTIAN (*Collins and Fount*)

THE CHRISTIAN CHALLENGE (*Collins*)

WHY PRIESTS? (*Fount*)

by Edward Schillebeeckx

JESUS: AN EXPERIMENT IN CHRISTOLOGY (*Collins*)

THE POPE FROM POLAND

AN ASSESSMENT

by Muriel Bowen, Nicholas Carroll,
Tana de Zulueta, Peter Hebblethwaite
and John Whale (editor)

for *The Sunday Times*

COLLINS
FOUNT PAPERBACKS

First published in 1980 simultaneously by
William Collins and Fount Paperbacks, London

© Times Newspapers Ltd 1980

Made and printed in Great Britain by
William Collins Sons & Co Ltd, Glasgow

CONDITIONS OF SALE

This book is sold subject to the condition that it
shall not, by way of trade or otherwise, be lent,
re-sold, hired out or otherwise circulated without
the publisher's prior consent in any form of
binding or cover other than that in which it is
published and without a similar condition
including this condition being imposed on the
subsequent purchaser.

Contents

'I have discovered in Rome
that it is not easy
to leave Krakow behind'

– John Paul II's first words
on his return there, 6 vi 79

1

An Old Magic

They gathered in vast numbers to see him – in Mexico, in Poland, in Ireland, in the United States, in Rome itself. It was one of the phenomena of 1979; and it was all the more surprising for being constantly renewed throughout the year. No other public figure drew anything like the same multitudes. Deliberate bids to advance their popularity were made during the year by the President of France (using the European elections) and the President of the United States (through the energy crisis). The ruler of Russia was an object of unusual curiosity, when he appeared in the West, because his health was failing. Britain (followed for a while by Portugal) took on a new Prime Minister who had the extra interest of being a woman. One Archbishop of Canterbury – himself the leading figure in a worldwide communion of Churches – prepared to give way to another. Pope John Paul II left all these people standing. Across the arid uplands of Mexico, where poverty was the universal fact of life and the Roman Catholic Church had done little to lighten its weight, crowds lined his route for eighty miles. In Poland, where religion had been actively discouraged by the State for a generation, congregations at the services he conducted were numbered in millions. In post-Christian America he was as much of a wonder as in holy Roman Ireland. Visitors from all over the world, the comparative sophisticates of the tourist class, so pressed to see him in Rome that his public audiences had to be first increased in frequency, then shifted out of doors, and finally deferred till late in the day to avoid jamming the traffic of an entire city. (They moved back indoors for the winter.)

The phenomenon was not totally new. Few things in the history of religion are. Massive papal popularity with the Catholic working classes went back at least to the start of Pius IX's long pontificate in the middle of the nineteenth century. But as revived by

John Paul II the acclaim was not confined to the working classes, nor even to Catholics. An English cabinet minister wrote of him in May 1979 in the language of a fan-club magazine: the Pope had star quality, his presence was majestic and electrifying, he radiated authority and strength, behind the soft folds of the papal robes were the muscles of an athlete. The writer, Norman St John Stevas, was a Catholic. Many ordinary journalists wrote in the same vein without that loyalty to affect their judgment; and they belonged to a profession not noted for easy adulation.

The renewed cult was not sufficiently accounted for by the Pope's gifts, considerable though they were. His past sporting activities – swimming, skiing, canoeing, cycling – were chiefly remarkable for being incongruous in a Church leader: there was no suggestion that he had done any of them with abnormal skill. He was a linguist; but he himself acknowledged that when he departed from Polish he needed the tolerance commonly extended to people not speaking their own tongue. His attractiveness of character was by no means without parallel in a profession which sets itself the highest of models. His voice, his presence, his timing, were effective: it would have been odd to become successively bishop, archbishop and cardinal without some such equipment. He had been a writer – of a play, poems, works of philosophy and moral theology; but it would be difficult to claim that his writings enjoyed any kind of fame before he became pope.

We come a little nearer the explanation for his huge popular success with the fact of his being Polish. Merely not to be Italian, in an office which the world had come to believe as irremovably Italian as the Appenines, would have given him a new claim on public interest. To be Polish made him a member of a country too small and distant to arouse hostility in Westerners, and one to which many of them felt positively sympathetic. Poland had been particularly wronged during the Second World War; many of its escaped servicemen had fought with Western armed forces; and an untroublesome Polish diaspora still flourished in the United States, Britain, France, Canada and Australia. More than all that, Poland was an unwilling Russian satellite: the new man had emerged from under the noses of the Russians. He was that loved figure, the underdog who had come out on top; he was the proof, to believers, that religion could yet survive in a deliberately godless climate; he could even be taken, by sanguine warriors of the cold war, as a sign that the days of the Russian empire in Eastern Europe were numbered.

Yet all this – the personal qualities, the accident of national-ity – would have meant little if the office to which Karol Wojtyla succeeded on 16 October 1978 had been anything other than the papacy. It was that which was being chiefly celebrated. The public fascination, extending far outside the simple-hearted Catholic devout, was there before John Paul II gave it a focus. It had been growing for twenty years, ever since Pius XII (the pope of the Second World War) had been replaced by John XXIII (the pope of the Second Vatican Council). It had then been a little dimmed by Paul VI's too-long persistence in office; but it was fully revived by the process of electing his successor, even before a name was known; and it contrived to find John Paul I un-discouraging, at any rate for the thirty-three days during which he survived. John Paul II inherited an office which was already the object of enormous international expectation.

It was the oldest and apparently the most durable human in-stitution in the world. Every schoolboy brought up on the essays of Macaulay knows Macaulay's picture of the papacy's longevity. 'She saw the commencement of all the governments and of all the ecclesiastical establishments that now exist in the world; and we feel no assurance that she is not destined to see the end of them all. She was great and respected before the Saxon had set foot on Britain, before the Frank had passed the Rhine, when Grecian eloquence still flourished in Antioch, when idols were still worshipped in the temple of Mecca. And she may still exist in un-diminished vigour when some traveller from New Zealand shall, in the midst of a vast solitude, take his stand on a broken arch of London Bridge to sketch the ruins of St Paul's.'

Macaulay wrote when the papacy was still a substantial tem-poral power, before the formation of modern Italy. There had been a change since then, true. After 1870 it lost its sovereignty to the new State; and although Mussolini tidied the position in 1929 by giving back to the Vatican a toy territory the size of St James's Park in London, John Paul I was recognizing the facts of inter-national politics when he declined to be crowned. It was only surprising that he was the first pope to make that change.

Yet there was another kind of power which was unaffected. The ceremony which John Paul I went through instead was the 'inauguration of his ministry as supreme pastor'. As an expression of the modern papacy's hold over the popular imagination, that came much nearer the mark than coronation would have done. The office had come to possess a straightforwardly religious, not a political, eminence. The one had moved in inverse relation to the other: as political weight had diminished, religious influence had advanced. 'Ultramontanism' – the tendency of Catholics in other countries than Italy to look for spiritual leadership 'beyond the mountains', in other words on the southern side of the Alps – had been steadily on the increase since the middle of the nineteenth century. As the Church came face to face with its lack of political impact, in individual countries as well as internationally, there was an increasing demand that at any rate in its own affairs it should be cohesive and decisively run. The great sign was the virtually unanimous approval in 1870, by the bishops gathered for the First Vatican Council, of a text declaring papal infallibility. The contribution of the Second Vatican Council, which ended in 1965, was to begin making the notion of the pope's spiritual leadership acceptable to thinking people of other Christian denominations and none at all. The Catholic Church was already the most populous of those denominations: if it were indeed brought up to date, as the Council seemed to promise, and if it tacitly acknowledged that it could sometimes be wrong and other believers right, then a measure of moral leadership far outside its normal boundaries might well be accorded to its head. Add to that the development, at about the same period, of television as a mass medium, tending by its nature to represent ideas in terms of personalities and able to deliver the pope's speaking likeness to many millions of homes, and the papal pedestal was raised higher yet. John Paul II's international acclaim became a natural development.

In a certain light, it could not be regarded as anything but heartening. It was a witness to the transcendental and the eternal. It was a recognition by millions, in the midst of their ordinary struggles to secure themselves for a few decades against cold and hunger and ill-health, that there was another kind of life to which they were heirs. Man 'thinks he was not made to die', and a new pope recalled a system of ideas which fostered that thought. If that was too solemn a reading of the massed charabancs in the purlieus of St Peter's, then at least they had a part in the perception which distinguished the 1970s from the 1960s – that plain materialism, the pursuit of progress through endless industrial growth, had not worked and showed no sign of working. The new papolatry may have been only partly religious, but it was a kind of cry for help. Man had not been able to help himself: perhaps God could help him. Perhaps, at any rate, it was unwise to neglect that possibility. John Paul II himself quoted in Warsaw the psalmist's claim that the fear of the Lord was the beginning of wisdom. If that was true, and if respect shown to the Lord's senior representative on earth was a first sign of the state of mind specified, then mankind might be groping its way towards a fitter frame of mind than it had been in for some time.

Yet that respect, that world-wide acclamation, had its discouraging side too. The forecast it suggested in many areas of life was 'no change'. How likely now was useful reform where it lay in the gift of Catholic leaders and teachers? The papacy was already a conservative autocracy. It was a monarchy unhampered by a parliament and served by a bureaucracy which reform had still not much opened to outside influences. Previous popes who had benefited from popular adulation – going back to Pius IX, who started (like John Paul II) in his fifties and ended as the architect of infallibility – had had their reactionary tendencies confirmed and strengthened. Criticized by a handful of dissident intellectuals, they had needed only to point to the mute approval of millions. From the start of his pontificate, John Paul II was licensed to go the same way. He lost no time in showing that he intended to uphold the Church's traditional teaching as he had received it. The cheers that continued to greet him could be taken as an encouragement to persist in that firmness. To what extent would he interpret them as such? How far, on the other hand, might his apparent rigidity be softened by his quickness of mind and the humanity of his personal dealings? Those were questions on which, during his first year in office, a great many people looked for light.

If his traditionalism persisted unmodified, its consequences were likely to be felt in several areas: in family life, in the organization of worship and pastoral care, in the content of faith. Given the size and prominence of the Roman Catholic Church, that would matter not merely to people inside it but to people outside, including non-believers. Birth-control was only the most vivid example among many. If the world's largest religious society continued to urge attitudes which made for an avoidable increase in population on a planet already gravely over-populated, then that concerned everyone whose supply of breathable air and drinkable water and eatable food was threatened as a result. John Paul II chose a visit to Latin America, one of the most miserably over-populated regions of the globe, as the occasion to show that he began his pontificate in a mood of opposition to any form of artificial birth control. This view of his was not new. Even before Paul VI had taken the same line in his 1968 encyclical *Humanae Vitae*, Bishop Wojtyla had set it out in a little book called *Love and Responsibility*; and he revised the book to emphasize his agreement with the encyclical (which he was subsequently credited with having influenced). Yet although he knew then that the encyclical and his own work went against the changing temper of the Church's advisers on the point, he put no new consultation in hand before he pronounced as pope in exactly the same sense.

The case for change over divorce and abortion was more disputed; but certainly there were pleas from within the Catholic communion that the system should become more openly flexible. Again, John Paul II gave himself no time to hear them. In Poland he dismissed abortion, in any circumstances; and as early as the Latin American visit he ruled out divorce. At the same time, in a continent where some of the few effective opponents of cruel governments were churchmen, he raised renewed doubt over the whole notion of social or political action by the Church.

On the conduct of the Church's worship and affairs, his line was similarly traditionalist. He made an early gesture of friendliness to the dissident conservative liturgiologist Archbishop Marcel Lefebvre. That could be defended as merely tactical; and certainly the Lefebvre affair died away thereafter. The new Pope was notably inflexible on the subject of priests: they must continue to be male, celibate, full-time and properly dressed. A whole range of reforms which might have saved their numbers and their morale was thus brushed aside. And these decisions, like the verdicts on birth control and the rest, were reached without any discernible consultation with fellow bishops. As a cardinal, Wojtyla had appeared reconciled enough to the principle of collegiality: it seemed less close to his heart once he became pope. An Italian Jesuit editor said of him: 'He listens to many, speaks with few and decides alone.'

As for the content of faith, he was no innovator there either. He appeared to personify exactly those doctrinal attitudes in Catholicism which Protestants found hardest to swallow: authoritarianism, opposition to free and rational enquiry, and yet readiness to accept unscriptural accretions if they aided popular devotion. Under him, the Holy Office was swiftly back in the business of anathematizing unorthodox opinion; and mariolatry flourished. In mainstream Catholicism, institutionalizing devotion to Mary was a nineteenth-century development; yet in the first three countries to which John Paul II travelled the cult was particularly strong – the first four, counting the Dominican Republic – and he actively encouraged it.

This approach to priesthood and doctrine might be thought of concern to believing Catholics only: if they approved it, as in the mass they appeared to, then no-one else had anything to say in the matter. Yet it could be expected to have an effect outside the Church as well as inside it. Among Catholics it was likely to trouble exactly those people, thoughtful laymen as well as professionals, on whose enthusiasm the Church depended if it was to continue a vital force. Among believers who were not Catholics it could not help dampening the impulse to ecumenism, to the reunion of all Christians in a single and necessarily flexible framework, which the Second Vatican Council had so recently encouraged. And among unbelievers it was in danger of confirming the view that Christian belief had nothing in common with the thought-forms of a scientific age, and so of limiting its extension and its helpfulness.

A single year could not foretell what would happen in an entire papacy, especially one which might well last a long time. John Paul II was 58 when he was elected, and six of his nine immediate predecessors had died in their eighties. But certain lines were early and revealingly laid down.

To some extent these attitudes were determined by his background; and it was quickly laid open, so that any interested member of those applauding crowds could understand what was being applauded. Because the mass media shared in the mass enthusiasm, more was known about him at the outset of his reign than about any previous pope. Within the space of a few months thirty books, and numberless feature articles and broadcast programmes, had left no stone unturned in the search for information about his past. There were not, in truth, many stones to turn: baptismal registers, school photographs, university records, Poland's own chronically unhappy history, a few of Wojtyla's own poems, recollections of those who had known him, his utterances as bishop and cardinal. The tone of much that was written and broadcast, as with a good deal of ecclesiastical journalism, was committed – committed to reverent approval; but the facts were clear enough.

His good brain was fostered by hard schooling – at Wadowice, in southern Poland, where he was born on 17 May 1920 and brought up. His teachers at the local high school were abetted by his disciplinarian father, a retired army officer: it would be possible to trace part of Wojtyla's authoritarianism to that source. For much of his youth his father was his only parent: his mother died in childbirth when he was nine; and a recent phrase of his own allows the view that his veneration for Mary dates from those motherless years. It was at school, too, that he took on his fondness for games and the outdoor life; while his voice and delivery began to be developed by elocution competitions, school plays, local folk festivals.

He went on to university at Krakow in 1938, to read Polish language and literature. The Jagiellonian university there was founded in the fourteenth century: John Paul II joins Copernicus and Dr Faustus in a trio of its most famous sons. From this milieu in particular he derived his most significant single attribute: his intense Polishness. Krakow, one of the country's old capitals, was a city where it was impossible not to be aware of Poland's past; and in 1938 and 1939 it was impossible not to be reminded how bitterly unhappy much of that past had been. Since 1772 Poland has been almost continually occupied by foreign powers. For 150 years it was not merely occupied but divided: rival invaders subjected it to three successive partitions. Its identity was re-established after the First World War, but not for long. On 22 August 1939 Germany made a treaty with the Soviet Union which amounted to a fourth partition. On 1 September, in the move which began the Second World War, Hitler invaded Poland from the west. Once the Polish forces were defeated, in a campaign lasting barely a fortnight, the Russians moved in from the east.

Krakow and Warsaw fell to the Germans. Wojtyla saw his university closed, the best of his countrymen degraded and murdered. Anyone with any pretensions to leadership in Poland was to be served the same way as Poland's Jews. Auschwitz, established on a bleak marsh not far from Krakow, was matched by Sachsenhausen, into which most of the Jagiellonian teaching staff disappeared. The one way to stay alive was to acquire an *Arbeitskarte* as a labourer. Wojtyla went to work in a stone-quarry on the city's edge. Yet the university's students and its few remaining dons still held together as best they could. Classes and activities continued surreptitiously. Wojtyla joined an enterprise called *Teatr Rapsodyczny* – Rhapsodic Theatre: its members recited Polish poetry and verse dramas for tiny audiences huddled in cellars or at the back of shops.

He had meant to become an actor by profession. It was a line of work which would use his special gifts in the service of his literary and nationalistic interests. But nationalism in Poland was inter-twined with Catholicism – a fact which made the Polish Church both widely followed and strongly conservative (since a creed consciously preserving a nation's history has every reason to keep its own links with the past in good shape). Wojtyla had always been a devout Catholic; and it was in those grinding first three years of war – in the struggle to keep some sort of native culture alive under a contemptuous invader, and to preserve the shreds of a tolerable existence for fellow labourers and fellow citizens, including Jews – that he conceived instead the intention of becoming a priest. These decisions are not to be documented in terms of cause and effect; but contributory incidents of that time included the death of his father, his surviving a serious accident when he was knocked down by a German lorry, and his introduction to the work of the sixteenth-century Spanish mystic St John of the Cross. It remained a lifelong interest.

In 1942, therefore, he shifted his secret studies from language to theology. His industrial work continued: in the Solway chemical works to which his stone-quarry was attached he carried buckets of lime about on a yoke across his shoulders. In the late summer of 1944 he finally exchanged his lime-whitened trousers for a black cassock. The Archbishop of Krakow, Prince Adam Sapieha, drew his seminarians permanently into his palace to protect them from the increasingly random savagery of the occupying German troops. For a while Wojtyla was a non-person, without official existence.

Ordained on 1 November 1946, he was given a brief reprieve from his disordered country. Its liberators from the Germans had been the Russians; the Yalta and Potsdam agreements had made them the new masters of a Poland shifted bodily westward into fresh frontiers. The Polish Church hardly benefited from the change. The Germans had correctly identified it as a centre of national resistance, and had fought it, killing some three thousand of its priests. The Russians realized that it would be an obstacle to the great task of building a socialist State: through their Polish instruments, their hand was hardly lighter. Wojtyla, as one of Sapieha's bright young men, was sent out of the country by the Archbishop to fill some of the gaps in his tormented wartime education. He went for two years to Rome.

He lived at the Belgian College with French-speaking seminarians, so the arrangement developed his French as well as his Italian; and his director of studies at the Angelicum University in Rome was a French Dominican called Réginald Garrigou-Lagrange, whose traditionalist approach reinforced the unyieldingness of the Catholicism that Wojtyla had learned in Poland. Garrigou-Lagrange had been a prime mover in the renaissance of spiritual theology between the wars, and remained an enthusiast for St John of the Cross, who was the subject of the thesis – written in Latin – for which Wojtyla won his Angelicum doctorate. (The Jagiellonian gave him a doctorate for it too.) At Sapieha's suggestion, he spent his final long vacation travelling in Belgium and France, where he was particularly interested by the efforts being made to recover for Catholicism the young urban working class.

He went back to Poland to embark on a thirty-year stretch of mingled pastoral and academic work. After a year as curate in a village outside Krakow he was appointed to a parish in the city itself. Here he began to establish himself both as a preacher – where his acting skills helped – and as a pastor, especially among young people. He played football, sang, skied with them. But he had not been in that post above two years before he was transferred to another Krakow parish where he would have more time for academic work. He collected a second doctorate from Lublin (where an independent Catholic university was financed by international Catholicism and the Polish diaspora). It was for a work on the significance for Catholic ethics of Max Scheler (an early twentieth-century Catholic philosopher who believed in the unique significance of human emotions, especially love, and the importance of saintly or heroic models for developing the moral life). He began teaching at the Krakow theological seminary, and organizing undergraduate activities: religious retreats, for example, in the discreet form of expeditions to the mountains. He became a visiting lecturer and then a professor at Lublin. It was two hundred miles from Krakow: Wojtyla travelled to and fro by train.

On 4 July 1958, ten years after his return from Rome, he became assistant bishop of Krakow: the youngest, at 38, of the eighty or so bishops in the country. He kept his connection with Lublin, but his work now lay mainly in Krakow again. He continued his pastoral work there among students and academics. He published plentifully, and with a widening range. The earliest version of his *Love and Responsibility* came out in 1960. In 1962, under a pseudonym, he brought out a meditation on marriage in drama form: part monologue and part dialogue, and called *In Front of the Jeweller's Shop*, it had been first written during his theatre days at the beginning of the war. (It was not performed until 1979, when there was a reading in Polish in London and then a radio broadcast in English from Dublin – on Radio Telefis Eireann – during the papal visit.) In 1963 he published in book form, and again pseudonymously, a selection of the verse which had been appearing in Catholic magazines for the past thirteen years. In 1969 appeared his big philosophical work, *The Acting Person*, an extension of his work on Scheler into a bold attempt to analyse the nature of man.

For Christians in Poland, the time did not encourage radical thought. The climate of relations between Church and State varied: it had been at its most menacing in the early 1950s, when Cardinal Stefan Wyszynski (the Polish primate), several bishops and hundreds of priests were in prison; but at the best there was always a drizzle of official harrassment. It was not an atmosphere in which churchmen could have felt safe in shifting their own ground. Hindrances were continually placed in the way of the holding of important services or the building of new churches. Religious training was restricted, both for schoolchildren and for seminarians; the Church had no access to television or radio, and Catholic newspapers were censored and kept short of paper, while atheistic propaganda abounded. The new bishop learnt to operate this system. He seldom engaged in trials of strength with the State; yet he knew – and local officials knew too – that the Church retained a strength of its own in the minds of the Polish people. He became an expert in what could and could not be done under communism; and up to those limits he knew how to press the Church's case.

He advanced swiftly in the Polish hierarchy. His superior, Archbishop Eugeniusz Baziak of Krakow, died in 1962. Wojtyla was made acting archbishop; and early in 1964 he was given the substantive rank.

His particular style of episcopacy was becoming known: notably his unconcern with his own comfort and status. When he met Cardinal Franz Koenig, Primate of Austria, at the Polish frontier in 1963, the first thing that struck Koenig was Wojtyla's shabby cassock and battered hat; the second, his friendliness and wide reading. This self-forgetfulness persisted. Cardinal Emmett Carter of Toronto tells a story of going to stay with Wojtyla in the old palace at Krakow in 1977. 'It was one of the most embarrassing things I ever did', says Carter. 'He insisted on giving me his room. Then I wanted him for something and I went all over the old palace. I couldn't find him; but I couldn't find another bed, either. I don't know where he slept. I asked him in the morning, but he brushed it aside. I was relieved to see him looking rested – I'd been awake thinking about him – as I'm quite sure the place didn't have another bed. I had a good look.'

Polish bishops had other things to think about. Carter found among them 'a tremendous sense of service and dedication to their people'. He also found Wojtyla 'very tough, very capable'. Koenig adds, of Wojtyla's private religious life: 'He told me once that he said the stations of the cross every day. Also when he has some special work to do he will place a table in his private chapel, close to the tabernacle, and work there.'

The instrument which furthered Wojtyla's reputation in the wider Church was the Second Vatican Council. He was in Rome (along with about a fifth of the Polish bishops) for all of its four sessions, held each autumn from 1962 to 1965. He made at least two noted speeches: he spoke with the authority of experience about the rightness (not always acknowledged by Catholics) of calling for universal religious liberty, and about the need to converse with atheism rather than simply condemn it. He contributed to the Council's most important document, *Lumen Gentium*, the 'dogmatic constitution' which recognized that the laity in its secular avocations was a crucial part of the Church. He regularly returned to Rome after the Council to take his part in work on its documents. (He wrote a book about it for his Polish flock called *The Foundations of Renewal*.) He was given his red hat by Paul VI on 9 July 1967 (and was careful not to divide the Polish episcopate by allowing the Government to show any more favour to him than to its old foe, Poland's other cardinal, Wyszynski). From that year on he attended all the gatherings of the Synod of Bishops, which met in Rome; and he was elected to its permanent council in 1971 and thereafter. He was numbered among the Pope's friends: in 1976 Paul VI invited him to preach the course of sermons at a Lent retreat for pope and Curia – Vatican officialdom. (The sermons were later published as *Sign of Contradiction*.) Within the college of cardinals he had become a recognizable figure.

Paul VI died on 6 August 1978, an invalid of 80. He was aware (it transpired a year later) that his departure would be 'a providential solution' for the Church; and yet he had believed retirement impermissible. That obduracy made the question of a papal retiring age inevitable for his successors. 'Bishops have to go at 75, after all', says Monsignor John Tracy Ellis, the American church historian: 'nobody again wants the spectacle of Pope Paul – ill for years, and not really able to carry on, before the good Lord took him.'

At the conclave to elect his successor at the end of August, non-Italians were in a substantial majority among the electing cardinals. There is evidence that Cardinal Wojtyla received a number of votes in early balloting. But another turn of events was needed before he came to seem the right man.

The papacy, like most elective offices, is filled on the principle of alternation. Each time, the electors look for a man who will spare them the shortcomings of the man chosen last time. Throughout this century, in consequence, there has been a seesaw between efficient men – diplomats, administrators – and holy men or pastors. Paul VI's training had been as a diplomat. This time the cardinals were looking for a pastor.

Even at that, their choice was a surprise. It fell on Cardinal Albino Luciani, the patriarch of Venice. He had succeeded to his Venetian eminence as being a well-liked local man and nothing more. He was intellectually unremarkable – although his book, *Illustrissimi*, a collection of newspaper articles, showed that he had a gift for popular communication. He had taken little overt part in the Second Vatican Council, though he had made friends with German and Belgian bishops there. His election was surprising on another count, for happening in a single day, as if the cardinals had been swept along on a pentecostal breeze; and the third and most surprising thing about John Paul I (the new incarnation he chose) was that he died just over a month later, on 28 September, of a massive heart attack. He was within three weeks of his 66th birthday.

The night before he died he had said to an aide: 'Isn't there a machine that reads paper and can bring it in line with the hours of the day?' He was overborne, it appeared, by the burdens of office in their simplest manifestation: the paperwork entailed. Short time as he had, it was long enough to give rise to the suspicion that he was out of his depth. The cardinals were bound to feel that mere holiness had been a disappointment. At the October 1978 conclave, the pendulum principle was called into operation once again. It was Luciani who gave Wojtyla his chance.

The regathered cardinals were gratified that there had been so much public recognition of Luciani's charm. That part of the specification stood. But this time they wanted an efficient man again, a man who was in no danger of being thought a simpleton as he faced a cruel and complicated world. (An upsurge of religious war in the Lebanon reinforced the feeling.) They also knew they needed a fit man.

A fit man suggested a comparatively young man; and that raised the spectre of Pius IX, appointed in 1846 at the age of 54 and still there, autocratic to the point of paranoia, thirty-four years later. Wojtyla was 58. Yet the difficulty vanished. In the early ballots a man a year younger, Cardinal Giovanni Benelli of Florence, was among the leaders. (He had been the number two figure in the Vatican Secretariat of State, and was certainly efficient.) His support turned out to be blocked by support for the other leading Italian, Cardinal Giuseppe Siri of Genoa. But a pope under 60 had been seriously contemplated. The way was open not merely for a non-Italian but for a comparatively young non-Italian.

The idea of a non-Italian pope had made ground at the August conclave. As it began, one cardinal took Wyszynski aside and said to him: 'It's time for a non-Italian pope – perhaps even a Polish pope.' Wyszynski retorted brusquely: 'Oh, I'm much too busy in Warsaw.'

More flexible minds than his were already ruminating on his junior colleague. Koenig in Vienna – a vantage point for surveying Eastern Europe – had had letters from Catholics in a number of different countries telling him it was time for a non-Italian. Then when he reached Rome for the August conclave he found bishops from South America and Europe talking about the possibility. 'I felt myself', Koenig says, 'that if that happened it could be Wojtyla.'

How had Koenig reached that belief? 'Well, when voting took place after the last Synod of Bishops in Rome for those bishops who would represent Europe, he came out top. That showed me he was very well thought of by a wide circle, not just by me.

'I had come to know him well since 1963. He often stopped off in Vienna on his way to Rome when he was Archbishop of Krakow. Sometimes he stayed a night. I had seen him as pope for quite some time. He's strongly gifted, with a clear mind. He's a careful person: what is the phrase I want in English? – He won't put his foot in it. He has good judgment – won't be rushed into things.

'He's a man who has travelled a lot: he knows foreigners on their home ground. That's very important today. He got the feel of foreign places before they knew him. That was useful and fortunate. Once you reach the point where people put out red carpets, getting the true picture is more difficult. Also he not only knows languages, he's got a command of languages.' Koenig himself conversed with Wojtyla mostly in Italian, sometimes in German.

This kind of backing was vital to Wojtyla's chances. To appoint an Iron Curtain pope was to risk giving a degree of offence to Moscow which would result only in worsened Church-State relations throughout Eastern Europe. Koenig was known to have a keen mind and an informed understanding of how to treat with Communist powers: he had handled the trouble in Hungary when Cardinal Josef Mindszenty took refuge in the American embassy in Budapest. He believed that, at any rate in Wojtyla's case, the risk was acceptable; and he allowed his belief to become known.

During conclaves, cardinals sit in order of seniority. The pattern is preserved even at meals, where they are grouped at long refectory tables. Koenig was at the same table as Wojtyla, a little further along on the opposite side, and seems regularly to have been sitting down before him. 'I always raised my glass to him when he came in', Koenig remembers: 'a sort of gesture of friendship.' Yet the Cardinal acknowledges that it could be seen as more than that. 'Well, yes: it was a toast.'

Koenig maintains that there is no rounding up of supporters in advance of conclaves – merely talks in small groups and between close friends. 'What everybody waits for is the first vote, to see the front runners.' Wojtyla, it appears, was not among them. The conclave had begun on the morning of Sunday 15 October. 'Many cardinals as they went in looked troubled. But I noticed in particular that Cardinal Wojtyla's face radiated perfect peace. He was not at all nervous.' He had no expectation of drawing the short straw. But by the middle of the second day, Monday, that had changed. 'He came into lunch looking very worried', Koenig recalls. 'He hardly raised his eyes. He seemed very confused. It was the way things were going.'

Koenig was himself sufficiently worried by Wojtyla's reaction to seek out Wyszynski after lunch. 'Do you think he will refuse?' Koenig asked. Wyszynski hushed him. 'There is no anxiety. I talked to him just now and told him he must accept if elected.'

There was another topic of conversation at that point besides the imminence of a result. It was the cold. Cardinal John Wright, an elderly American in a Vatican post, disclosed (before his death the following year) that there was already dissatisfaction over the beds: 'indescribably awful', he called them. (They were from the emergency supply kept for Rome hospitals.) To this was now added the chill of Roman autumn nights – and a shortage of blankets. 'It was absolutely bitter', said Wright. 'The funny thing was that at lunch everybody was talking about the cold. Then we had a pope; and one of the first things he said to the assembled cardinals was "I want you to stay with me here tonight in the Vatican: we will pray together." '

Koenig testifies that even at this stage the election 'was a great surprise to many of the cardinals'. The story is taken up by Cardinal John Krol of Philadelphia, himself the son of a Polish immigrant to the United States and a long-standing friend of Wojtyla's. (They converse in Polish.) 'We were all waiting for the Pope to return', Krol recalls. 'He had gone to put on his white cassock. When he came back we were expecting him to take his place at the top. Instead he walked straight down to the seat he had occupied before the election.' (As a function of the date of his appointment, it lay between Michele Pellegrino of Italy and Justinus Darmojuwono of Indonesia.) 'The cardinals were very moved by the way the Pope ignored the chair set out for him and sat in our midst.'

Krol remembers that there was still 'an atmosphere of surprise among the cardinals, especially the Italians'. Partly in response to it, partly knowing Wojtyla's predilections, Cardinal Terence Cooke of New York said to Krol: 'You must sing.' After a moment's hesitation, Krol launched into a Latin number called '*Plurimos annos plurimos*' (a wish for long life) which he had often sung with Wojtyla. Several other cardinals joined in.

'The singing seemed to catch on', Krol pursues. 'There were calls of "Sing 'The Mountaineer', sing 'The Mountaineer' "

That's a great favourite of the Pope's. The song is called *"Goralu, czy ci nie zal"* in Polish, and goes "Mountaineer, do you not regret leaving your beautiful hills?"; and it goes on to say "You leave them for the sake of bread". After I had finished, the Pope said "Sing it again." Then Cardinal Wyszynski said "Instead of singing 'For the sake of bread' sing 'for the Lord's sake'." So I sang it that way. Others joined in. Then the Pope said "Sing it once again." '

The marked man of the moment was Wyszynski. The old warrior passed over for his junior is a classically awkward figure. Koenig records what happened. 'When Wojtyla was elected, and all the cardinals filed up to kiss the fisherman's ring, there was much watching to see what would happen when it was Wyszysnki's turn. But the Pope would not let him kiss his ring: he rose from his chair and embraced Wyszynski on both cheeks. It was a very touching moment.'

Krol offers a prediction about what sort of pope Wojtyla will make. 'My own conviction is that he'll make up his own mind. He'll be the boss. He won't be overwhelmed by the experts — though he'll use their knowledge. Of course, he's very expert himself. That, I'd say, was the big influence in his election. People had seen him in action in the Synods. He's got a very wide grasp of complicated issues.'

He had accepted office, among the cardinals, in Latin. He made a short and successful speech to the crowd in St Peter's Square in Italian. In the next few days, at receptions for journalists and for dignitaries from other Christian denominations, he deployed every other language he knew. The first year of his ministry to the city and the world, *urbi et orbi*, was well begun.

In human as distinct from astronomical terms a year is an arbitrary division of time. Yet John Paul II's first year in office had a unity which marked it off. It was given shape by the three great journeys which punctuated it: to Mexico after less than three months, to Poland after a little under eight, to Ireland and the United States after nearly twelve; and the enormous public interest they aroused made them events that deserved recording for themselves. More than that, the year provided unusually full evidence about the ideas with which the new man began his course.

The journeys themselves called forth statements of position: it would have been impossible to visit Latin America without discussing the Church's social action, Eastern Europe without considering the relation between Christians and Communists, the United States without noticing the demands by a great many Catholics for a liberalization of the rules that bound them. Besides the journeys, the Pope made use of other opportunities. He was quick into print with his first encyclical, published after five months in March 1979. He entered with very little delay into the controversy which promised to be among the sharpest of his pontificate, about the priesthood – who should belong to it, and on what terms: his long 'Letter to all the priests of the Church' reached them in April. His main Vatican appointments were made in May, and his first batch of cardinals in June, after the return from Poland. Within a year, it was possible to discern the areas where he would have effect and the areas where he would have trouble.

All these items of evidence – the journeys, the documents, the appointments – shed light on the man and his method and his message. But there is something else to be considered before them; and it occupies the next two chapters of this book. The first striking thing about John Paul II, before he so much as opened his mouth, was that he was not Italian. There had not been such a pope for four and a half centuries. He belonged instead to a nation far older than Italy, and one which left a much deeper mark on him than being Italian would have done. That mark was on the books and poems he had already written before his election; and they in turn were indispensable evidence towards a grasp of what he wrote as pope. There could be no understanding of his papacy without an understanding of his Polishness, and of the writings of his Polish period.

2

The Black Madonna

On 18 October 1978, two days after his election, John Paul II addressed the diplomats accredited to the Holy See. Speaking in French, he said that the Church valued cultural, historical and linguistic diversity and regarded such differences as an enrichment. He added that 'the particular nature of our country of origin is from now on of little importance; as a Christian, and still more as pope, we are and will be witnesses of a universal love'. He seemed to be saying that we should disregard the fact that he is a Pole.

Speaking to young people in Gniezno on 3 June 1979, the second day of his Polish journey, he used very different language. He dwelt at some length on the *Bogurodzica* (Mother of God – a late medieval Polish literary text). It is not only a poem, he said, but 'a profession of faith, a Polish *credo*'. He then went on to speak of Polish culture generally, which combines Christian inspiration with deeply felt humanistic values. He quoted Adam Mickiewicz, the nineteenth-century romantic poet: 'A civilization truly worthy of man must be a Christian civilization.' And he concluded: 'You are hearing these words from a man who owes his own spiritual formation from the beginning to Polish culture, its literature, its music, its plastic arts, to Polish schools, Polish universities'. He said nothing of St John of the Cross. He could not have laid greater emphasis on his Polishness.

The contrast between the two statements is striking. Yet perhaps the paradox of being Polish and being universal is more apparent than real. John Paul II is proud of his Polishness. But he does not regard it as a limitation. It is simply his way of being inserted into the human race. His philosophy stresses that the human person is 'embodied': he must sit somewhere, either on the schoolbench at Wadowice or the canteen of the Solway chemical factory or the chair of Peter. It follows that the only way to find one's place in the world is through a particular culture: to deny that is to deny the human condition. But once given a firm and clear identity through that culture, the human person is capable of becoming open to others and to other cultures. Without that openness he will lack integrity; but without the rootedness in a particular culture he will lack identity. Wojtyla, then, values both rootedness and openness. 'He is not', said one of his friends, 'a cosmopolitan, but he does have a sense of "cultural collegiality".'

It can be seen, for instance, in the way he has systematically set about learning languages. It is the way a Pole breaks out of intellectual isolation. Furthermore, to be Polish means to have a sense of being different and also, to some extent, to feel neglected. This sense of being different permits him to appreciate difference in others – a specific requirement for the papal office: since its role, as defined by the Second Vatican Council, is 'to preside over the whole assembly of charity, and protect legitimate differences' (*On the Church, 13*).

Nevertheless, any attempt to understand and assess John Paul II must try to come to terms with the Polish factor. This, on his own admission, has made him what he is. He has been shaped by Polish culture. He uses that term comprehensively and in two senses: for him it includes both high culture (music, painting, poetry) and common culture – the assumptions that people automatically make, the 'long tradition' (to use Raymond Williams's term) that they share in. And the Polish common culture fuses literature and Christianity, national and religious consciousness, to a degree hard to match elsewhere.

This makes life difficult for the Polish Communist Party. For the basis of its claim to legitimacy is that a new Poland, radically different from anything that went before, came into existence with the advent of socialism in 1944. When John Paul II returned to Poland in June 1979, the government was orchestrating a campaign to persuade Poles to celebrate '35 years of socialism'. There were posters on the walls and fluttering banners. Edward Gierek, First Secretary of the Polish Workers' United (which means Communist) Party, welcomed the Pope in the Belvedere Palace and outlined the achievements of those 35 years. In Marxist theory what went before was pre-history, a mere run-up to the splendours of the present. John Paul II in his reply pointedly ignored this theme, congratulated Gierek on rebuilding the royal palace in Warsaw 'as a symbol of Polish sovereignty', and recalled the thousand years and more of Polish history.

Christ is built into Polish culture. Preaching in Victory Square in Warsaw on 2 June the Pope quoted the eighteenth-century preacher Piotr Skarga: 'This old oak tree has grown as it has, and not been knocked down by any wind, since its root is in Christ.' There are thus two competing versions of Poland's past.

Wojtyla has always stressed that the Polish people, and especially the young, have a right to their past. Where this past is ignored or travestied by the official media and the educational system, one of the tasks of the Church is to put that right. It becomes the place where truth may be spoken without fear. So the cultural battle becomes in many ways more important than the philosophical or ideological conflict – or rather, it is itself the philosophical conflict, but expressed in terms of the nation's values. This was a theme to which Cardinal Wojtyla frequently returned in his preaching. In his Corpus Christi sermon in Krakow in 1978 he summed up what he had been saying for many years:

> Ours is a difficult and glorious past, a past that has wrung tears from whole generations, a past in which generations were shackled and bled . . . We will not tear ourselves away from our past! We will not allow our past to be torn away from our souls! It is the essence of our identity even today. We want our young people to be familiar with the truth and history of our nation. We want the inheritance of our Polish culture to be passed on without distortion to a new generation of Poles. A nation lives by the truth about itself. Above all it has the right to expect that truth from those who teach.

– A truth it does not always get, was the unstated implication. It was characteristic of the Wojtyla style in Poland to use understatement: he would assert a principle boldly, and let his hearers draw their own conclusions. Unlike Wyszynski, he did not heap abuse on his opponents.

But the conclusion to that Corpus Christi sermon was unambiguous: an educational system based on atheism could not do justice to Polish history and culture, which for Wojtyla formed a seamless garment.

There are special reasons why Poles should have long memories and a keen sense of the past. As Wojtyla remarked in a recent article, thinking of the shifting and (in the nineteenth century) obliteration of Polish frontiers, 'Several generations of Poles had to have their identity-cards stamped with the seal of another State, although they lived in the land they were born in'. In these circumstances it was natural that memories of the past, suitably gilded, should compensate for the bleakness of the present.

Poles remembered the conversion to Christianity of Mieszko I, prince of the Piast dynasty, in 966. It was the origin of the bond between nationalism and Catholicism. The foundation of the State and the conversion to Christianity coincided – a fact that the Polish bishops stressed in 1966, the year of the millennium. They recalled the glories of the cathedral of Gniezno, the first Polish capital, where the early kings of Poland had been crowned: to this day the Primate of Poland has the title of Archbishop of Gniezno. Krakow, where Wojtyla had lived and worked, possessed its own set of memories. In the sixteenth century it had been the capital. Economic life flourished; Polish armies were victorious in the east. (Between 1610 and 1612 they even occupied Moscow.) Artists and scholars flocked to Krakow and its famous university. Though the Counter-Reformation triumphed in Poland, there was a tradition of tolerance there – extending to Jews – which was not found elsewhere in Europe at that time. The Inquisition never existed in Poland. Yet after notable victories over Swedish Protestants, who invaded Poland from the north in the seventeenth century, the country went into a decline which made it an easy victim at the end of the eighteenth for the first two partitions. It was the second which wiped Poland off the map.

When an independent Polish republic reappeared in 1918, it soon found itself at war with the Soviet Union. Three months after Karol Wojtyla was born, the Red Army stood at the gates of Warsaw. It was flung back in a battle known not unjustifiably as 'the miracle of the Vistula'. The date was 15 August, feast of the Assumption of Our Lady. The republic lasted, precariously, until the first day of the Second World War; and when 'liberation' from the Nazis came in 1944, it did not exactly take the form the Home Army had fought for. The dominant fact of Polish life from then on was the looming presence of the Soviet Union, the 'friendly ally' to the east. Any suggestion that Communism, as an ideological system, was wanted or welcomed in Poland is difficult to sustain. It came to Poland because the Red Army liberated the country and because the Yalta agreement had accepted the theory of spheres of influence in post-war Europe. The result was that it was unconvincing in Poland to speak of revolution, which in Marxist theory is the decisive and legitimating act that establishes socialism. Poles know that as applied to them this theory is false.

Instead the story of Poland strongly suggests that nationalism and religion, in combination, are more important influences than class conflict. And these memories of the past are not dead facts in a history textbook. They remain very much alive and operative; they provide a permanent frame of reference for interpreting the present. In Northern Ireland the past weighs down upon the present and blocks progress. In Poland the sense of the past is liberating. The sermons of Wojtyla admirably illustrate this point and show how the Polish factor affects his thinking. As a preacher, he constantly reanimates the past in order to derive lessons for the present.

His whole treatment of Church-State relations, for example, is coloured by the story of the martyrdom of St Stanislaw, one of his predecessors as Archbishop of Krakow. The circumstances were murky, the resemblance to the Thomas à Becket story uncanny. In a pastoral letter of 9 April 1972 Wojtyla showed that he was familiar with the views of secular historians who presented Stanislaw as a meddlesome priest whose political hands were not entirely clean. But by 1977 he had abandoned such scholarly inhibitions and made the leap from the eleventh to the twentieth century without batting an eyelid. His pastoral letter dated 8 May declared:

> St Stanislaw has become the patron saint of moral and social order in this country . . . He dared to tell the King himself that he was bound to respect the law of God. The age-old veneration for St Stanislaw is, in fact, a confession of the truth that the moral law is the foundation of social order. He was also the defender of the

freedom which is the inalienable right of every man, so that the violation of that freedom by the State is at the same time a violation of the moral and social order.

Wojtyla returned to the theme as pope. Stanislaw keeps his relevance to modern Poland. He is a perpetual reminder that no one, be he ever so high, is above the moral law. John Paul II had originally intended to visit Poland in May 1979, when the nine hundredth anniversary of Stanislaw's martyrdom was due to be celebrated. The Polish authorities asked him to choose a less politically provocative date. The Pope agreed. But the Government gained nothing, and had acted naïvely, since there was available in any case a rich store of symbolic occasions on which the message about the moral law and human rights could be proclaimed.

Devotion to Mary is something else that Wojtyla owes to the Polish long tradition. It is so natural to him that he would be surprised that anyone should remark on it. Even in his briefest statements he alludes to Mary. On the fateful 16 October 1978, when he had received the majority needed to be elected pope, he was asked the ritual question: did he accept? His reply was: 'With obedience in faith to Christ, my Lord, and with trust in the Mother of Christ and of the Church, in spite of the great difficulties, I accept.' In his first speech from the balcony of St Peter's shortly afterwards, there were two references to the Madonna. He concluded his encyclical, *Redemptor Hominis*, with a peroration which is a request for prayer 'together with Mary the Mother of Jesus, as the apostles and the disciples of the Lord did in the upper room in Jerusalem after his ascension' (section 22). Likewise in his Letter to Priests, dated Passion Sunday 1979, he 'entrusts all priests to the Mother of Christ who, in a special way, is our Mother, the Mother of priests' (11). He explains that 'in the ministerial priesthood there is the wonderful and penetrating dimension of nearness to the Mother of Christ', and adds a personal touch: 'If I may be permitted to speak here of my own experience, I will say that in writing to you I am referring to my own personal experience'. That is the observation which seems to connect his veneration for Mary with his childhood loss of his mother; Mary represents the feminine element in his life. (The intriguing rumour of a clandestine wife who died at the hands of the Gestapo is a fabrication.)

Some Catholics find this cult of Mary excessive; some Protestants dismiss it as unscriptural, superstitious and even, at the limit, blasphemous. Yet Wojtyla's mariology stays within Catholic orthodoxy. There is a link, not always perceived, between mariology and the Church's view of itself. For Mary was the first to say 'yes', *fiat*, to the divine plan, and from that possibility of co-operating with the divine plan the Church is born. The Second Vatican Council had developed a sober, scriptural mariology in which Mary no longer appeared as a remote goddess on a distant pedestal but as the type or model of the faith of the Church. She is with the Church, not above it. She is honoured as the first of believers. ('Blessed is she who believed that there would be a fulfilment of what was spoken to her from the Lord', Luke 1.45.) She was present at two of the decisive moments in the foundation of the Church: she stood at the foot of the cross, and she was among the disciples in prayer after the ascension. In his preaching Wojtyla constantly returns to these two incidents. It is fair to say that he has tried to bring Polish mariology back to its evangelical and theological foundations. His mariology coincides with that of Vatican II. If there remains a difference of emphasis, this is because Wojtyla and the Council had different starting-points. The Council was trying to meet the legitimate objections of Protestants by restoring mariology to the 'hierarchy of truths' and bringing out its theological point. Wojtyla, on the other hand, started from the Polish tradition and tried to breathe theological life into it.

In this tradition Mary is hailed as 'Queen of Poland'. Other nations – Mexico and Ireland, for example – have made comparable claims. But elsewhere the metaphors have been drained of life or become pious clichés. It is difficult realistically to think of England as 'Our Lady's dowry', though this term was once enshrined in popular piety. In contrast, 'Our Lady, Queen of Poland' is still operative. When Wyszynski welcomed John Paul II at Warsaw airport, he exclaimed: 'May the Virgin Mother of God open wide to you this her kingdom, devoted without reservation to the successor of St Peter upon the see of the bishops of Rome'. To speak of Mary in those terms makes a point about where true sovereignty lies. President Henryk Jablonski had to listen impassively to this suggestion that his mandate and authority were secondary. He is, after all, merely president of the State, while Mary is presented as Queen of the nation; and in a country which has twice disappeared from the map, and where the nation nevertheless managed to subsist without the State, the distinction is an important one.

Devotion to Mary forms a continuous thread in Polish history. The *Bogurodzica* is ascribed by tradition to St Adalbert, the first apostle of Poland, though literary historians place it in the fifteenth century. It was sung on the eve of battles. It has been sung, and is still sung, at the great shrines of Poland – Piekary Slaskie, in Silesia; Czestochowa, where the famous painting called the Black Madonna is honoured. These shrines sum up the spirit of Polish Catholicism. It is a mass religion and a popular religion. Millions flock to those places every year. If the Church is a pilgrim Church, on the road, *in via*, then these great pilgrimages give concrete expression to that truth.

The Polish shrines were places where, even during the partitions, 'Our Lady spoke Polish'. In the early nineteenth century Tsar Alexander I ordered the fortifications round Jasna Gora (Bright Mountain), the monastery at Czestochowa, to be destroyed. No doubt he knew of the occasion on 18 November 1655 when the monastery had been successfully defended by a handful of monks and a few noblemen against a vastly superior Swedish force. In thanksgiving for this victory, on 1 April 1656 King Jan Kazimierz had dedicated the whole country to Our Lady, Queen of Poland, and pledged himself to work for social justice among his people. The Polish parliament had given the monastery the title of Jasna Gora of Victory. The consecration of the nation to Our Lady has been repeated at other decisive moments of Polish history, notably on 26 August 1956, just as the country was emerging from Stalinism, when over a million people took the 'Jasna Gora oath of the nation'. It had been specially composed by Wyszynski as part of the ten-year scheme designed to prepare the millennium celebrations. Pilgrimages, consecrations, anniversaries, mariology, all in a popular and national context – these are the elements that have given shape and coherence to Polish Catholicism. They still do.

Cardinal Wojtyla had a special relationship with Czestochowa. It was in his Krakow archdiocese. He preached there on many occasions, rarely missing the feast of Our Lady, Queen of Poland, on 3 May. Those sermons make curious reading for a non-Pole who might fail to grasp the code-language in which they are written. In 1977, for example, he stressed that Mary was Queen of all Poles, including those abroad and in exile: her sovereignty was broader in scope than anything the Government could claim. He reminded his hearers that King Jan Kazimierz had made his famous vow in distant Lwow, now in the Soviet Union: the reminder contained a hint of Polish revanchism, still not entirely reconciled to the loss of eastern territories – and, under the Communists, a taboo topic. More important still, he recalled the second part of the Kazimierz vow: to work for social justice. Had that promise been fulfilled? Only in the constitution of 1791, swiftly overwhelmed by the realities of occupation.

Once again, he was speaking in code. His hearers would understand that he was commenting indirectly on the new constitution that had been bitterly debated earlier in 1977. There were two main grounds of complaint. The 1977 constitution declared that the permanent alliance with the Soviet Union was the basis of the Polish State: even those who agreed that this was *de facto* true saw no reason why it should be enshrined *de jure* in the constitution. Another clause made citizens' rights dependent on the performance of duties; some citizens would thereby be more equal than others. That was why Wojtyla always laid such great stress on the inalienability of rights: they were not a gift from the State for the well-behaved.

On 3 May 1978, preaching for the last time at Czestochowa before he became pope, he pointed out that in four years' time would be celebrated the 600th anniversary of the arrival of the mysterious painting in Jasna Gora. But his main theme was more theological. The Gospel reading of the day was John 19, where the dying Jesus entrusts the beloved disciple, John, to his mother ('Woman, behold, your son') and his mother to John ('Behold, your mother'). Wojtyla interpreted the text as a statement about the adoptive sonship of all Christians. For John is here a 'representative figure'. This fits in with Jewish modes of thinking. By becoming the spiritual son of Mary, Jesus's mother, John becomes the brother of Jesus; and this astonishing claim holds for all Christians. It is for the very reason that they are the brothers of Jesus that they can speak of Mary as their mother.

This is not an eccentric piece of exegesis. It is also advanced by reputable biblical scholars like the American Raymond E. Brown. It is a good instance of the way Wojtyla has tried to put a Christian and theological context into popular piety. Mariology, understood in this way, is not a separated cult: it points to Jesus. Halina Bortnowska, the Catholic authoress who has been Wojtyla's Polish editor, says: 'A man like Wojtyla will never exploit popular religion as a means – to achieve popularity, for instance. So under John Paul II popular religiosity will be practised in all simplicity and protected against the destructive scorn of those who reduce it to mere folklore. It will also be delicately pruned to become more clearly christocentric and less purely ritualistic.'

John Paul II constantly tries to convert popular religion. This process he calls 'catechesis'. In his sermon to young people in Warsaw on 3 June 1979 he defined his attitude to popular religion:

> My fellow countrymen, I desire that my pilgrimage through this Polish land, in communion with all of you, should become a living catechesis, the integration of that catechesis which entire generations of our forebears have inscribed into our history. May this be the catechesis of all the history of the Church and of Poland, and at the same time the catechesis of our age . . . The fundamental task of the Church is catechesis. In this way an ever more conscious faith is gradually introduced into the life of each generation, through the common efforts of the family, the parish, the priests and pastors of souls, men and women catechists, the community, the mass media and traditions. In fact the walls of the bell-towers of our churches, the crucifixes at the crossroads, the holy paintings on the walls of houses – all these, in some sense, are part of catechesis.

The goal of preaching the Gospel is thus an 'ever more conscious faith', as contrasted with inert, conventional, non-operative, merely 'sociological' faith. John Paul II takes as his starting point not some ideal, non-existent *tabula rasa* but the actual convictions of his hearers. The consistent application of this principle would mean adopting a different approach in different countries, provided the local tradition had been identified. Ireland and Mexico are not Poland.

In Poland he accepted and used the link between Christianity and Polishness. This could lead to remarkable juxtapositions. In the same sermon, after quoting 1 Peter 2.9 ('You are a chosen race, a royal priesthood, a holy nation, God's own people'), he added 'All together we form also "the royal race of the Piasts" '. The Piasts were the first Polish dynasty. In his May 1978 sermon at Czestochowa, after presenting John as a representative figure, he had gone on to consider each individual Pole as a representative of the whole nation: 'In the heart of every man there happens something that belongs to all men. No one is alone, no man is an island. The entire nation passes through the heart of every Pole. We cannot live apart from this: it shapes our soul.' It was a simplified version of his philosophical positions. Philosophy is only possible because of our common humanity, because we have comparable experiences. But there is no abstract humanity: there are people and nations.

An intense patriotism results. From the nineteenth century onwards, patriotism has so often slid over into destructive forms of nationalism which exclude other people, be they foreigners or Jews. In Wojtyla's old diocese lay Auschwitz: he did not need to be reminded of the excesses of nationalism when allied to a perverted ideology. But he distinguishes between patriotism and nationalism. Addressing 'all his fellow countrymen without exception, whatever their philosophical views', he wrote in a letter shortly after his election:

> The love of the motherland unites and should unite us, since it stands above all differences. It has nothing in common with narrow nationalism or chauvinism. It is a right of the human heart. It is the measure of human generosity – a measure tested many times over in our far-from-easy history. Dear fellow-countrymen, it is not easy to give up the possibility of returning to the

motherland, 'To those fields strewn with flowers, where silvery wheat and golden rye are blossoming', as Mickiewicz wrote . . . But since such is the will of Christ, it must be accepted.

But his patriotism, deep though it is, has nothing in common with 'my country, right or wrong'. It is a patriotism not of pride but of compassion and service. For his Victory Square sermon on 2 June 1979, the temporary altar looked directly across, along the red carpet, to the tomb of the Unknown Soldier. John Paul II said on that occasion:

In how many places in our native land has that soldier fallen! In how many places in Europe and the world has he cried with his death that there can be no just Europe without the independence of Poland marked on its map! On how many battlefields has that soldier given witness to the rights of man, indelibly inscribed in the inviolable rights of the people, by dying for 'our freedom and yours'!

He was already moving away from a narrow and exclusive patriotism. The principles of human rights and self-determination asserted in Poland applied also to the rest of mankind. John Paul II went on to remove all traces of militarism from his meditation on the Unknown Soldier and to relate the Polish experience to the passion of Christ:

I wish to kneel before this tomb and to venerate every seed that falls into the earth and dies and thus bears fruit. It may be the seed of the blood of a soldier shed on a battlefield, or the sacrifice of martyrdom in concentration camps or prisons. It may be the seed of hard daily toil, with the sweat of one's brow, in the fields, the workshops, the mines, the foundries and the factories. It may be the seed of the love of parents who do not refuse to give new life to a human being and who undertake responsibility for bringing him up. It may be the seed of creative work in the universities, the institutes of higher learning, the libraries, the places where national culture is developed. It may be the seed of prayer, of service to the sick, the suffering, the abandoned, 'all that of which Poland is made'.

All that in the hands of the Mother of God, at the foot of the cross on Calvary and in the upper room of Pentecost.

It was like a complex prose poem on the theme of John 12.24 ('Unless a grain of wheat falls into the earth and dies, it remains alone; but if it dies, it bears much fruit'), linked with the ancient patristic idea that 'the blood of martyrs is the seed of the Church' and then set in a modern context. This yoking together of disparate meanings is characteristic of Wojtyla's style. It is highly personal, and yet it takes up the most ancient traditions. When it comes to patriotism, the Polish government is at a disadvantage. It is stuck in the groove of anti-Nazism. Wojtyla has unimpeachable anti-Nazi credentials, but he can also evoke a store of associations which add a new dimension to patriotism.

Must the weight of the Polish long tradition result in a distorted vision of the rest of the Church and its many problems? That tradition is, not surprisingly, conservative, and '35 years of socialism' have contributed powerfully to confirming conservative attitudes. Everyone today claims to rejoice that the active persecution of the Church in the Stalinist period is no more. But the way society is ordered, and its basic theory, have not changed: religion is the product of the alienations of capitalist society. In socialism those contradictions have been, allegedly, removed, and therefore religion is ultimately doomed to disappear. That is what the official ideology says. The fact that this theory is massively refuted in Poland poses a problem that Marxist thinkers have been most unwilling to face. Communism has not destroyed the Church in Poland. What it has done is to make an already conservative Church more conservative still.

Wyszynski gloried in that. 'We want a Polish theology for Poles', he wrote to the 1971 congress of Polish theologians 'written from the standpoint of the East for a community living in the East'. The implication was that Western theology should not be imported into Poland. The progressive ideas of French and Dutch theologians might look fine on paper, but they had emptied the churches. In embattled Poland, where the Church was always potentially under threat, where its legal existence was still not guaranteed, there was every incentive to close the ranks, to discourage theological speculation, to insist on the most literal orthodoxy. The monolith of the Party and the monolith of the Church reinforced each other. They needed each other like the two sides of a Gothic arch.

A distinction has to be made between Wyszynski and Wojtyla: there were differences of emphasis between them. But on the three controverted questions which racked the Church elsewhere – clerical celibacy, the position of women in society, and sexual morality – it was impossible to drive even a very thin wedge between them.

The Polish Church is a clerical and hierarchical Church. The whole vocabulary of 'Church-State relations' suggests that 'Church' means the bishops. Nor is there any drive to 'declericalize' the Church. Clerical dress, for instance, is insisted on because it makes the priest 'visible', and marks out his sacred status in an officially secular world. He will be friendly with many families, if he is a good priest; and no one enjoyed more than Karol Wojtyla the round of carol-singing visits at Christmas time But the priest keeps his distance, maintains a certain reserve. In the Letter to Priests of Palm Sunday 1979 John Paul II brackets together 'declericalization' and 'secularization' (though they are not the same). He notes that sometimes the laity may call for a clergy who will be in every way 'like themselves', but warns: 'Those who call for the secularization of priestly life and applaud its various manifestations will undoubtedly abandon us when we succumb to temptation. We shall then cease to be necessary and popular' (7).

Again, women who wish to be ordained are unlikely to have any better luck than married men with the same hopes. Kalwaria Zebrzydowska is another Polish shrine where Cardinal Wojtyla preached regularly. It has separate pilgrimages for men and women. While the sermons addressed to men do not attempt to speak to them specifically as males, those addressed to women presuppose certain immutable feminine characteristics. At the 1976 pilgrimage for women, Wojtyla's theme was that 'woman's vocation is to give life to new men':

Your vocation is to fashion the human community. What is more simple? And yet without it every community would be deprived of the roots of its own humanity. The community of the family is the strength of the nation and the State, of the Church and humanity. It owes its cohesion to you . . . Woman is the heart of the family. We know that a man is dead when his heart stops beating. Likewise the family dies when its heart stops beating.

It remained to enquire whether the hearts of Polish families were beating soundly. The practice of birth-control and abortion suggested that in some places they were beginning to falter.

No doubt most of the women at Kalwaria Zebrzydowska shared those views. Wojtyla was not telling them anything they did not know, but he brought his characteristic touch of poetry ('Woman is the heart of the family') to renew a familiar theme. The Polish attitude to women is one of chivalry. John Paul II has a special affection for Queen Jadwiga, a foundress of the Jagiellonian University. (Watch for her canonization.) He is certainly not opposed to the education of women, and women have played an important role in Polish Catholic intellectual life. But he starts from the theory of complementarity, allegedly the fundamental reason for their exclusion from the priestly ministry. There are God-given characteristics expressed through nature. And anyway, ordaining women is against tradition.

Since Wojtyla has a traditional view of womanhood and gives such a central place to the family, it should not be a matter for surprise that he also defends traditional sexual morality. Divorce and abortion – perhaps birth control is a different case – are odd ways of encouraging family life. The traditional view is not mere obscurantism. In a country where the Government aims at total social control through its monopoly of the mass media and the educational system, the family – along with its ally, the Church – remains one of the last bastions of freedom. At home you can pray, play Bach, think forbidden thoughts or say that Kazimierz Kakol (Poland's Minister for Religious Affairs) is an ass. The family represents in Poland the only available alternative society (again, along with the Church). This also helps to explain why Wojtyla has always laid great stress on the family as 'the domestic church' and as 'the school of a deeper humanity' (both phrases borrowed from Vatican II).

There is another reason why Polish bishops must be expected to defend traditional sexual morality: it is one of the points at issue in their conflict with the State. Since it is the State which claims to encourage feminine emancipation (though in practice this means merely the right to go out to work as well as running a home) and to permit or in some cases promote the feminist triad of divorce, birth-control and abortion, then the Church will inevitably tend to resist these developments and to do so in the name of both tradition and civilization. Why should the Church side with the opposition? Why should it do the devil's work for him? Its policy will be to hold on until such time as the unwisdom of the Government's positions becomes apparent to all.

So it is beyond question that John Paul II is deeply rooted in the experience of the Polish Church. To that Church he can speak with remarkable effectiveness. By that Church he has been fashioned. But an important qualification must be added. Despite the uniqueness of its experience, the Polish Catholic Church has always cherished the link with Rome, and through Rome with the universal Church. Certainly Poles have sometimes been impatient with the Vatican. Made to wait for over a week for an audience with Pope Pius XII, who absurdly suspected him of collusion with the Communists, Wyszynski said at a Rome press conference that if the Church in Poland was called 'the Church of silence', what he found in Rome was 'the Church of the deaf'. And Cardinal Wladislaw Rubin, secretary of the Synod of Bishops, once said that 'Rome needs Poland more than Poland needs Rome'. But these suspicions tended to vanish with a Pope as sympathetic to Poland as Paul VI was. (His first diplomatic mission had been to Poland in the early 1920s.)

The Polish bishops were not isolated. Their window on the wider world was the Second Vatican Council; unlike other East Europeans, they took a full part in it from the start. No Polish bishop was busier there or in the subsequent Synods than Wojtyla. That also implied that he was released, and seen to be released, from Polish narrowness.

It is the paradox with which this chapter began. One is inserted into the universal Church only through a local Church. One starts by being oneself, and then, only then, can one be open to others.

It is here that Wojtyla must be distinguished from Wyszynski. He was twenty years younger. He knew that to the outsider the Polish Church, with its crowded Masses, its vast pilgrimages, and its traditionalist approach to the questions that have agitated the Church elsewhere in the developed world, appeared old-fashioned and – a still more devastating charge – 'pre-conciliar'. He worked hard to rebut this charge, and did all he could to implement the Council in his Krakow diocese. The diocesan synod became a vast enterprise of adult education in which as many of the laity as possible were involved. That meant that he was not complacent. He accepted the conciliar teaching that 'the Church is always in need of purification' (*On the Church*, 8). Wyszynski's censors had once excised it from a book on the grounds that it came dangerously close to Luther's statement that the Church was in constant need of reform (*ecclesia semper reformanda*).

True, Wojtyla emphasized that implementing the Council was a matter of Christian renewal rather than *aggiornamento*. But that simply means that he was concerned with revivifying Christian life through the virtues of faith, hope and charity rather than with any programme of reform. The Polish Church never shared in the 'liberal agenda' developed elsewhere, which said that if only birth-control were permitted (on grounds of conscience), women and married men ordained, and the clerical caste put in its place, then all would be well in the Church. Wojtyla has not believed in the liberal agenda either. But that does not mean that he can be dismissed as 'pre-conciliar', for the same can be said of Paul VI.

What the Council meant for Wojtyla can be summed up in two essential attitudes: collegiality and a new style of leadership. The two are connected. He has been a man who listens, who believes that problems should not be put up to a higher level if they can be solved where they are, who values decentralization.

But that does not quite settle the matter. Another term of abuse that is frequently applied to the Polish Church is 'triumphalistic'. The triumphalist is secure in his faith. Doubt never enters his head. As for ecumenism, the triumphalist interprets it as weakness. ('Anglicans only began to be interested in ecumenism', said the late Archbishop Cyril Cowderoy of Southwark, 'when they discovered that their churches were empty.') Is the Polish Church triumphalistic? Once again a distinction needs to be made between Wyszynski and Wojtyla. Wyszynski enjoyed being triumphalistic. He adopted a haughty, aristocratic tone towards the Government, which he periodically lectured. He could not see the relevance of ecumenism to Poland. He was uninterested in liturgical reform, apparently believing that Polish peasants understood Latin. The 'kiss of peace', he suggested, turned the church into a salon. On all these points Wojtyla was more subtle. He believed that dialogue should replace confrontation, welcomed liturgical reform, and was committed to ecumenism (in so far as is possible in Poland, where partners in dialogue are hard to find). Year by year the octave of prayer for Christian unity was celebrated in his diocese. It was concluded by an *agape* or lovefeast in the Dominican church in Krakow in which the cardinal always took part. But the suspicion of triumphalism remains.

There is another way of looking at this question. The Polish experience of faith differs from that of Western Europeans and Americans. The Churches of Western Europe, and to a lesser extent of America, have been plagued in the past thirty years by feelings of guilt. They have been given to defeatism and breast-beating because they have 'lost the workers', failed to preach a relevant message to urban man, and scandalously exploited the third world. The Church in Germany has the added burden of knowing that its resistance to Hitler was, with heroic exceptions, feeble. The Polish Church, on the other hand, has none of these reasons for a sense of guilt. It has not lost the workers, despite a State ideology which presents them as 'new men' to be liberated from their superstitious past. It does not feel guilty about Third World countries, since – apart from the missionaries it has annually exported – it has not been allowed to have any contact with them. And its record of resistance to Hitlerism is unchallengeable. On the contrary, it has been a victim Church, and a victim Church that has somehow survived and flourished in face of terrible odds. This different experience produces a different psychology of faith. It issues in a faith that is serene, confident, unhampered by self-doubt; but it is saved from smugness because it has been tested in the crucible of persecution. This analysis (which was suggested by Halina Bortnowska) throws light on the spiritual attitudes of John Paul II.

One further question needs to be raised: why, after 455 years of Italian popes, a Polish pope? Why, that is, in the divine scheme of things, for it is part of Catholic doctrine that the Spirit continues to be at work in the Church (though not exclusively in the Church) and in particular through the Petrine office. Most of us would be content to leave such questions in the lap of mystery. But many Poles, including John Paul II himself, have pondered this particular riddle and suggested the outline of an answer.

Within four days of his election, John Paul II was writing a letter to the Polish people. At one point he addressed Wyszynski personally:

> Let me tell you quite simply what I think. In Peter's see today there would not be a Polish pope – that pope who begins a new pontificate full of awe but also full of confidence – were it not for your faith, which never feared prison and suffering, for your heroic hope, for your total confidence in the Mother of God, for Jasna Gora, and for that whole period of the Church in our motherland that has been associated with your ministry as bishop and primate.

The tribute to Wyszynski was sincere. But the thrust of the letter is to claim that it was the Polish experience itself which had somehow led to John Paul II's election. This experience was of exemplary value for the whole Church. In his election Poland itself was honoured.

He was yet more explicit in his remarks in Warsaw on Victory Square, when he had had time to meditate more deeply on the meaning of his election. He raised the question brutally, knowing that it would be in the minds of many of his hearers. Exactly why a pope from Poland? The whole passage is worth quoting:

> Leaving myself aside at this point, I must nevertheless ask along with you why, precisely in 1978, after so many centuries of a well-established tradition in this matter, a son of the Polish nation was called to the chair of St Peter. Christ demanded of Peter and the other apostles that they should be his 'witnesses in Jerusalem and in all Judaea and Samaria and to the end of the earth' (Acts

1.8). Recalling these words of Christ, have we not the right to think that Poland has today become the land of a specially responsible witness? The right to think that from here – from Warsaw, and also from Gniezno, from Jasna Gora, from Krakow and from the whole of this historic route that I have so often in my life taken and that it is right that I should take again during these days – one must proclaim Christ with humility but also with conviction? The right to think that one must come again to this very place, to this land, along this road, to read again the witness of his cross and resurrection?

Though put in the form of a series of questions and of no dogmatic value, this remarkable statement, when teased out, suggests that we have a Polish pope because the Polish nation has suffered in a terrible and unique manner. There was a deliberate echo of Luke 24.26 ('Was it not necessary that the Christ should suffer these things and enter into his glory?' – another question rather than a statement). In other words, John Paul II was suggesting that the sufferings of Poland were now compensated for by the election of a Polish pope. Centuries of humiliation and oppression were now put right.

This was an idea that would never occur to a non-Pole. But it was not uncommon in Poland. The 88-year-old Helena Szczepanska, who had known Karol Wojtyla as a baby and watched over his pram in her courtyard, expressed the same idea when, to her astonishment, she became a television star: 'This is our reward for so many sufferings, deportations, massacres, all the indescribable torments of the twentieth century. We have been rewarded for not having lost hope.'

The notion of the papacy as a reward may seem far-fetched and untheological. But the idea that Poland has an exemplary destiny, and that its appalling sufferings linked it in some mysterious way with the passion of Christ, is frequently found among the Polish romantic writers. Adam Mickiewicz came to believe that the experiences the Polish nation had undergone resembled the stations of the cross, and that the partition of Poland in 1795 could be compared to Christ's first day in the tomb, while the bloody crushing of a revolt in 1831 was the second day. Resurrection, which could only be hoped for, lay somewhere ahead.

3

Thoughts of the Heart

Wojtyla, then, thinks Polish. Polish history and culture have provided him with a stock of references and symbols by which he can illumine the present. This means that when he is addressing not merely Poles but the whole Church, and potentially the whole world, his language becomes more abstract and difficult. He cannot fall back on the symbols and images which have been his stock in trade. When he can no longer appeal to Our Lady of Czestochowa or to the experience of Auschwitz or to the Blessed Maximilian Kolbe (a priest who died there) or to St Stanislaw a certain air of abstraction creeps in to his treatment of Mary, or reconciliation, or the priesthood, or human rights.

But Wojtyla is also a philosopher by professional discipline. He has therefore given thought to the problems of language and communication. In his message for World Peace Day (1 January 1979) he has a characteristic passage on language:

> Language is made for expressing the thoughts of the heart and for uniting people. But when it is the prisoner of prefabricated formulas, in its turn it drags the heart along downward paths. One must therefore act upon language in order to act upon the heart and to avoid the pitfalls of language.

This may sound odd in Anglo-Saxon ears. What he means is that if our language habitually speaks of us and them, of insiders and outsiders, of group and class struggles, then we will be unable to perceive the world except through this distorting prism. As Wittgenstein said, 'The limits of my language are the limits of my world'. One of the tasks of the Church will be to make a new language – and therefore new perceptions – possible. John Paul II concludes this section: 'Leaders of the nations and of the international organizations will have to learn to find a new language, a language of peace: by its very self it creates new room for peace.'

Both these quotations have a quaint and abstract feel. They have been translated from the Polish in which the Pope thinks and writes: they may have passed through Italian or Latin. They make use of concepts that are unfamiliar to us. Yet to Wojtyla they are part of a highly developed intellectual synthesis that he has developed over the last thirty years. They recall articles published long ago. When he speaks of the heart, for example, he is not thinking sentimentally: he is evoking the biblical meaning of heart, which is continued in the Polish literary tradition. The heart means the human person on the deepest level. People are not disembodied intellects or ghostly wills. The heart is the ultimate in human personality. (Cardinal Newman was in the same tradition: his motto was *Cor ad cor loquitur* – 'Heart speaks to heart.')

Likewise the concept of 'making room' or 'leaving space' is one that recurs again and again in Wojtyla's poetry and philosophy. It represents his aspiration towards a life that is uncluttered, unencumbered, unconstrained – an aspiration towards freedom. No wonder he likes mountains. The image is filled out by others: opening windows, abolishing frontiers, not being afraid. It goes without saying that these images are not specially Polish. They are universal.

This characteristic vocabulary can best be made intelligible by setting it in the context of Polish culture and by examining his philosophy and poetry. There will be three stages in learning to understand it. How was Wojtyla influenced by Polish high culture? Is he a serious philosopher and what does he say? And finally, why should he bother to write poetry?

As an undergraduate he read Polish language and literature. His preferred authors were and remain the group of romantic poets who flourished in the nineteenth century: Adam Mickiewicz, Zygmunt Krasinski, Juliusz Slowacki, Aleksander Fredro and (increasingly) Cyprian Norwid, who influenced Wojtyla's own poetry. If Polish were as accessible a language as French, they would be as well known as Hugo or Baudelaire.

The Polish romantic poets differed among themselves, not surprisingly, but they had three features in common. They shared a concern for what another Slav, Feodor Dostoevsky, called 'those cussed eternal questions' – the meaning of life and death, the mystery of suffering and evil, the endless quest for redemption. They did not regard poetry as a merely aesthetic exercise. They anticipated the twentieth-century existentialists, who also grappled with fundamental problems of human existence. Secondly, they wanted their language to be above all an authentic expression of the soul or the heart. They were not embarrassed by feelings. The music of Chopin is a lyrical and musical confirmation of their attitudes. Finally, they were Polish nationalists who dreamed of the restoration of Poland to its people. This meant that they were at least culturally Catholic, even if their actual relationship with the Church might ebb and flow.

With the defeat and dismemberment of Poland in 1939, these writers became important once again. The Poles needed their romantic poets. For history seemed to be repeating itself, not as farce, but as an even more terrible tragedy. When John Paul II denounces 'ideologies', he is not talking about theories: he is speaking from his own painful experience of systems which claim to inaugurate a new man, an era of humanistic development, and yet in practice lead to tyrannies in which opponents are treated as non-persons. Under the Nazis the Poles were to be reduced to a slave-race. Intellectual and artistic activity was banned as unnecessary for so inferior a people.

In this context the theatre became a form of cultural resistance, a defiant declaration that Poles could think and feel for themselves. The Rhapsodic Theatre with which Wojtyla was associated, founded by his Wadowice friend Mieczyslaw Kotlarczyk, was partly an experimental form of the theatre in which the spoken word had priority over everything else; but it was also a way of keeping hope alive through the darkest days. Kotlarczyk has recalled the atmosphere of these clandestine performances before small groups of fifteen or twenty: 'Unforgettable Wednesdays and Saturdays, despite terror and arrests. The rehearsals of works by the greatest Polish poets went on, often in a dark, cold kitchen, sometimes with just a candle or two. But we firmly believed in our survival; we were sure we would reach the frontiers of freedom, always faithful to our idea of the theatre.'

The effects of Wojtyla's youthful passion for the theatre have been abiding. He learned to speak in public. (Sir John Gielgud, who happened to be filming in Poland during the Pope's visit, much admired his skill.) He learned to ponder the mystery of appearance and reality; the actor assumes a role and yet must remain himself (cf his poem 'The Actor'). He learned about the discipline required for effective theatre. He later wrote:

> The Rhapsodic Theatre needed great subordination of the actor to the dictates of the poetic word. This became particularly evident when the word expanded in fault-lessly delivered choral passages. A group of people unanimously, as it were, subjected to the poetic word has a sort of ethical significance: solidarity and loyalty to the word.

The theatre, moreover, was a way of proclaiming spiritual freedom, whatever regime happened to be in power. The Rhap-sodic Theatre had re-opened in public after the war, only to be closed down again in 1952, the year before Stalin's death. And the theatre was a gesture towards that Christian civilization of which the Polish romantics had dreamed. That dream still had point in post-war Poland. For now the options were sharp: the official State ideology of atheism, or Christianity. But in these new circumstances, it had to be a Christianity that was intellectually responsible and reputable. Nothing less than solid philosophical work could meet the new challenge.

This seems to have been what brought Wojtyla to the study of philosophy. The transition from the committed theatre of Kotlarczyk to philosophy was not difficult. Both activities were concerned with existential questions. Wojtyla does not seem to have been much concerned with Marxism, perhaps for the reason given by Leszek Kolakowski as long ago as 1957: Polish Marxism 'did not have any intellectual content but only an institutional content'. It was an instrument of power and social control rather than a serious interpretation of the world. Stalin had debauched Marxist language. But the Orwellian newspeak which pervaded Polish life raised acutely the age-old questions of moral philosophy to which Wojtyla began to turn his attention in the 1950s. What does it mean to be good? What is the good of good? What makes up authentic human action? And authentic language? These are the questions that dominate his philosophical thinking. Clearly they are not specifically Christian questions.

Any reflective person must ask them if he wants to get beyond what Socrates called 'the unexamined life'. Wojtyla's philosophical approach prepared and equipped him for dialogue with all men. It made him interested in the common ground that can be found among the most diverse people.

But he developed his personal philosophical style only gradually. Max Scheler, on whom Wojtyla wrote his second doctoral thesis, was a Catholic philosopher formed in the phenomenological school founded by Edmund Husserl. Husserl's slogan was 'Back to the Object' (*Zurück zum Gegenstand*). Phenomenology began as an attempt to overcome the idealism which had split the body from the mind. It tried to banish dualism by focusing as intensely as possible upon the objects thrown up by consciousness and discovering their inter-relatedness. It was a method rather than a doctrine (though some Husserlians quickly turned it into a dogma). That is precisely why it could prove fruitful in areas untouched by Husserl. Scheler had tried to apply the method to provide a basis for ethical theory.

Wojtyla enquired in his thesis whether Scheler had succeeded in providing a satisfactory basis for specifically Christian ethics, meaning the complex web of norms and values found in the New Testament. He concludes that Scheler fails; the thesis points out where. First, Scheler tries to construct his ethics on the perception of values and the appreciation of models (i.e. good people). But, says Wojtyla, that remains a purely theoretical position unless one recognizes that such an ideal embodiment of values actually exists and can be encountered; and the Gospels say that it does exist in the person of Christ. They present a practical ideal. Secondly, ethical values are grasped in Scheler through feelings and emotions, by intuition rather than by any rational process. Christ, Scheler suggests (following Pascal), is a 'genius of the heart' whose personality proves contagious and who strengthens the ethical dispositions found in all men. Wojtyla thinks this too subjective. Christ is not merely a 'genius of the heart' or a moral exemplar. His ethical teaching has content as well as style. It leads to the perception of an objective moral order and an objective moral good.

Thirdly, Scheler's system remains a general description of moral experience. It does not descend to details; it does not help in the solution of particular moral problems. Fourthly, 'conscience' in Scheler cannot provide any precise moral norms. His tendency to remain on the level of description leads him to exclude concepts such as commandments or rules and, in the end, duty. But, argues Wojtyla, there can be no morality at all without some sense of duty. Fifthly and finally, Scheler remains unclear on the relationship between morality and religion, and consequently between philosophy and theology. In a truly Christian system of ethics – which is what Wojtyla is looking for – there is an intrinsic link between morality and religion in the sense that an act is judged good or bad in so far as it is or is not a response to God's will.

So Wojtyla's overall judgement on Scheler is negative. Nevertheless this brush with modern philosophy did not prove fruitless. Wojtyla gathered from it a keen sense of the importance of values in moral philosophy, and concluded that his work had at least made clear 'the indispensable place of phenomenological experience in ethical studies.' The method of approach was right, even if the conclusions were not. He was able to agree with Paul Ricoeur, who said that 'rethinking Husserl' implies both 'thinking with and thinking against Husserl'.

Wojtyla's later book, *The Acting Person*, is nothing less than an attempt to rethink Husserl and to use the phenomenological method to do what Scheler had failed to do: provide a philosophical starting point for Christian ethics. Chapters were tried out at various philosophical congresses over the years. The work germinated and grew slowly, in dialogue with others. That says something about Wojtyla's tenacity of purpose: one can think of few other bishops who either have or make the leisure to engage in serious philosophical activity, if they read at all. (The late Cardinal John Heenan of Westminster once said that given the choice between reading a book or visiting a hospital, he would always visit the hospital.) Why did Wojtyla bother?

His own straightforward answer to this question is that he was impelled by a desire to understand men. 'Man' is one of those words that glow with a peculiar intensity in Wojtyla's writings. 'With what reverence the apostle of Christ pronounces the word "man" ', he said at the end of the sermon at his inauguration Mass. *The Acting Person* starts from the premise that although contemporary science has vastly extended the range of human knowledge, it does not seem to have deepened our understanding of man as a person: 'Having conquered so many secrets of nature, the conqueror must have his own mysteries ceaselessly unravelled anew' (p.21). To this Wojtyla adds a second motivation which has an almost Chestertonian flavour. The study of man is neglected, he suggests, because we take man for granted: 'He risks becoming too ordinary even for himself . . . . It was . . . to oppose the temptation of falling into the rut of habit that this study was conceived. It was born out of that wonderment at the human being which, as we know, initiates the first cognitive impulse' (p.22).

Moreover, although his philosophical work is not directly oriented towards theology, he explains that the sessions of the Second Vatican Council 'stimulated and inspired his thinking about the person'. He rejoiced in the conciliar statement that the Church cannot be bound to any particular political system, 'for she is at once a sign and a safeguard of the transcendence of the human person'. And he trusts that his own reflections will contribute towards solving 'the existential problems of man in the contemporary world' (p.22 and n.9).

The word 'existential' is important here. Despite the daunting technicality of some of his chapters, he is not concerned with abstract problems. He is not writing yet another book which is merely theories about theories. He will tackle directly what it means for a human, embodied person to act in the world. He is concerned with man's becoming (hence his constant use of the terms 'dynamic' and 'dynamism'), with the unfolding or realization of human potential.

The portrait of existential man in all his complexity builds up slowly in *The Acting Person*. Wojtyla's concern is to make a complete statement. This leads him to reject both idealism and materialism as partial statements which truncate man. He makes room for the body, the emotional life, thinking, the subconscious, the biological impulses of which we are so rarely conscious. All the time he is trying to say what specifies the human person. Ordinary language permits us to distinguish without difficulty between 'something' and 'somebody'. When we say 'somebody', we acknowledge that we are in the presence of a human person.

The human person is free and makes choices. In so doing he may be said to 'make himself', to become more lucid, more aware, more responsible. For Wojtyla the effect of human actions on the person is as important as their effect on the outside world. Once performed, they do not sink without trace. Decisions, made in the light of values, mark a person for life. One can trace here the origins of the value Wojtyla sets on commitment – whether in marriage or in priestly and religious life. As he says: 'Every authentic, whole-hearted "I will" actualizes the proper self-governance and self-possession of the person' (p. 147). Basic commitments also have an integrating role: they gather together the multiplicity of disparate acts. They bind a life together, give it coherence. Hence Wojtyla's emphasis on 'fidelity'.

The most fascinating chapter of *The Acting Person* is the last (unarrestingly called 'Inter-subjectivity by participation'). This is where he was heading all along the journey. This explains on a deeper level why he bothered. The starting point is simple enough: human persons do not live in isolation. The full meaning of human activity is not discovered until we recognize that 'man acts together with others'. Persons are only fully themselves in a community.

But 'acting together with others' can go wrong and become harmful to the person. Two extremes are to be avoided. 'Individualism' rejects social responsibility, drops out and concentrates on self-fulfilment or self-preservation; but it cannot be the way to true fulfilment as a human being. The opposite extreme is 'collectivism', which sets out to check and curb the person, to subject him to its norms, by coercion if need be; and that, too, damages the human person.

It is legitimate to translate these abstractions into political terms; and Wojtyla, without writing a treatise on political philosophy, provides a sketch for one. What he calls 'individualism' is the equivalent in political terms of *laissez-faire* liberalism, while 'collectivism' has taken the well-known forms of Nazism and Communism. What both these extreme positions overlook is that the human person requires society to fulfil himself; society must leave him enough room for his self-fulfilment. Lacking an authentic idea of 'acting together with others', they also lack the correlative idea of 'community', a form of social organization in which participation is taken seriously. By the same token they also lack any sense of the common good: individualism is not concerned with it, and collectivism has decided in advance what it is. But the common good always lies ahead and beyond. It is like a half-seen horizon towards which we must move, step by step, day by day, choice by choice.

What practical political attitudes result from these distinctions? Wojtyla suggests that both 'solidarity' and 'opposition' are needed as necessary components if persons are to be fulfilled. Solidarity means not evading social responsibility by dropping out, locking the door and letting the world go hang. Solidarity is both a duty imposed and a right to be claimed. But opposition is also a duty and a right. It is not cussedness, or a systematic refusal to play the game according to society's rules. It does not mean cutting oneself off from the community. On the contrary, those who oppose 'seek their own place and a constructive role in the community' (p.286). They want to draw attention to aspects of the common good that have been neglected or forgotten. Wojtyla gives the example of parents whose views on education differ from those put forward by the State. In all this he is defending what the French *nouveaux philosophes* call the right to interrupt and interject. The answer to 'Big Brother is watching you' is 'But we are watching Big Brother' (the principle behind Charter 77 in Czechoslovakia, set up to monitor infringements of the Helsinki agreements on human rights as signed by the Soviet Union).

Wojtyla's grappling with the problem of solidarity and opposition (which he tactfully refrains from calling dissidence) no doubt reflects his own experience of living under a Communist Government in Poland. He does not wish to abdicate his responsibility for what was happening in Polish society (solidarity); but the right to differ from the official ideology is also asserted (opposition). From this particular experience he draws a criterion by which any society may be judged: 'The structure of a human community is correct only if it admits not just the presence of a justified opposition but also that practical effectiveness of opposition required by the common good and the right of participation' (p.287). In other words toleration of dissidents (opposition) is the first stage; but they have also a right to be involved in the decision-making process.

This principle is the more justified by the ways in which solidarity and opposition can go wrong and thus become 'inauthentic'. When the personalistic basis of solidarity is forgotten, when belonging to society is no longer a matter of free and renewable choice, then solidarity slumps to the level of mere conformity. Wojtyla might almost have a particular Communist bureaucrat in mind in his excellent paragraph on conformity:

> If it still denotes man's assimilation with the other members of a community, it does so only in an external and superficial sense, in a sense devoid of the personal grounds of conviction, decision and choice. Thus conformism consists primarily in an attitude of compliance or resignation, in a specific form of passivity that makes the man-person to be but the subject of *what happens* instead of being the *actor* or *agent* responsible for building his own attitudes and his own commitment in the community. Man then fails to accept his share in constructing the community and allows himself to be carried with and by the anonymous majority (p.289, author's italics).

Conformity, in short, is a surrender to the prevailing climate of opinion. It is set against the 'surrender to the perceived good' which Wojtyla has defined as the essence of morality. He does not discuss the motives which lead to conformity, but clearly it represents the easy and most advantageous option. 'Opportunist', a Polish academic said recently, 'is the dirtiest word in our language.'

It is not difficult to see how the principle of solidarity can thus go wrong. But how does opposition become inauthentic? It happens, says Wojtyla, when it goes beyond the right to interrupt and becomes an attitude of systematic non-involvement and non-commitment. Such an attitude might be justified, he concedes, as a form of protest in desperate situations, 'but even if there are valid reasons to justify its being adopted by the individual these same reasons become an accusation of the community insofar as it has caused it' (p.291). We may translate: if I have been driven into this position by the State's denying me any right to participate in society, then the State shares the blame for turning my legitimate right of dissent into outright rejection.

But Wojtyla does not conclude *The Acting Person* with a catalogue of woe. He concludes positively with a vision of what could happen when people 'act together' authentically. Then they would discover, he says, that the other is their neighbour. The evangelical commandment of love is mentioned not as an argument from authority (which would have no place in a philosophical work) but because it reflects a general human truth: to love my neighbour as myself presupposes that I can only fulfil myself in the love and service of others who share with me a common humanity, a common personhood. Wojtyla's *envoi* is the suggestion, profoundly un-Marxist, that the deepest form of alienation is to be found in a lack of neighbourliness and in the end a lack of love. The feeling of alienation cannot be ascribed simply to 'man's relationship to nature, the system of production and distribution of material goods, the blind pursuit of progress' (p.297). It lies deeper than that.

So Wojtyla's work as philosopher bears directly on his thought as pope. He may have left philosophy behind, in the professional sense, but it is the author of *The Acting Person* who also wrote the encyclical *Redemptor Hominis*. Many of the obscurer passages in the encyclical take on their full meaning only in the light of his previous work. His reflections on 'alienation' in *Redemptor Hominis* (section 15), puzzling in isolation, become clear if seen as a development of what he says in chapter 7 of *The Acting Person*. Even more Husserlian and 'personalistic' in tone is the language used in section 14 of the encyclical, where we read that 'each man is all the unrepeatable reality of what he is and what he does', and that man 'writes this personal history of his through numerous bonds, contacts, situations, and social structures linking him with other men'.

Cardinal Heenan used to have an imaginary interlocutor called Mrs Murphy of Manor Park. What would she make of all this? No doubt she is simply happy that the Holy Father exists and smiles, and is not much concerned about what he actually says. But there is a problem of communication within the Church. It flows from having a pope who is a genuinely independent thinker, whatever the content of his thinking. Professor Michael Dummett of Oxford – whose philosophical and Catholic credentials are unimpeachable – is not altogether happy with the late-Husserlian philosophical style adopted by Karol Wojtyla. It proceeds by pronouncement rather than by argument, it is sparing of examples, it fails to state rival positions and to give the reasons why they are unacceptable. It is thus unnecessarily obscure. That does not mean that it is mistaken. The praiseworthiness of Wojtyla's philosophical aims can be acknowledged. Philosophy often utters simple truths in complicated terms. But Wojtyla's practice does raise the question of whether the Church has to learn Husserlian language in order to understand its Pope.

The answer must be no. The Roman Catholic Church has not gone phenomenological just because the Pope happens to be interested in that philosophical approach. Beyond the immediate problem of communication, though, complicated by difficulties of exact translation and perhaps even further by journalistic attempts at crisp summary, lies the more serious problem of the relationship between philosophy and theology. The two are always in dialogue. The classic example is St Thomas Aquinas, who in the thirteenth century took over Aristotle and incorporated many Aristotelian ideas into his all-embracing Christian synthesis (with some help from the Arabs). Twentieth-century theologians have often been urged to 'do for x what Aquinas did for Aristotle', where x stands for Marx or Heidegger or Wittgenstein. In Wojtyla, x equals Husserl.

This puts him out on a theological limb. But it also permits him to acknowledge the importance and the validity of attempts to enter into dialogue with other philosophers. In *Redemptor Hominis* he speaks of 'a certain pluralism of methodology' which leaves room for many different approaches (19). What is important is that he should have seen his task as a Catholic philosopher as something more than simply repeating Thomist theses in traditional language. His professors at the Angelicum had been content with that kind of repetition; he broke away from it. He grapples with Husserl and Scheler to find a modern language for the preliminaries of faith and to release theological language from being a ventriloquist discourse echoing round an ivory tower. In a Poland dominated by official Marxist philosophy, he shows that there is an alternative way of philosophizing that Christians do not have to fear. His method could be applied to other contemporary 'partners in dialogue'.

A different approach to *The Acting Person* is also possible. One can look not merely at the individual theologian's choice of a partner in dialogue, but at what this particular choice tells us about the man. Wojtyla was drawn to the Husserlian style because it helped him personally and enabled him to 'integrate' all the different aspects of his life. He was 'driven on', spurred by that 'internal dynamism' he finds in the human person; and at the same time he was 'drawn' by the values of truth and goodness which he sees as bounding the human horizon and pointing beyond it. Moreover, both the push and the pull, the drive and the attraction, are part of the process of becoming a truly integrated person. He is all of a piece with his personalistic philosophy. He is not afraid of the body, not alarmed by what the subconscious may throw up, keenly aware of the way responsible, interpersonal decisions and commitments are arrived at. He will keep his word. There will be no gap between private convictions and public image.

His personalistic philosophy, finally, teaches him openness to the new along with fidelity to commitments, a willingness to follow the evidence (his chief reason for rejecting or disregarding Marxism is that it does not obey this principle), and a readiness to learn from experience in an ever-renewed surrender to truth. For all these reasons it is difficult to say that his thought is merely conservative.

There is another way of checking the application of Wojtyla's thought to his life. He wrote poems. Once more, they are all of a piece with *The Acting Person*, even though many of them precede it by almost twenty years. In an obvious sense, poetry and philosophy are contrasting or even opposed activities: philosophy takes the long way round, makes claims to rigorous rationality, is not afraid of lengthy exposition and development; poetry works more directly and intuitively through image and evocation. The interesting thing is that Wojtyla should have been impelled to write poetry at all. It is as though the very inadequacy of the philosophy, the sense that all is straw, gives birth to the poems. One of his poems (in *Easter Vigil*, p.23) is called precisely 'Thought's resistance to words'. It is worth giving in full, since it rehearses many of the themes of *The Acting Person*.

Sometimes it happens in conversation: we stand
facing truth and lack the words,
have no gesture, no sign;
and yet – we feel – no word, no gesture
or sign would convey the whole image
that we must enter alone and face like Jacob.

This isn't mere wrestling with images
carried in our thoughts;
we fight with the likeness of all things
that inwardly constitute man.
But when we act can our deeds surrender
the ultimate truths we presume to ponder?

It is difficult to judge poetry in translations, even good ones.
(These are by Professor Jerzy Peterkiewicz of London
University.) The best course will be to consider the patterns and
clusters of images that recur, in whatever version. 'Man' is in
the foreground of Wojtyla's poetry, described, addressed,
apostrophized. Once again, as in the philosophy, man is seen in
all his dimensions, and three successive poems bring out the perils
of one-sidedness ('Man of emotion', 'Man of intellect' and 'Man
of will'). But 'we never see spirit – eye mirrors thought' (p.53),
and so Wojtyla concentrates on the bodily manifestations of
spirit: 'the shoulder's tension' in work, the profile, the eyes (tired,
reddened, fever-shot), the hands. He sees the body as sculpted
gradually through work, action and choices: 'Hands are the
heart's landscape' (p.26).

But man here is seen in precise settings. He is poised between
alienation and participation. The worker in the car factory, for
example (p.40), is robbed of the fruit of his labours; he cannot
find meaning for his life in the 'smart new models' he turns out:

I am not with them at the controls
on sleek motorways; the policeman's in charge.
They stole my voice; it's the cars that speak.

But like the weary typist and the armaments factory worker, the
car worker and the other 'alienated' characters who appear in
Wojtyla's poems are potentially related to Simon of Cyrene, who
helped Jesus carry his cross. They can enter another dimension,

find 'heart-space', be caught up in the brightness of sunlight and flashing water that is never far away. They can glimpse 'participation'. The third section of 'The quarry', a long poem which reflects Wojtyla's wartime experience of work, is called 'Participation' (p.31), and it ends:

> There is silence again between heart, stone and tree.
> Whoever enters Him keeps his own self.
> He who does not
> has no full part in the business of this world
> despite all appearances.

But this reference to God is not presented as a complacent 'solution', as though the pious young Polish priest-poet had already fully realized the lines of St John of the Cross: 'You have gone out into everything I love, And everything I love has come to rest in You'. There is tension in some of the poems, and it is not easily resolved. 'The quarry' (p.29) shows outrage and compassion in conflict. What is the truly human response to man's inhumanity to man? To learn from anger, he says,

> Your speech must not break at the lever's tension:
> the fulcrum of anger and love.

There will be no cheating, no manipulation, no feigning noble sentiments not yet possessed. The conclusion of the poem — 'The greater the anger, the higher the explosion of love' (p.33) — is not an empty formula but a hard-won conquest. 'The quarry' is a remarkable poem about work, its dignity and indignity, about suffering and pain, about children and the future, about the difficult victory of love. The explosive charges in the quarry are used to evoke the energy which charges the whole universe.

The same image is picked up again ten years later in 'The birth of confessors', (p.52), where images of force, energy, mountain streams, electric currents and dynamism flow organically together. The first section of the poem is called 'A bishop's thoughts on giving the sacrament of confirmation in a mountain village'. For Wojtyla, confirmation is a release of the energy of the Holy Spirit. What he writes here gives us some understanding of his idea of the ministry:

The world is charged with hidden energies
and boldly I call them by name.
No flat words; though ready to leap
they don't hurtle like mountain water on stones
or flash past like trees from sight . . .

I am a giver, I touch forces that expand the mind;
sometimes the memory of a starless night
is all that remains.

'I touch forces that expand the mind': the continuity of Wojtyla, the all-of-a-piece quality already noted, is admirably expressed by that phrase. Everything he has done, philosophy, poetry, ministry, is directed towards the same end: that of helping man to grasp the full dimensions of his existence. He is an enabler.

English readers may see a parallel with Gerard Manley Hopkins ('The world is charged with the grandeur of God'), though there is no question of direct influence. Polish critics trace the influence of Cyprian Norwid. The English poet, Peter Levi, writes of Wojtyla's poetry: 'It is quite unlike socialist poetry, and it is perfectly modern, courageous, individual' (*The Tablet*, 7 April 1979, p.346).

The doggedness of Wojtyla – another word for it is fidelity – throughout his life is striking. In his youth he had a dream: there would be a Catholic renaissance in which poetry, the theatre, the novel and philosophy would all make their contribution to a new and modern synthesis of faith and art. This dream was found elsewhere in Europe and America in the 1930s and 1940s. In France, Paul Claudel, François Mauriac and Georges Bernanos (not to mention the half-American Julien Green) showed that Catholicism could inspire plays and novels which the secular world had to take account of. Etienne Gilson and Jacques Maritain were Catholic philosophers whose work appeared in lay journals. England had Graham Greene and Evelyn Waugh. Germany had Gertrud von le Fort and Edith Stein, a Carmelite nun who had been a pupil of Husserl and who died in Dachau. Faced by the totalitarianisms of Hitler and Stalin, Catholicism seemed a viable intellectual option. Wojtyla's version of the Catholic renaissance had of course a Polish nuance, but it was not narrow.

The Second World War drove the dream underground but at the same time made it more necessary than ever. Polish intellectual life was officially abolished. In particular, the clergy were to be given special attention. 'Priests will preach what we want them to preach', said an order from Hitler to Hans Frank, his Governor General in Poland, on 2 October 1939, 'and if any priest acts differently, we will make short work of him; the task of a priest is to keep the Poles quiet, stupid and dull-witted.' The whole vocation of Wojtyla can be seen as a rebuttal of that suggestion. For him the task of a priest would be to keep Poles intellectually alive and alert. 'I touch forces that expand the mind' takes its origin here. In post-war Poland the same task remained equally urgent. Wojtyla's vision of a Christian culture (the cultivation of the whole man – body, mind, heart, feelings) was denied all public expression. What went under the name of culture had to serve narrowly political ends.

Meanwhile, elsewhere in the Church, dreams of a Catholic renaissance had largely evaporated. The difference can be measured in the different response to two encyclicals: *Humani Generis* in 1950 and *Humanae Vitae* in 1968. *Humani Generis* was a condemnation of what was then known as 'the new theology' associated with French Jesuits and Dominicans. Theologians like Henri de Lubac and Yves Congar were forbidden to teach. (Twelve years later they became experts at the Council.) Catholic intellectuals were shocked and shaken, but they did not protest. They discovered hidden wisdom in the encyclical: for the moment they could not quite state it, but it no doubt existed. *Humanae Vitae*, on the other hand, aroused a storm of protest. That was not merely because its subject – contraception – was of more immediate concern to lay-people than the theological deviations denounced by *Humani Generis*: it was because the whole notion of 'being a Catholic' had changed. A typical remark from the Catholic renaissance period was that of Bernanos: 'The Church does not need reformers but saints.' But by 1968 being a committed Catholic often meant having an agenda for reform – an attitude stimulated by the Vatican Council.

A bishop in Poland, Wojtyla was fully committed to the implementation of Vatican II. At the same time, many of his attitudes seem to derive from the Catholic renaissance mentality:

his confident, non-breastbeating faith, his optimism, his tendency to brush aside talk of crisis, and above all his priorities. For him the most urgent priority is that Christians should realize in their lives the mystery of Christ, the Second Adam. He is concerned with faith, hope and charity, these three. The questions which have agitated the Church in the post-conciliar period seem less important. That is why, suddenly and unexpectedly emerging as pope in 1978, he bursts on to the world scene as both an anachronistic and a challenging figure. He can be made to serve nostalgia or to boost hope.

4
Santidad

A country with certain marked similarities to Poland is Mexico. It is a country where religion is outlawed. It is nevertheless a country where popular Catholicism, centred on Mary, spreads wide and deep. Partly for that reason, it is a country where the Catholic Church bears its part in resisting a hard-faced regime. Chance offered Mexico as the new Pope's first point of pilgrimage; and he did not refuse.

It was no bad place to start. Mexico could stand for Latin America, and Latin America for a suffering world. In Central and South America live somewhere near half the world's Catholics; and most of that half is in misery. Unfairness in the distribution of wealth, a recent analysis claims, has actually increased under the influence of agrarian and industrial conglomerates; and this inequity is maintained both by violence from the forces of order and through state control of education and the media.

That analysis was published in January 1979 not by a sociologist or a politician but by a cardinal: Paulo Evaristo Arns. Arns is a Franciscan who is archbishop of the world's largest diocese, with nine million souls – Sao Paulo in Brazil. With ordinary opposition voices stifled, the chief critics of authoritarian Latin American governments – in Chile, in El Salvador, in Ecuador, in Nicaragua – have been churchmen. The intellectual basis of their criticism has been the theology of liberation.

Liberation theology began in the 1960s as an attempt to give Christian doctrine meaning for the Latin American poor. Salvation was expressed in terms of liberation; the sin chiefly aimed at was social sin – oppression, injustice. Liberation theologians argued that if you sat where the poor sat, you would read the Bible with a fresh eye. Moses would be rediscovered as a political leader, the *Magnificat* as a manifesto. God would be found to be on the side of the poor: to see him as the guarantor of an unjust social system was to turn him into an idol which deserved to be smashed.

Many of these ideas, and the language which clothes them, are borrowed from Marxism. Certain liberation theologians identify the Gospel poor with Marx's proletariat. They talk of class war. They deploy the standard Marxist argument for violence: that it is needed to counterbalance the built-in violence of unjust societies. They insist, though, that theirs is a critical Marxism. Into Marxist orthodoxy they introduce the idea of reconciliation; but it is a reconciliation which will come only after the revolution. They commonly explain that while they accept Marx's critique of capitalism, they reject his atheism.

Liberation theology is more than merely academic. The practitioners are already down in the dust of the arena. In particular they foster institutions which they call *communidades eclesiales de base* – basic church communities. Arns, who has founded hundreds, defines them as 'families which in general live together and have a community centre: they meet there to consider what they can do in common – but always in the Gospel spirit'. A new society, even a new Church, is to be built from the ground up. There are believed to be about 100,000 such communities in Latin America as a whole. Gustavo Gutierrez, the man who gave liberation theology its name, organizes them throughout the suburbs of Lima, in Peru. Leonardo Boff, a Brazilian theologian to the left of Gutierrez, says: A commitment to faith must have its political manifestation. My experience of this has been the basic communities, which reflect the word of God but also have a political aspect – political in the sense of a search for a juster society.'

Many bishops, notably in Brazil, contend that this is ordinary and indeed inescapable pastoral activity. 'Do you think I have any choice but to accept the basic communities?' asks a Brazilian bishop with 86 priests for over two million people. Many politicians, on the other hand, see the communities as nests of subversion; and the forces of order take their line from the politicians. Arns compiled a long list of attacks by the authorities, in Brazil alone, during the decade 1968-78, on the priesthood: arrests, torturings, assassinations, kidnappings, trials, expulsions, intimidations, threats of death, together with irruptions into church buildings and censorship of church publications. In El Salvador, the Inter-American Human Rights Commission found that the Catholic Church was being 'systematically persecuted': and Archbishop Oscar Arnulfo Romero offered supporting evidence of priests regularly killed by the police.

That extremism is matched by extremism on the other side. The memory of Camillo Torres, the Colombian priest killed fighting as a guerrilla in the jungle, is still very much alive. In the early part of 1979, priests were fighting with the guerrillas in Colombia, Nicaragua and Argentina.

Not by any means all ecclesiastics in Latin America, still less in Rome, have been happy with this departure from the Church's ancient tradition of political quietism. The theology of liberation which underpinned the change had been first aired at a conference of Latin American bishops at Medellin, in Colombia, in 1968. The conference had been opened by Pope Paul VI; and he had dealt with the issue with careful even-handedness. But the bishops had broadly endorsed the new approach. In the decade that followed, fresh military regimes were established, and certain of the clergy had been further radicalized. The argument had grown louder, the division deeper. A successor conference to Medellin was arranged for 1978 at Puebla de los Angeles, a hill town in Mexico. Again it was to be attended by the pope. It was delayed by two popes' successive deaths; but at last a new date was set. The gathering was to be inaugurated by John Paul II at the end of January 1979.

The Puebla conference was therefore a highly significant occasion. Events in Latin America had re-involved the Catholic Church there in one of the oldest dilemmas of Christianity: how far should it maintain that 'the powers that be are ordained of God', even when they were unscrupulous; to what extent should it try to change them, especially if that called for unscrupulous means? Radical churchmen hoped that Puebla would provide a ringing and conclusive endorsement of liberation theology; and they hoped that the lead would be given by the new Pope himself. Conservative theologians, on the other hand, looked to see liberation theology snubbed. Their leader among Latin American bishops was Alfonso Lopez Trujillo, a Colombian bishop who was secretary general of the conference; and he was backed at the

Vatican by Cardinal Sebastiano Baggio, president of the pontifical commission for Latin America and one of the conference's co-presidents.

The two sides were evenly matched. In a preliminary skirmish, Lopez Trujillo and Baggio produced a preparatory document for Puebla which was dominated by the fear of the Church's incurring further persecution. It condemned Marxism as much as unfettered capitalism, and showed a certain sympathy with military regimes: their ideology could be 'abusive', but they had come into existence 'as a response to social and political chaos'. The liberation men, furious, declared the document an insult to the seven hundred martyrs of the past ten years. The protest was influential enough to elicit a revised version which met some of the criticisms.

The Pope's weight in one side of the scale or the other could clearly be decisive. The judgement of Puebla would be crucial to the future relation of Church and State in Latin America. It could determine Catholicism's future even more widely: John Paul II, reflecting on the high proportion of the world's problems concentrated in the region, quoted early in his pontificate and with approval the observation that 'the future of the Church will be decided in Latin America'. And Puebla would set an ineradicable mark on the new man's own papacy. It was his first sortie from Italy; it would be the occasion of his first important public statement; and nobody knew which side he would come down on.

On 25 January he left Rome. Pausing for a few hours in the Dominican Republic, in the West Indies, he was to fly on to Mexico City. One of his first calls there was to be at the country's most noted shrine.

At midnight on the eve of the Pope's arrival, the sanctuary of the Virgin of Guadelupe in Mexico City was already ringed with policemen and milling with people. Beyond the gates and the police checks, both the old and the new sanctuaries looked out on the darkness. The picture of the Virgin of Guadelupe – magically imprinted, the belief goes, on the blanket of a Mexican Indian she appeared to – no longer hangs in the sixteenth-century basilica; it has been transferred across the esplanade to a spacious new concrete building, circular, split-level, and looking like a sports centre. There is even a conveyor-belt to ensure a fast flow of pilgrims past the modest-looking picture of the miraculous Virgin. The old shrine is threatened with subsidence, and it now stands alarmingly askew, a deep crack running down its facade.

Inside, the old church was full of bright lights, music and voices. Men were playing guitars and shaking maracas, while the rest of the crowd prayed, sang and sometimes wept. Leading the prayers were two priests. From inside, the basilica seemed even more crooked than from outside; its old chandeliers hung out of true, and concrete pillars had been put in to hold it up. There were people sitting on the steps of the altar, and on either side were the carved wooden seats built for the canons. Nearby stood a large white marble statue of a dead dignitary. To the visitor pressing a little closer there suddenly appeared, standing amongst the seats, a life-size image of John Paul II – his arms wide open, a rosary in his hands, and smiling at the humble worshippers praying around him. He looked as if he might speak at any moment; the wax image, with its real red robes, seemed strangely lifelike near the white stone of the statue. In a din of music and a burble of voices the service proceeded. Mexico was greeting its pontiff.

The next day it was one o'clock on the dot when John Paul II stepped out of his plane into the bright sunshine and rarefied air of Mexico City. The airport had been closed all day to other air traffic. Three thousand Mexicans were packed into two specially built platforms, and even President José Lopez Portillo had thrown Mexico's ferociously anti-clerical traditions to the winds and was waiting on the tarmac with his wife. No sooner was the Pope's sturdy white figure framed in the orange door of the Aeromexico DC-10 than a full-scale *mariachis* band – traditional local musicians – swung into the great Mexican favourite, *'Cielito Lindo'* ('pretty little sky', addressed to a young woman). It was a cliché, but nobody cared. This pontifical tour was to be the greatest show, the biggest fiesta ever.

John Paul II's sense of spectacle proved equal to his hosts'. He stalked down the gangway and fell on his hands and knees to kiss Mexican soil. (It had become a traditional gesture. He had done it the day before in the Dominican Republic; Paul VI had done the same at Medellin. But it never failed of its effect.) Just as he bent down a gust of wind caught his white cape and blew it unexpectedly over his face. Helpers rushed forward; soon the Holy Father, disentangled, was beaming at the cheering crowds, the sombreroed band, the President, the first lady and her bouquet of red roses.

The President did not stay long. He welcomed the 'distinguished visitor' and left. That was the highest dignity the Pope could be received in; not as a head of State. He had come to the one Latin American country which constitutionally forbids 'religious propaganda'. Acknowledging no church, Mexico does not recognize the Vatican.

The Pope was left to the welcome of his bishops. They were in black trousers, in contrast to his long white robes; Mexican law forbids all priests and nuns to wear religious habits outside consecrated ground. The Pope himself had been granted special dispensation to travel about the country in his pontifical robes. Within minutes, the nodding bishops were overwhelmed by a crowd of photographers and the faithful. The Pope's small white skull-cap almost disappeared in the throng. While policemen did what they could to disengage him, Bishop Paul Marcinkus, the Vatican's athletic Chicago-born chief of finances, threw himself into the fray and began shoving back the crowd by main force.

John Paul II found time to distribute innumerable blessings, kiss two small children and try on a Mexican sombrero. They were routines of which he never tired: during his tour he repeated the scene for the benefit of dozens of Mexican infants and tried on every possible sort of headgear. Nor did he turn a hair when asked to board the strange vehicle which was to carry him in triumph through Mexico City. It looked like a single-decker bus with the roof sawn off; the radiator was draped in Vatican yellow and white for the occasion. (Elizabeth II of England had already ridden in it on her State visit to Mexico in February, 1975; and the Pope himself had only lately been gliding about the Dominican Rebublic in a canopied snow-white golf cart.) He took up his position standing behind the driver, with a metal bar to lean on, while his entire retinue of twenty was accommodated in the rows of seats behind. The machine sailed incongruously down the Mexican highways like a barge down the Grand Canal.

Before the grand motorcade could get fully under way the

atmosphere at the airport was briefly spoilt by a scuffle round the two open trucks laid on to accommodate the press. They turned out to be hopelessly inadequate. More than a thousand journalists had been accredited to follow the Pope. Official passes and allocated places were ignored as the trucks were stormed by photographers and cameramen. Even a few amateurs with their Instamatics leapt on for the ride. The scene became hysterical when the police fired a couple of tear gas grenades at the trucks. In the subsequent confusion a photographer for Associated Press was led away, visibly in pain. Later in the day the police made it clear that their heavy boots and long truncheons, too, were not just for show. Thirty people, including several journalists, had to be treated by the first-aid attendants in the cathedral square.

A hundred thousand policemen and soldiers had been mobilized for the Pope's visit, including a thousand snipers strategically placed on rooftops – not to speak of the twenty helicopters patrolling the city. Two thousand doctors and six thousand auxiliaries manned first aid posts. Altogether it was a tremendous outlay for a secular State to provide on the occasion of a visit from a religious leader.

Preceded by motorcyclists riding in formation, flanked by young policemen in black suits and running shoes who trotted beside him all the way, and followed by another bus and several limousines, the Pope entered Mexico City at a stately pace. Pictures of the entire visit were being broadcast live on two separate television channels, with the compliments of Banamex and Bancomer, Mexico's biggest banks; but it seemed to make no difference to the crowds. Everybody wanted to see '*el Santo Padre*' in the flesh. The sheer numbers were daunting. Mexico City has twelve million inhabitants, and some two million more visitors had poured into town. The traveller from old Europe could hardly help being struck by the number of young people. Half the population of Mexico is under fifteen. The Pope, who loves children, was followed the whole way by a horde of them, all running as close to his open vehicle as they could get.

Every inch of the road from the airport to the city centre was lined with cheering, waving crowds. It was a continuous shout of '*Viva el Papa*!', a shower of confetti and fresh flowers, a wall of outstretched hands and eager faces. As he moved slowly through the streets on his chariot, the white, open-armed figure seemed to be repeating a mythical return – the return of Quetzalcoatl, the legendary Aztec god who was to sail back from the east and come into his own here in this upland capital. The white Pope brought his own *mysterium* with him. 'Welcome John Paul II, representative of Christ on earth', ran some of the posters. There were photographs of the Pope, and yellow and white flags, tied to every house; there were more people crammed into every balcony, perched on every rooftop. John Paul II, standing throughout the trip, tried to acknowledge them all. He seemed astonished, moved and delighted.

Visitors to Mexico City are always advised to take it easy in their first few days. The high altitude can induce dizziness or a thumping of the heart. The Mexicans call it *la turista*. Would the Pope, people wondered, be immune to *la turista*? By the time he had reached the splendid sixteenth-century cathedral built by the conqueror Hernando Cortés on the site of the Aztec pyramid of the sun, John Paul II was beginning to show signs of fatigue. Once inside he made his way only slowly to the altar, as many of the four thousand guests clapped and women in black lace mantillas tried to kiss his hands. Later, while the archbishop made his welcoming speech, the Pope's head was bowed; he seemed to be breathing with difficulty. Next to him stood the Vatican's schoolmasterly chief of protocol, Monsignor Virgilio Noè, always ready to adjust the pontifical vestments or whisper a reminder in the pontifical ear.

Outside, two hundred thousand people were massed in the grandiose Zocalo Square. It had been laid out by Cortés as a worthy centre to an empire which then stretched from Panama to Vancouver. The entire square was a sea of heads. Some of the people there had spent the night on the cold paving-stones so as to catch a glimpse of the Pope and hear him say Mass. Most of them were poorly dressed; children in frayed trousers and bare feet scuttled between their legs. A man with no buttons on his shirt was selling photographs of the Pope at ten pesos each – double the price on previous days. Large numbers of nuns, taking advantage of the Government's temporary tolerance of all things religious, had turned out in veils and habits. A young man peered through a carefully made cardboard periscope at the carved stonework of the cathedral's main door, through which the Pope had just passed.

The Mexicans were waiting for the Pope to address them for the first time. Though they would only hear his voice over the loudspeakers, it would be the voice of *su Santidad,* his Holiness himself, who had come all the way from Rome and had passed in front of their eyes. 'You are Peter!', they had chanted; innumerable crucifixes had been held up to be blessed as he came near them.

It seemed to mean little to them that this pope was Polish. Any pope was already an infinitely exotic figure. For others, however, a Polish pope was an event of definite political significance. The anti-Communist lobby was congratulating itself even before the Pope had arrived. 'He will leave the Marxist priests standing in their underpants', ran one newspaper headline. How could a pope who had suffered Communist persecution for thirty years, argued the paper's editorial, fail to be a sworn enemy of Communism and Marxism? In the cathedral square itself a large banner had been stretched above the heads of the crowds: '*Marxismo no*', it read. It was a reminder of the central dispute which the Pope had come to adjudicate.

Once he had begun talking, seated in front of the resplendent baroque altar, he no longer showed signs of fatigue. His voice rang out in a speech devoted above all to Mexico's patron, the Virgin of Guadelupe, and to the significance of Mary's religious example – all of it read in perfectly pronounced Spanish. He raised a cheer by extending the Polish motto, '*Polonia semper fidelis*', to Mexico: '*Mexico siempre fiel*' – words which by the end of his visit had become a regular chorus.

In this first speech there was already more than a hint of what the Pope's instruction to his Latin American bishops would be. He deplored theological 'deviations'. There was no such thing as a 'new Church', he told his listeners; following Vatican II the Church 'has new aspects, but is still essentially the same'. Further-more, he said, in a clear reference to one of the key tenets of the theology of liberation, the Church is not born 'from the people'. Along with fidelity to the papacy, he demanded that the Catholics of Latin America should subscribe to his own version of the re-lationship: it was the Church which must build a people who wished to grow in faith, hope and fraternal love. Liberation theology was turned on its head: the people were to be born from the Church.

A papal blessing was read out on the cathedral steps: the papal truck was in motion once more; the police on their Harley Davidsons took up their positions in a roar of engines, their blue lights flashing. The crowd began to scatter down the empty streets. Many of the women and girls wore yellow and white: they had put together anything they could – T-shirts, skirts, trousers – just to be able to wear the Vatican colours in honour of the Pope. They milled past Sanbourn's, a department store where a pair of nail-scissors costs a day's ordinary wage. Inside, a very different crowd of people was drinking at the soda fountain. Further on a young man in rags played a solitary trumpet while a silent doll-like baby girl with a thatch of black hair nursed his hat on the pavement.

An entire floor of a first-class hotel had been turned into the press centre for the Pope's visit, again by courtesy of Banamex (which includes the Vatican among its shareholders). Officially the Government was washing its hands of the entire event. Accreditations were in the hands of the conference. Flanked by numerous young Banamex ladies dressed in black, white and yellow, but quite unprepared for the task, one priest and three or four nuns (all in plain clothes) tried to cope with the demands of a thousand journalists. It took six hours to get accredited. No queue lasted for more than half an hour, inevitably degenerating into a free-for-all. People argued in three of four languages; every kind of national prejudice was aired. The Vatican correspondents, used to a more sheltered life, clamoured for their guardian angel, Padre Pierfranco Pastore of the pontifical commission for social communications; but he could do nothing for them.

Passes were distributed on the eve of every event. On one occasion a nervous girl in a tight bun started to read out the publications whose lucky representatives were to be admitted to some event. The first name on the list – as if in caricature of religious journalism – was 'Ave Maria Press'. 'Ave Maria Press!' burst out a French photographer. 'I'll have seen everything on this trip – everything except the Pope. Ave Maria Press!'

At the airport, a boy and girl had emptied at the Pope's feet a blanket full of roses. It was an allusion to the story of the Virgin of Guadelupe. Mexicans call her '*la Morenita*', 'the dark one'; and anthropologists identify the 'sweet lady of Tepeyac' with the old Aztec goddess Tonantzin. Guadelupe is certainly an Indian, a Mexican Virgin. According to legend, in the very first years of the Spanish conquest she appeared to an Indian, Juan Diego, asking him to tell the local bishop to build her a shrine on that very spot, Tepeyac. The Spanish bishop demands proof that Juan Diego really has met the Virgin. She returns and sends the Indian into the mountain to pick roses. Having filled his *manta*, or Mexican blanket, with roses he takes them to the bishop's palace. There, in front of the bishop, he empties the blanket; on it is imprinted the Virgin's image. The story ends with the bishop kneeling to the Indian.

The Pope's visit to this national symbol, this image of the Virgin, was for most Mexicans the high point of his visit. On the eve of his departure from Rome he had said – and it had made Mexican headlines: 'I look forward above all to prostrating myself before the Virgin of Guadelupe.' His sermon at the shrine was also to be the formal inauguration of the bishops' conference.

The police – there were forty thousand of them in the area – estimated the crowd round the sanctuary at a million people. Occasionally it would surge forward and the tall wire fence would bend ominously while the police rushed in, letting their truncheons fly. The heat was stifling; women and children, white from heatstroke, were passed bodily over the fence and hurried away on stretchers. The ambulances and Red Cross flags seemed to give the Mexicans a sense of occasion. Later the evening papers gleefully reported that the first-aid stations had attended 'two thousand faintings'. This was the measure of a real event, with casualties on an Aztec scale.

While the Pope spoke, and the sun poured down on the thousands of people outside, the street sellers did a brisk trade in paper hats, parasols and the Pope's picture around the fringes of the crowd. Women fried and rolled tortillas, the thin maize pancakes which are the staple food of Mexicans, stuffed with anything from beans to shreds of meat but always spicy. Others hawked alarmingly green or purple water-ices, or little dishes of chopped tropical fruits. The Pope himself was to have a two-hour lunch before addressing local nuns and clergy. Nobody seemed to mind the prospect of several hours' wait, just for the sake of catching one more glimpse of *su Santidad*.

The sanctuary itself was a blaze of vivid colours: craftsmen from the nearby town of Tlaxco had decorated the facade of the old basilica with a colossal frieze of flowers, its curlicues outdoing the carved stone scrolls of the Spanish baroque. But the Pope spoke in the building opposite, the new home of the figure in the blanket; and there was no more than a thin border of flowers along its concrete balcony.

His sermon was a characteristically enthusiastic celebration of Mary. This was the stuff of Mexican popular religion; but of religion for the people there was less encouragement. His doubts about the message of Medellin were becoming more apparent. 'Ten years have passed', he said; 'and there have been interpretations which have been sometimes contradictory, not always correct and not always beneficial to the Church.' He was even more categorical in his message to Mexican nuns. They had made him impatient with an excited welcome and repeated cheers as he tried to read his speech; he had raised his hands to stop them, as though objecting to their female volubility. 'Remember', he told them, 'that you are the mystical brides of Christ.' He reproached them for substituting action for prayer, for pursuing above all 'socio-political' ends and even 'radical ideologies'. He suspected them of 'seeking new horizons and experiences', and of not always choosing their company 'according to evangelical criteria'.

Having advised the nuns to pray more, the Pope then received the Mexican clergy. With them too he was to the point: 'You are priests and members of religious orders, not social or political leaders . . . Let us have no illusion that we will serve the gospel if we "dilute" our charisma by showing an exaggerated interest in temporal problems.' For the liberationists, the omens were not good.

The Pope's third day in Mexico was for most of the correspondents crowded together in the Mexico City press centre the most crucial day of all. They had foregone the visit to Puebla;

they would miss the sight of that splendid baroque town filled to the rafters with visitors from the countryside for miles around, the old houses hung with flags and the people dressed to the nines to welcome the Pope. That was no more than local colour: the journalists could see enough of that on television. They were waiting for the Puebla speech – the words which might set the tone not just of the bishops' conference but of a whole pontificate.

It landed on the journalists' table several hours before he read it to the assembled bishops. Hundreds of heads were instantly bowed over the typewritten pages, and an unusual silence spread over the room. Then came the first comments; one of the Italians let his fist bang on the table. 'We're back in the Middle Ages!' he exclaimed. There were murmurs of disappointment when journalists reached the paragraph explaining the Pope's dissatisfaction with certain 're-readings' of the Gospels which in fact only caused 'confusion'. Clearly the Pope's prime target was the theology of liberation. True liberation, he said, was liberation from sin, and the notion of a Church 'born from the people' and manifest in the poor looked suspiciously 'ideological' – that is, Marxist. There was no doubt in anybody's mind: the Pope was sharply pulling in the reins.

The most passionate reactions were from the Italian Vatican correspondents. Coming from a country where it is hard to disentangle religion and politics and the Vatican inexorably casts its shadow over affairs of State, they had been in a fever of anticipation to read the speech 'which would give the key to the new pontificate'. Between them they represented every current of Catholic opinion; and while some congratulated themselves on what they saw as a healthy call to order in a continent running amuck with guerrilla priests and political bishops, a progressive shook his head with concern because the Pope was denigrating 'the most innovative theologians in the world'. There it was in the text: the idea of Christ as a political figure, it roundly declared, did not tally with the Church's catechesis – its teaching.

By now in Puebla the Pope was making his way with difficulty through the narrow streets. The crowds prevented his reaching the cathedral square, where he had meant to make a brief speech; instead his convoy headed straight for the Palafoxian Seminary, on the outskirts of town, where the conference was being held. Here the Pope prepared to say Mass for the 300,000 people gathered on the seminary's football pitch. The front rows were all filled by priests, nuns and guests with invitations; behind stretched open ground for the people, marked '*pueblo*' on the notice boards. The sermon was yet another hint of the hard line to come, though more related to European than Latin American conditions. The Pope exhorted his Indian and peasant listeners not to get divorced; recently passed divorce laws in various Latin American countries, he said, 'mean a new threat to the solidarity of the family'. He called on Governments to make 'socio-familial policies' their main priority – though in this area the Church is as much of a defaulter as Governments: in Mexico, as in many other Latin American countries, half the babies are born to unmarried parents. Finally, in spite of a Mexican bir'' 'ate which doubles the population every ten years, he stressed his vigorous opposition to birth-control. An intelligent, audacious, persevering socio-familial policy, he said, 'should not be understood as an indiscriminate effort to reduce the birth-rate at any cost – what my predecessor Paul VI called "reducing the number of guests at the banquet of life" '. Family policies, in other words, were not to be confused with family planning.

After lunch the Pope made his way to the seminary's assembly hall. He took his seat at the middle of a long table – not raised above the bishops, as had been the custom of Paul VI on similar occasions, but level with them. On either side sat the presidents of the conference. One was Baggio, the Vatican conservative; the other was Cardinal Aloisio Lorscheider, who is (like Arns) a Franciscan and a liberal. The bishops themselves had not yet seen the speech.

John Paul II drew up his chair in a business-like manner and began reading his message in a clear, measured voice. It was a very different tone from his speeches and addresses to the people; his voice neither rose nor fell, nor did he pause or look at his audience. In public he had been the 'smiling Pope'; now, with his broad head bent over his notes, he seemed to be chairing a board at the opening of an important meeting.

He told the bishops that the conference must take as its starting point the conclusions of Medellin, 'with all that is positive in them; but', he added, underlining the Spanish word, *pero*, 'without ignoring the incorrect interpretations which have at times been made'. As he read on there were visible signs of dismay amongst some of the bishops. Several of them began hastily taking notes. At points Lorscheider seemed aghast; Baggio, on the other hand, was looking calmly into the middle distance.

Most international press comment, as based on dispatches from the Mexico City press centre, reflected that picture. The liberals had lost. An editorial in *The New York Times* found that the Pope 'spoke out flatly against the concept of "liberation theology" '. In the left-wing Paris morning paper *Le Matin*, Claude Manceron called up the pope of the Second World War as a parallel. 'Pius XII without the constipation' was his verdict on John Paul II. 'Guaranteed by one of the most cheerfully conservative popes of modern times, dictators of all stripes will be able to massacre, torture and imprison in peace – as long as it's done in front of the papal portrait and the crucifix.'

This general judgement was unduly severe. Certainly it was an abstract speech. It contained no mention of a theology of 'signs of the times', as taken up by the liberation men from John XXIII and Vatican II – the belief that God can speak not only through the accepted sources but through events and trends which have to be discerned in the light of the Gospel.

The Pope had nevertheless not condemned the theology of liberation: he had proposed an alternative form of it. Liberation theology, as developed in Latin America, was scrutinized and found gravely wanting. But at the same time the concern for social justice expressed by liberation theology was validated and confirmed.

The criticism of liberation theology was acute and showed a good knowledge of the literature. John Paul II asserted, as a central principle, that the primary mission of pastors was to be 'teachers of the truth, not a human and rational truth, but the truth which comes from God'. This ran counter to one of the main theses of liberation theologians, which is that 'truth which comes from God' cannot be discovered outside the political and social world in which they are embroiled. A separated spiritual truth has no meaning for them. The Pope's concern for orthodoxy as paramount was unsympathetic to liberation theologians because they stress the equal claims of what they call 'orthopraxy': it is not enough to proclaim the Gospel faithfully, it must be lived – or rather, you cannot truly proclaim it unless you live by it (by identifying with the oppressed). As against that, the Pope declared: 'Over and above unity in love, unity in truth is always urgent for us.' He also reacted against the tendency of the liberationists to say that the starting point of theology is the given situation. Against this source of theology, the Pope reasserted the traditional sources, scripture and tradition.

Just as emphatic was his rejection of the 're-readings' of the Gospel that had been proposed. They were the result, he said, 'of theoretical speculations rather than an authentic meditation on the word of God'. His dismissal, though, of the political view of Jesus as 'not tallying with the Church's catechesis' was mildly phrased. He did not say that it was either misleading or un-scriptural.

The Pope recalled that in his very first speech in office he had said that a concern for sound ecclesiology would be central to his pontificate. That was why he attacked as erroneous the position which suggested that a distinction could be made between the in-stitutional or official Church, which is judged and condemned, and a new Church, 'springing from the people and taking con-crete form in the poor'. Preaching the Gospel, he explained, is not an individualistic activity, and it is not subject 'to the dis-cretionary power of individualistic criteria and perspectives but to that of communion with the Church and her pastors'. The Pope had an explanation for these deviant views. They were the product, he suggested, of 'familiar forms of ideological con-ditioning'. In his vocabulary, that meant Marxism.

So far, so negative. The most fundamental principles of liber-ation theology were challenged. Yet all this was qualified by the final and positive section of the speech. John Paul II's basic Christian humanism came out in his second part. Though the Christian message was primarily about God and his action in the world, he suggested, it said something correlatively about man: it enshrined an anthropology. The Pope examined a paradox which the *nouveaux philosophes* like Maurice Clavel had also pondered: that we live in an age which has poured forth endless rhetoric about man and liberation, and yet in practice never have so many actual men been enslaved and tortured. John Paul II had no doubt about the answer. Humanism required a more than human dimension to protect man against tyranny. Atheistic humanism led directly to a paradox: 'It is the drama of man's being deprived of an essential dimension of his being, namely his search for the infinite, and thus faced with having his being reduced in the worst way'. The clear implication was that 'liberation', understood in a secular context, led straight to its contrary: enslavement. Against this the Pope set 'Catholic social doctrine', which insisted on the dignity of every human person: 'This complete truth about the human being constitutes the foundation of the Church's social teaching and the basis also of true liberation.'

The rest of the speech developed this idea and showed its practical application. From the liberationists the Pope turned to the dictators. He denounced the way in which 'the growing wealth of a few parallels the growing poverty of the masses'. He recognized the world's interdependence: 'Internal peace and international peace can only be ensured if a social and economic system based on justice flourishes.

In Mexico itself there were two further glosses which made it clear that the two sides were not implacably opposed. One came from the liberationists; the other from the Pope. Leading liberationists – seeing little alternative, perhaps, when the people they championed had just welcomed the Pope so rapturously – claimed that they had no quarrel with him, nor he with them. 'We are innocent', protested Gutierrez himself. 'We have done no "re-readings". I believe that the Pope was referring to what is being done in certain European circles.' The Pope had said that the Church was born 'of our response in faith to Christ': Gutierrez and others chose to take that as another way of saying that the Church was born of the people. How then could one identify, Gutierrez was asked, the specifically Christian kind of liberation theology which was all the Pope approved? 'As far as I am concerned', he replied, 'it is commitment to liberation according to the Gospel which is important. Commitment is the real work; theology is what you do in the evenings, when you're tired.'

In private, a Venezuelan liberationist was more frank. Shown the Pope's most specific condemnations of his theology, he replied: 'There is a saying from colonial days, when the King of Spain sent his orders out to America: "*Se acata, pero no se cumple*" – "We acknowledge, but we do not accomplish".' Yet even that was not a disagreement with the Pope himself. The blame was laid on figures like Baggio; the Pope was absolved with the recurrent formula: 'He is badly advised.' He could not after all know the full facts.

Alex Morelli, a French Dominican, said: 'My attitude is that the Pope and the hierarchy are talking in a realm of ideals. The reality is too dramatic, too tragic to be ignored.' His parish is in Ciudad Netzahuacoyotl, the world's largest shanty-town, just on the edge of Mexico City. Mile upon mile of shabby huts line roads which are choking dust in the dry season and deep mud in the wet. Because the area is a dried-up salt lake nothing grows: there are no trees, no plants, no birds. With the population multiplying all the time, no administration can contend with the problems of poverty, ignorance and disease. Morelli himself actively favours birth control. In his Church of the Immaculate Conception, a single cement-walled room, a leper in a reading from St Mark was swiftly identified by both priest and congregation – in a service a few days after the Puebla speech – with the outcast poor. 'The Pope has an idealist, spiritual reading of the scriptures', said Morelli afterwards. 'The fact is that the reading of the poor – and it's not me who suggests it to them – is materialist.'

The Pope's own gloss on his apparent anti-liberationism was delivered the day after the Puebla speech. It came during a visit to the Southern Pacific region of Mexico.

'When the Holy Father arrives', shouted an excited priest into a microphone, 'I want you all to say "Welcome Fisherman" in Polish. Ready? One, two, three. *Viva el Papa*! . . .' On a dry, empty hilltop near the southern town of Oaxaca, 15,000 Indians stood patiently in the burning sun. Many of them had spent the night there after travelling for up to four days, some from as far as Guatemala. Behind an improvised heliport and a large bright orange dais stood the empty ruins of a Dominican priory. One could see nothing else for miles around except the bare, rolling hills.

A large jet plane crossed the blue sky and disappeared in the valley below. 'That's him! The Pope's plane has arrived!' bawled the priest, almost beside himself, waving his straw sombrero. Soon four helicopters came flapping out of the sky, the largest, a white one, in the lead. It tore up clouds of dust and terrified the pigeons sent up in welcome.

The crowd remained silent in spite of the cheerleader's efforts. Throughout the speeches people milled about, buying drinks or sticky lumps of the local brown sugar to suck. Others simply wandered off.

Up on the dais, against the background of a geometric orange and yellow pattern which made the occasion look like an encounter of Zapotec princes, John Paul II was welcomed by the eleven bishops of the Southern Pacific area, all of them with wide straw hats above their black soutanes and crimson sashes. Most of them were forthright exponents of the most socially committed recommendations of Medellin. The year before they had published a document on the problems of evangelization in their area which had been considered too radical for acceptance by the rest of the Mexican bishops. The Southern Pacific area is the poorest in Mexico; conditions there are dramatic enough to radicalize most priests. Between seventy and eighty percent of their parishioners are peasants, and more than half of those have either no land at all or not enough to subsist on. Sixty percent are defined as 'indigenous', still speaking their own language rather than Spanish.

The bishops let the figures speak for themselves: life expectancy in the area is 53 years and infant mortality 58.8 per thousand, among the highest in the world. What alarms them, though, is the fact that 'not only is the poverty terrible, but people are growing poorer'. They blame all this on 'our system, which has generated new forms of economic exploitation and political manipulation. There have been ideological aggressions, cultures have been destroyed, even religion is used to dominate.' The bishops notice that the tendency is for land to be concentrated in very few hands; agricultural reforms, government grants, even new irrigation schemes operate to the advantage of the major landowners; votes can be bought for no more than a hat or a food parcel; landowners use armed bands to protect their property, and violence from the police or the army goes unpunished. Oaxaca is the only state in Mexico under martial law.

It was against this background that Estabán Fernandez, a peasant half the year and a labourer the other, stood up to make his welcoming speech in Zapotec: '*Datu Gunibatu . . .*', he began, but his words were very much to the point once translated: 'You said that we, the poor of Latin America, are the hope of your Church. Well, look at how that hope lives. They have pushed us out into the harshest mountains. In the land which belonged to our fathers and grandfathers we are treated as strangers.' Fernandez is a catechist, one of those lay workers and interpreters without whom it would be impossible for the mainly Spanish-speaking priests to work at all. He lives in a village in the mountains to which the best access is a seven-hour ride on horseback.

Fernandez won a warmer response from the visitor than he could have expected. An anodyne papal speech had already been issued to the press; but whether because the Pope had by now glimpsed the reality of the way the poor lived in Mexico, or because he had been effectively briefed on the region he was now in, he put the original text aside in favour of a new and more radical address. Its strongest passages were quotations from past papal encyclicals, notably *Populorum Progressio*, Paul VI's 1967 essay on development (which *The Wall Street Journal* had called 'souped-up Marxism'); but that did not diminish their effect. In these rural areas, said John Paul II at Oaxaca, the worker had the right not to be deprived of the little he had; the right to expect that the barriers of exploitation would be destroyed; the right to effective help towards the development which his status as a son of God deserved. This was therefore a time for swift and bold reform. He went on:

> The Church defends the legitimate right to private prop-
> erty, but it teaches with no less clarity that, above all,
> private property always carries with it a social obli-
> gation, so that material possessions may serve the
> general goal that God intended. And if the common
> good requires it, there must be no doubt about ex-
> propriation itself, carried out in the proper manner.

The phrase for 'social obligation' was *hipoteca social* – literally a social mortgage, with the implication that the mortgage-

holder, and therefore the real owner, was the community; and it
reverberated round Latin America.

After the speeches came a display of traditional dances called
Guelagetza, which means 'offering'; and at the end of each dance
the dancers filed up the steps of the dais to lay their offerings at
the Pope's feet – an image of the Virgin, baskets of fruit, sweets,
brightly embroidered stoles which the Pope promptly put round
his neck. The offerings are a pre-Christian propitiatory tradition.
Particularly taken with a spectacular feather-dance, 'The Pope
likes to watch the poor dance', he said. The compliment failed of
its effect: the dancers were in fact genteel young women from the
town organized into a troupe by the Ministry of Tourism.

On his way down to the town of Oaxaca the Pope stopped to
bless the old and sick gathered together in the sixteenth-century
church of Santo Domingo. As he crossed the threshold of the
church he paused to take in the rows of stretchers and
wheelchairs, the sick people and white-coated doctors all waiting
in the splendid painted nave, its walls bright with a gold-and-
white geometric pattern. (That was another pre-Christian echo in
Mexican Christianity: it recalled the designs on Mexico's ancient
ruins at Mitla.) Without waiting to reach the altar, John Paul II
began blessing the people he passed. 'How are you?' he asked
each in turn. 'We all wept', said one of the doctors afterwards.
'We were very worried because of the number of sick people with
delicate heart conditions which could worsen under strong
emotion; but nothing happened. He had that effect on
them . . .'

(The importunate sick were an inescapable feature of the whole
tour. A Dutch journalist sprained his ankle and had to hobble
about on crutches. At one stop the police thrust him into a pen
full of cripples and told him to wait his turn to be blessed with the
others.)

The Mass celebrated on a dais outside Oaxaca cathedral even
included a full-scale brass band. The crowd in the square was so
dense that many of them perched in trees. Law and order were
better secured than at Puebla: besides the police, young men in
white T-shirts with yellow armbands held back the faithful with
long, menacing-looking poles. As the service drew to an end the
trombones blared gaily; several priests came through the wrought-

iron grille to begin distributing Communion among passing nurses or enthusiastic women who had to leap over the poles to reach it; and a priest led a rousing song known as a *porra* to celebrate the Pope. Singing *porras* for dignitaries is in fact a novelty: shouts of '*A la via, a la vao, a la bim, bom, ba*' were once reserved for football stars; but now it was '*El Papa, el Papa, ra, ra, ra*!'

It was John Paul II's last day in Mexico, and the Mexicans were doing all they could to make it memorable. He was woken at dawn by a *mariachis* serenade under his window. Then began the most crowded schedule of the entire visit. The papal nuncio's house in a quiet suburb of Mexico City, where he was staying, was besieged by enthusiastic crowds waiting for their last glimpse of the Pope. They were disappointed, because he made his way by helicopter – nearly two hours late, after an unscheduled meeting with Central American diplomats – to the Basilica of Guadelupe to address 50,000 students from the Mexican Catholic Universities.

He sheltered from the sun under a black umbrella to speak to the crowd of students below. Having read his speech in Spanish – a Catholic university must offer more than scientific education, it must offer 'a moral and Christian training' – he spoke impromptu in the same language. He sometimes confused it with Italian, adding at one point: 'I am glad that the Pope still has to learn. It would have been easier for me to speak Polish, but I don't think it would be very easy for you to understand.' The students were delighted.

Outside an enormous crowd, clearly not made up of students, was pressing against the gates of the sanctuary. Some of them tried to climb over. A soldier perched on the railings shouted: 'Get down! Get down, I say, or I'll kick you down!'

Then there was a brief word for journalists – 'yours is not an easy life' – and a display of horsemanship to be sat through (during which a flock of young women riding side-saddle in frothy white dresses performed an *escarmouche* with the standard of the Virgin of Guadelupe) before it was time for the ride back to the nunciature on the way to the airport. As his open truck drove in, the Pope saw a little boy dressed in a friar's habit. He picked him

up and held him high, as he had done with so many other
children; but the truck carried on through the gate and the little
boy disappeared with the Pope. The pious *promesa* expressed by
the habit – that if the child recovered from an illness he would
grow up to take orders – seemed to have been spectacularly fulfilled. His grandmother had tears of relief in her eyes when the
gate opened again and a security man came out bearing her grand-
son.

In the same crowd outside the Pope's residence an elegant
woman held up a simple rosary and repeated with delight: 'It was
the Holy Father's. I had offered him mine, which was of coral
and gold, but he thought I wanted it blessed. I told him to take it.
When he understood he put his hand in his pocket and said:
"Take a far humbler one." '

At the airport, one of the motorcycle police who had escorted
him all the way fell on his knees for a pontifical blessing. His
friends tried to stop him; but the Pope blessed the bowed,
helmeted head. 'I do not want to leave any Mexican with his hand
outstretched', the Pope said as he boarded his plane. 'It hurts me
to leave.' As the plane took off, thousands of people stood on
Mexico City rooftops flashing pocket mirrors up at the sky in a
spectacular goodbye.

Even that was not the end of the Mexican journey. The plane
travelled north across snow-capped peaks to Monterrey, almost
on the border with the United States. It was nearly sunset by the
time the Pope's helicopter landed beside the high bridge from
which he would speak to the people of Monterrey. The visit had
not been on the original schedule; it had been added after the
Pope's arrival in Mexico, following pressures from Mexican in-
dustrialists. The Holy Father, they argued, would get the wrong
impression if he visited only historic towns like Puebla and
Oaxaca. Monterrey is modern Mexico. The local employers had
given their work force a day off to see the Pope; it cost them 200
million *pesos*, they claimed, but it was 'a present to the Holy
Father'.

As the Pope walked down the bridge, swept by a cold north
wind, he kept passing from side to side to acknowledge the
endless cheers and shouts of welcome. It was the largest single
crowd he had addressed in Mexico; and it drew from him, when

he spoke, a kind of epitome of his Mexican message. There was a place for reform, yes – 'daring innovations to overcome the grave injustices inherited from the past'; but there was also room for a little plain Christian spirit on both sides. The Church should offer its help 'to employers and workers so that they became aware of the immense reserves of goodness which they have within themselves'. Alluding to the flow of Mexican 'wetbacks' who cross without permits into the United States in search of work, he said that Mexican employers were wrong to take advantage of this safety-valve to pay low wages and hold down welfare benefits; but he reminded the workers that they too had certain obligations, and he warned them against 'alien ideologies'. It was not hard for his hearers to guess that he meant Marxism. He had already told them that he was put in mind of his own days as a worker in his 'dear, far-off Krakow'.

'But let us not just stick to man', he concluded. He had brought a message of love: 'the love of God, the Virgin Mary, the Church and the Pope. I leave you the greetings of a friend: to all of you, to your children and families, a brother's embrace.'

The Pope's aim had been to see that when the revolution came in Latin America it would be a Christian revolution. He hoped that Latin American society could be changed in the direction of greater fraternity and fairness – without violence, in the light of the Gospel, undistorted by ideological manipulation. That would be the highest test of his Latin American achievement. But there was a more immediate check: how was his Mexican magisterium, or teaching, received by the professionals of his own Church? The effect could be directly measured in the rest of the Puebla conference.

Most Mexicans were quite unaware of the bishops' meeting. Once the Pope had left, the show was over. They began to reminisce, with a touch of national pride, about the six Mexican days of '*Juan Pablo Segundo*'. It had been six days of religious reprieve. In the daily struggle for survival it was a luminous intermission, not a serious prospect of change.

Yet for the bishops in the Palafoxian Seminary at Puebla, the effort to apply the Pope's words to their daily work was only now beginning. It was not the sort of event designed to raise great crowds; there was nobody to be seen waiting outside the tall steel gates on a dusty suburban road in Puebla except three of the numerous security men who double-checked every visitor and journalist. The Seminary is a modern building set in large grounds, with a domed observatory on the roof – 'to watch the evolutions of the angels', said a Mexican journalist who was sunning himself on the steps.

Reporters who cover religious affairs become more engaged than other kinds of journalists. Political reporters come in the end to regard all politicians with the same scepticism. Among religious journalists, on the other hand, commitment springs eternal. At Puebla, most of it was on the liberal side. The bishops met in private, and only encountered the press if they chose to advance down a glass-walled corridor to the wooden counter behind which the press was penned. Bishop Helder Camara, the Brazilian progressive, was a favourite. When his tiny, frail figure appeared at the counter on his seventieth birthday, the entire contingent of Brazilian journalists began singing 'Happy Birthday to you! Happy Birthday, Dom Helder . . .' He acknowledged the ovation with hands raised, and hurried away again. Another cult-figure was Lorscheider, also of Brazil (and a linguist in the Wojtyla class). The general *bête noire*, on the other hand, was Lopez Trujillo. He kept his head down, after a most embarrassing disclosure the very day after the Pope had left for Rome. On 1 February the Mexican newspaper *Uno Mas Uno* published a letter from Lopez Trujillo to a Brazilian colleague, Archbishop Luciano Cabral Duarte. Its authenticity was never denied, and there was no comment from its author. The letter was chatty and personal, simply addressed 'Dear Luciano'. It started with Lopez Trujillo's rejoicing in the election of the new Pope because 'he has begun by speaking out very clearly' against the 'deviations' which Trujillo believed the Latin American Church to be plagued by.

If anyone had any doubts as to where Lopez Trujillo's own sympathies lay, the letter would have dispelled them. For him, the conference at Puebla was to be a real battle. 'Prepare your bomber planes', he wrote to Cabral Duarte; 'you must start training the way boxers do before going into the ring for a world championship. May your blows be evangelical and sure.'

The letter showed him to be an effective, but not invincible, wire-puller. The conference president, it said, had promised 'something like a call to order' for the far-left liberation theologian, Boff. On an episcopal appointment, Lopez Trujillo wrote: 'When I arrived in Rome, Dom Aloisio had already obtained the nomination of the bishop of whom we had spoken. When I complained, they told me that it would be balanced by the nomination of another bishop with a very reliable line.' But he deplored the fact that Father Pedro Arrupe – the General of the Jesuits, the 'Black Pope' – had been invited to Puebla 'thanks to the pressure of others'.

According to *Uno Mas Uno* reporters, the letter had been carelessly left in the blank part of a cassette tape containing an interview prepared by Lopez Trujillo in answer to a journalist's written questions. 'He was so suspicious he had to write his own interview', one of the reporters said, 'so serve him right.'

In public, the assembled bishops never betrayed their differences. Everyone – even the liberation theologians, who had been excluded from the conference itself – declared that they had the highest hopes for the outcome of the meeting. And all of them, from the most conservative to the most radical, proclaimed absolute agreement with the Pope. There had been sustenance in his speeches for both sides.

The Lopez Trujillo letter was tactfully ignored by his colleagues. Only rarely was the discreet chorus of assent broken. During the first official press conference the representative of the French Episcopal Conference for Latin America, Ludovic Revillard, appeared on the speaker's dais to explain accusations of his which had appeared in a published interview, to the effect that representatives of the Roman Curia were arrogantly trying to put pressure on members of the conference in order to make them fall into line. 'I can only refer to my own experience', Revillard said. 'I belong to a working group with eleven bishops, of whom four are cardinals either belonging to or nominated by the Curia. It's just that it's difficult to contradict a cardinal.' Altogether, besides Cardinal Baggio, there were twelve Vatican nominees with voting status in the conference – all of them, as Lopez Trujillo would have said, 'very reliable'.

On the central question of the poor, there was ostensibly no division. Everyone was for them. 'We want the poor to know that they are our brothers', said Cardinal José Maurer of Bolivia from the dais, 'and because he is poor, the humble man is closer to God than a millionaire.' The Cardinal went on to talk about the statue of the Virgin in his cathedral 'covered in pearls, gold and other priceless things; and in front of this Virgin, so rich in jewels, is a poor peasant woman, with her baby – her *babita*, as we say in Bolivia – tied on her back. And this woman hasn't even got five pesos to buy milk or medicine for her child. I am sure that, if she could, the Virgin would give away not just one but many of her jewels.' Maurer delivered his speech looking like a prince of the Church off-duty, dressed in a black pullover and smoking a large cigar. Journalists cheered when he told them how he had sold his Mercedes in aid of a housing project for the poor.

In one of their reports, though, the bishops stressed that their commitment to the poor was 'preferential but not exclusive'. It was a quotation from the Pope; and it was significant, because an exclusive commitment to the poor – evangelization with the poor as its starting point and their 'liberation' as its end – is a tenet of liberation theology. These allusive redefinitions, which corrected liberation theology without ever actually mentioning it, cropped up again and again. The Pope's message, the influence of the Vatican, was to that extent taking effect.

On the first Sunday of the conference, as on most Sundays after the eleven o'clock Mass, Bishop Sergio Mendez Arceo was standing on the steps of his fort-like cathedral at Cuernavaca – one of the oldest churches in Mexico, built in austere Gothic. Mendez Arceo had become the *enfant terrible* of the Mexican episcopate. He had spoken up for Freud at Vatican II (urging the Church not to risk another 'Galileo affair'); he had been a patron of Ivan Illich (the 'de-schooling' man, whose 'cultural centre' was in Cuernavaca); he had tolled the bells of his cathedral in mourning for the death of Salvador Allende, the leftist president of Chile; he had organized church collections in support of strikers.

That Sunday he was dressed in a simple green vestment, with abstract appliqués in coloured cotton stitched round the hem; and his shaven head towered above the crowd. His manner was gentle but authoritative as he talked of Puebla. Lopez Trujillo? '*Un hombre malefico*', he said – a man who does harm. 'He is a friend of mine', Mendez Arceo added with a smile: 'it is a sign of friendship to speak the truth about a man.' Yet he believed that, in spite of Lopez Trujillo, the Puebla conference was working well. 'It's all a question of interpretation, of exegesis.'

This emphasis on 'exegesis' was Mendez Arceo's key to the conference. The most important thing, for him as for the theologians of liberation, was the way in which both the documents of the Puebla Conference and even the Pope's speeches left certain margins for interpretation. Rather then admit any conflict, all the Bishop wanted was room for manoeuvre; and he seemed likely to get it.

On the Pope he was cautious. He had had a twenty-minute audience with him in Rome, yet still said 'I don't know him; but he seems a very thoughtful man. He prepared his visit and his speech very carefully.'

During that audience, Mendez Arceo had said: 'You will have heard a lot about me, both good and bad.' The Pope's answer had pleased the bishop: 'What counts is the person.' The Pope had also recognized Mendez Arceo on his arrival at Mexico City airport, saying in spite of the crowd and the hubbub 'We've met before.' Don Sergio is the first to recognize John Paul II's gift for dealing with people: 'He is a good demagogue – in the best sense of the word.' Nonetheless he regretted that the Pope had changed the original plan, which was that he should spend a little time at Puebla, where a room had been specially prepared for him, so as to speak to the bishops individually: 'He preferred the masses.' Another reproach concerned John Paul II's inordinate devotion to Mary; the innumerable references to the Virgin of Guadelupe were 'altogether too much. But what can you do? That's the way the Poles are.'

Mendez Arceo was confident that the bishops would make their decisions quite independently of the pressures of the Vatican or even of the Pope. When it was pointed out to him that many of the bishops at the Seminary were simply echoing the Pope, he did admit that 'unfortunately we are far more "papolatrous" here in Latin America than elsewhere. It all goes back to the days of Spanish rule, when the kings of Spain governed the Continent on the strength of concessions granted by successive Renaissance popes.' Yet of the Pope's speech he felt that 'it's all a question of hermeneutics, the key which is used to interpret it. As the Pope didn't actually condemn the theology of liberation as such, one can, one can . . .' He broke off. 'It's all relative, you see.'

To get through the work of the conference, the delegates were divided into commissions or working groups. The distribution was done partly by choice, and partly by dispensation from above. The most strikingly packed was the commission on 'action within the national and multinational company'. Of its eighteen members, ten were not from Latin America at all: there were two Vatican nominees, two papal nuncios, two Canadians, an American, an African, and the representatives of a Swiss and a German charity.

A few observers were also admitted; and at least one of them, Father Wilhelm Saelman from Holland, was distressed by what – from a clear ideological standpoint – he observed. 'I was shocked', he declared. 'Not only do they not subscribe to the analysis which sees the multinationals as the authors of poverty and under-development, but they declare that Latin America is on the road to industrialization and that the Church wishes to associate itself with development and urbanization. These cities of millions of people, poor in every way, places which are impossible to live in – they say they are a good thing! We know that the purpose of these organizations, the multinationals, is not the welfare of South Americans, but making money. In so far as this is the case, we should declare ourselves their enemies. The bishops all declare they are the voices of the people,' Saelman went on, 'but when you ask them what the people are saying, somehow all you hear is what the Pope said. I think the bishops are all taking refuge in what the Pope said, are following it and that's all. Personally, I feel that true collegiality means the Pope should have spoken last.'

The quiet city of Puebla had become an international political theatre; and the action was not all at the Palafoxian Seminary. The cafés in the arcades round the cathedral square looked like a who's-who of the political left in Latin America. One afternoon Mrs Allende could be seen, frail and ladylike in a flowered frock, sipping coffee while her daughter talked to friends. A Brazilian girl reporter, recognizing the widow, rushed up and embraced her, almost in tears.

A Mexican Catholic news agency of progressive bent named CENCOS – the only speech of the Pope's which it put out in full was his address to the Indians and peasants of Oaxaca – transferred its offices to the arcades. The resultant forum became known as 'anti-Puebla'. Gutierrez could be found there, giving interviews. Another CENCOS guest was Ernesto Cardenal, priest, poet and self-confessed fighter on the Nicaraguan guerrilla front (and Minister for Education and Culture after the successful Nicaraguan revolution six months later, product of a rare alliance between guerrillas and bourgeoisie.)

'The Pope is quite right when he says the clergy shouldn't get into politics', declared Cardenal. The audience packed into the small conference room smiled. With his white beard, shoulder-length hair, black beret and khaki shirt, Cardenal looked like a revolutionary sage. He spoke with absolute conviction: 'I used to be a poet. I became a priest, and love of God led me to revolution. I have never gone in for politics.'

He was there to denounce the cruelty of the then Nicaraguan dictator Anastasio Somoza, a man so unpopular as to be 'at war with his own people', and by reading two eye-witness accounts of recent massacres Cardenal reduced the room to horrified silence. He had hard words, too, for the Vatican nuncio in Nicaragua: 'While the city of Leon was being bombed, the nuncio was drinking cocktails at a party given by Somoza himself. I hope', he added, 'that the new Pope will change pontifical policy. The previous Pope died without ever uttering a word about the massacres taking place in Nicaragua, and the people resented him for it. It was Paul VI who gave the President the title of "great Christian statesman" – a message which the Archbishop of Managua, Miguel Obando Bravo, never passed on to Somoza, for fear of ruining the Pope's image in the eyes of the people.' Finally, Cardenal quoted Torres, the guerrilla priest who died fighting for revolution in Colombia: 'Revolution,' said Camillo Torres, 'is effective charity. The bishops' conference, just by condemning politics, can't stop us clothing the poor, feeding the hungry and teaching the ignorant. That is what we call revolution.'

Cardenal declined to say Mass in the square in front of Puebla

university, so as not to break the law which forbids religious
ceremonies in public places. There was a concert instead. Students
from the university still protested against it under the rallying cry
of '*Christianismo si, Communismo no*'; and they handed out
leaflets urging the citizens of Puebla to reject 'the enemies of the
Pope'.

Up at the Seminary, a comparable performance to Cardenal's
was mounted by Arrupe, the General of the Jesuits, who had
offered to give a press conference by himself. The hall was packed
when the small frail man, dressed plainly in black, took his seat
alone at the speaker's table. Beginning with an introduction on
'these Jesuits who have such mixed reputations', he took occasion
to stress his order's 'fourth vow': 'that of absolute fidelity to the
will of the Roman Pontiff'. In that spirit, and basing himself on
Paul VI's encyclical *Populorum progressio,* Arrupe became the
only participant at Puebla who publicly recognized the legitimacy
of political violence in certain situations. He did so with great
care, reading from notes and speaking slowly. It was an important
statement because – as was well known to the Jesuit Provincial
for Nicaragua – there was at least one member of the Society then
fighting with a liberation front.

First he stressed the virtues of pacifism, justice and fraternal
love. He went on: 'Revolutionary violence can be legitimate in the
case of a prolonged tyranny, in situations where basic human
rights are being trampled on. I am quoting the words of the Holy
Father, so don't accuse me of being a revolutionary. But a person
who chooses to resort to violence puts a very great weight on his
conscience. Certainly nobody outside the country can judge
whether or not such a situation exists there.'

The conference was slowly approaching its end. At a party the
bishops gave for the press in the glass corridor which the journalists had tried so hard to enter, Lopez Trujillo was asked whether
he was pleased with the Conference. 'Very,' he answered,
'because everything is taking place in the greatest freedom.' Did
he think he might organize another? 'I don't know.' He added
with a smile, 'I am also a pastor, you know. I have a diocese in
Colombia which is small but very famous. It's called Medellin.'

Cardinal Munoz Duque, also from Colombia, amiable and a

little cross-eyed, explained his satisfaction with the Pope's Puebla speech. 'I did not expect the Holy Father to be so clear.' And did he think there was consensus in the assembly? 'I will answer you on two levels', he said. 'As a man of faith, I know that the Holy Ghost is always present on such occasions and brings consensus. Of course, as a human witness, I recognize certain differences of opinion; but we are certainly working towards consensus.'

The consensus, in the end, was attuned to the Pope's wishes. The magisterium had been received. The work of the conference issued in a book-length 'final document' which gathered up the reports of the various commissions. The prose was balanced; but on each issue the balance tipped down towards the conservative side.

The document urged Catholics to take up the cause of the poor as if it were their own, quoting Matthew 25:40: 'as you did it unto one of the least of these my brethren, you did it to me.' It even recognized in certain Latin American countries 'a situation of social sin' – a phrase identified with liberation theology. But a sentence which in so many words rejoiced in 'the benefits of a theological reflection on liberation, as arose from Medellin' was struck out in the final voting. Since Medellin the brakes were going on.

Again, the basic communities were 'one of the Church's great reasons for joy and hope'; they were 'the expression of the Church's special love for the ordinary simple man'; but the Marxism which nourished them was repeatedly condemned, and fear of it was offered as a reason why unrestrained capitalism had not been more effectively confronted. The Christian faith did not despise politics; but all political systems and ideologies must be interpreted and illuminated in the light of the Gospel.

In a gesture of humility which the Pope himself had noticeably not made, the document acknowledged that not all leaders of the Latin American Church had 'identified themselves sufficiently with the poor' or dissociated themselves enough from the rich and politically powerful. Yet the fate of the document gave little sign that anything had changed. It passed to the permanent secretariat of the Consejo Episcopal Latinoamericano – CELAM; and there, so the liberationists claimed, more than five hundred alterations were made to the text. Neither the number nor the direction of the changes ought to have been a surprise. At the end of March, CELAM had elected a new president: Lopez Trujillo. His successor as secretary general, Bishop Antonio Quarracino of Argentina, was a man of like views; and one of the two new vice-presidents, Cabral Duarte of Brazil (recipient of the Lopez Trujillo letter), was if anything further still to the right. The pace of change in the Latin American Church was certainly not speeded by the Pope's visit to Puebla.

5

Magisterium

John Paul II is no laggard when it comes to putting pen to paper. His first encyclical, *Redemptor Hominis*, was published within five months of his election and written even earlier. (John XXIII waited two and a half years before his first encyclical, *Mater et Magistra*, appeared; and Paul VI delayed for over a year before publishing *Ecclesiam Suam*.) The first encyclical of a new pope is nearly always taken, rightly, as in some sense programmatic: this is what is on his mind, this is the most urgent task facing the Church, this is the way ahead for the future.

But in addition to being precipitate, John Paul II has also been prolific, and a whole stream of documents has flowed from his pen in his first year. The sermons and addresses delivered on his travels in Mexico, Poland, Ireland and the United States would have been work enough for a lesser man; yet besides them there are three documents, impressive by their scope and bulk, which deserve consideration in some detail. They are the Message for World Peace Day (1 January 1979); *Redemptor Hominis* (4 March 1979); and the Letter to Priests (8 April 1979). Each of these documents had a very different fate. The Message for World Peace Day was unjustifiably ignored (no doubt on the grounds that popes are expected to be for peace); the encyclical was widely misunderstood; and the Letter to Priests gave rise to controversy and obloquy.

One of the principal functions of the papal office is to manufacture documents; and certainly one of the chief activities of the Roman Curia, the pope's bureaucratic staff, is preparing, scrutinizing and vetting them. There are minor triumphs to be celebrated when this positive phrase is included or that misleading word left out. But the Curia is disconcerted by John Paul II. He does most of his writing himself. His philosophical background gives him a regard for authenticity which means that he is unlikely to put his name readily to documents written by some other hand. Karl Rahner, the most influential Catholic theologian, has been critical of this way of going on: the pope is not writing private documents and should enlist theological help (from, naturally, the right quarters). The matter is important because the pope, any pope, teaches mainly through the documents he issues. They are his chief means of communicating with the rest of the Church, and the principal expression of his magisterium, his teaching. The pope may travel, give audiences, be seen on television, but the written text remains the main source for a study of the content of his teaching. This is the way he fulfils the mission entrusted to Peter (Luke 22.32): 'strengthen your brethren'.

Exactly how he does this has varied in the course of history. A whole thesaurus of literary forms has flourished: letters, whether pastoral, apostolic or encyclical; briefs and bulls; constitutions and decrees. Theologians have to distinguish carefully between these different forms, since they are not all on the same level or of the same weight. In the period between the two Vatican Councils (from 1870 to 1962) there was a tendency to inflate the value of all papal utterances. Critics spoke of 'creeping infallibility', by which they meant that the concept of infallibility, which applied only in the most rare and stringent circumstances, had been abusively extended to cover day-to-day pronouncements which did not merit so lofty an accolade. In fact there has been only one instance of the specific exercise of infallibility since it was laid down by Vatican I: the definition by Pius XII in 1950 of Mary's assumption into heaven. His successor, John XXIII, seems to have thought infallibility a rusty weapon; at any rate he insisted that the decrees of Vatican II should not be so qualified. And Paul VI never described any of his teachings as infallible – not even the controversial encyclical *Humanae Vitae* in 1968. It would be more accurate to speak of 'vanishing' than of 'creeping' infallibility.

The documents so far published by John Paul II mark another shift. Earlier Vatican documents seemed to emanate from a computer which turned good ideas into an ungainly gobbledegook that only skilled minds could interpret. John Paul's documents are highly personal. If they are sometimes obscure, that is not because they are written in Vaticanese, but because his philosophical background is unfamiliar. All his documents, including his encyclical, are written in the first person singular. That is no trivial change. It means that he does not intend his own personality to be submerged in his office. Pope though he may be, he will remain a man, marked by his own personal history and experience, who addresses his fellow men. His documents are a personal witness.

That is the tone of his Message for World Peace Day. It is difficult to say anything novel or arresting about peace. Since the pontificate of Pius X the word 'peace' has tolled like a bell through papal encyclicals and addresses. Yet despite these pontifical exhortations, two world wars and innumerable lesser conflicts have raged unchecked. Talk about peace always runs the risk of combining rhetorical inflation with a sense of powerlessness; and popes can come to resemble puzzled headmasters who berate their uncomprehending charges for their totally unreasonable behaviour. But within pontifical peace-talk one can distinguish different styles, from the 'impassioned, anguished appeal' favoured by Pius XII to Paul VI's trust in the art of diplomacy. ('To despair of diplomacy', he told the diplomats accredited to the Vatican in 1968, 'is to despair of man.') John Paul II's approach, as revealed in his Message, is more like John XXIII's in *Pacem in Terris*, his 'last will and testament' (set to music by Olivier Messiaen, the only encyclical for which the experiment has been tried). Both stress our common humanity. John Paul II speaks less like a diplomat and more like the ethical philosopher that he is by training. The final chapter of *The Acting Person* provides his starting point. It is concerned with the person and the community. Conflicts and eventually wars come about where communication has broken down; man's God-intended destiny is for dialogue.

John Paul II makes a complete break with the baroque rhetoric of the impassioned appeal and writes with a realistic sense of the difficulty of the peacemaking enterprise. Conflicts do not occur only because people are wicked. They have 'structural' causes. They come about because the 'imperatives' which prevail in international affairs are military or political, and because economic and commercial 'interests' demand the continued manufacture and stockpiling of dangerous weapons. The result is that

> The arms race then prevails over the great tasks of
> peace, which ought to unite peoples in a new solidarity;
> it fosters sporadic but murderous conflicts and builds up
> the gravest threats. It is true that at first sight the cause
> of peace seems to be handicapped to a crippling extent.

He also realizes that not all those who talk about 'peace, *détente*
and the rational solution of conflicts' mean what they say. 'Peace
has become the slogan that reassures or is meant to beguile.' It is
not, on the whole, internationally respectable to advocate war.
Peace is paid the last tribute of vice to virtue: hypocrisy.

Peacemaking is not easy. There are no short cuts. But John
Paul II accepts the 'challenge' of working for peace. The Church
can make a contribution precisely because it is concerned with
human motivations. When not led astray by false imperatives or
illusory interests, human beings can recognize a set of simple principles on which they could all agree:

> Human affairs must be dealt with humanely, not by
> violence. Tensions, rivalries and conflicts must be settled
> by reasonable negotiations and not by force. Opposing
> ideologies must confront each other in a climate of
> dialogue and free discussion. The legitimate interests of
> particular groups must also take into account the
> legitimate interests of the other groups involved and the
> demands of the higher common good. Recourse to arms
> cannot be considered the right means for settling con-
> flicts. Inalienable human rights must be safeguarded in
> every circumstance. It is not permissible to kill in order to
> impose a solution.

These are far-reaching axioms, and not without novelty. The final
principle seems to rule out the possibility of the 'just war'. One
could quibble and say that 'to kill in order to impose a solution' is
essentially the act of an aggressor, whereas the theory of the just
war supposes a defensive posture which seeks only to repel the
enemy. But whatever casuistry is brought to bear on this simple
statement, it does seem that the Pope has taken a step towards
Christian pacifism.

The axioms come from two connected sources. John Paul goes
on: 'Every person of good will can find these principles of

humanity in his or her own conscience. They correspond to God's will for the human race.' In other words, there are two convergent starting points for international ethics. One can either begin from below, with the human conscience – and conscience is an attribute of every human person, whatever philosophical positions he may otherwise adopt. 'Should' and 'ought' can never be banished from human discourse. Or one can begin from above, from the divine plan, from Christian revelation. Wherever one starts, the result is the same. That implies a further point: to be a Christian (i.e. to allow oneself to be guided by revelation) and to be responsibly human are one and the same thing. This principle underlies section III of the Message, which is devoted to 'the specific contribution of Christians'.

In one sense there is no specific contribution of Christians. As peacemakers – and 'Blessed are the peacemakers' is the refrain of the Message – they do not have to say or do anything different. What they have to do is to undergird the best efforts of their secular contemporaries. They possess no special knowledge, no privileged expertise. But what they can legitimately claim is a clear sense that the human effort to achieve reconciliation between peoples coincides with the divine intention for mankind. As the Pope says, 'it corresponds to an initial call by God to form a single family of brothers and sisters, created in the image of the same Father'. If this aspiration is anonymously present elsewhere, so much the better. The Bible, as John Paul II points out, offers an image of the tragic failure of peacemaking efforts: the Tower of Babel. It represents the chaos which follows when diversity is regarded as a reason for opposition and hostility. But Babel, with its hubbub of competing languages, is countered by the image of Pentecost, when people understood each other in their own language. The New Testament is all about peace and reconciliation. Christ is 'our peace' (Ephesians 2:14), and he breaks down the walls that divide hostile and warring brothers. He restores lost fraternity. John Paul II concludes, not that the Church provides the model of peacemaking, but more modestly: 'By reconciling us with God, he (Christ) heals the wounds of sin and division and enables us to produce in our societies a rough outline of the unity that he is re-establishing in us.' A rough outline; no more.

But that is, or ought to be, enough to impel Christians to work for peace with complete commitment. John Paul II develops the peacemaking task under three heads: bringing a vision of peace, speaking the language of peace, and making gestures for peace. There is no action, first, without vision, without some sense of how my particular bit of peacemaking – which may seem derisory – fits in with the whole. John Paul II tries to bring peacemaking home: 'The individuals and families who by accepting and respecting each other gain their own inner peace and radiate it; the peoples, often poor and sorely tried, whose wisdom has been forged on the anvil of the supreme good of peace' – these are the builders of peace from day to day. The importance of finding a 'new language for peace', second, is that stereotypes and clichés obstruct the vision and wreck the chances of peace. They carve the world up into 'us' and 'them' and so 'strangle both social charity and justice itself'. Marxism, though not mentioned by name, is condemned here because it makes a virtue of class hatred: 'By expressing everything in terms of force, of group and class struggles, and of friends and enemies, a propitious atmosphere is created for social barriers, contempt, even hatred and terrorism and underhand or open support for them.' If attitudes are to be changed, one has to go to work on language. The Pope proposes an alternative language which does not rule people out in advance (as class enemies or blacks or Protestants). It is characterized by 'a readiness to listen and to understand, respect for others, a gentleness which is real strength, and trust. Such a language puts one on the path of objectivity, truth and peace.' Third, there are 'gestures for peace', actions which break down barriers and lead to reconciliation. 'It is the practice of peace', says John Paul II, 'that leads to peace.' His hope is placed in young people, who do not share the inherited prejudices of their parents and who want to get to know other people 'in meeting fraternally without regard for frontiers, in learning foreign languages to make communication easier, and in giving disinterested service to the countries with the least resources . . . You are the hope of peace.'

John Paul II is not advocating 'peace at any price'. He knows perfectly well that a sense of injustice is the root cause of so many conflicts. That is why he adds that 'there is no peace without justice and freedom, without a courageous commitment to promote both'. Was he thinking of Poland? Yes, but not exclusively: 'What happens in a country's internal social life has a considerable bearing – for better or worse – upon peace between nations.' This is aimed at the argument – heard from Czechoslovakia to South Africa – that outsiders should not meddle in what are purely 'internal matters'. In an interdependent world, that argument is invalid.

The Pope realistically recognizes the fact that history is in large measure a record of wars and conflicts. But he invites us to 're-read history'. What the re-reading will show, he says, is that even when violence was necessary, all else having failed, 'the factors of life and progress found even in wars and revolutions were derived from aspirations of another order than that of violence'. It is the only just-war or just-revolution theory he admits – and it is retrospective. In the present, he urges the leaders of the nations to 'make gestures for peace, even audacious ones, to break free from vicious circles and from the deadweight of passions inherited from history'.

What John Paul II has to say to the leaders of the world is in essence what he said at his inaugural Mass. Do not be afraid. Trust your people. As he puts it: 'I dare to encourage you to go further. Open up new doors to peace. Do everything in your power to make the way of dialogue prevail over that of force.' And his philosophical positions both permit and encourage him to consider the defence of humanity as an aspect, whether recognized or not, of the fundamental Christian task. There are not two worlds, one sacred and the other profane, but only one, and we are all in it together.

> We know that, without losing its natural consistency or its peculiar difficulties, our journey towards peace on earth is comprised within another journey, that of salvation, which reaches fulfilment in an eternal plenitude of grace, in total communion with God. Thus the Kingdom of God, the Kingdom of Peace, with its own source, means and end, already permeates, but without dilution, the whole of earthly activity. This vision of faith has a deep impact on the everyday action of Christians.

All the Latin American speeches on the political involvement of the Church should be seen in the light of this Teilhardian statement. The efforts towards peace and justice to which he summons the Church cannot be identified with the establishment of the Kingdom of God on earth, but neither can they be separated from it.

Little attention was paid to the Message. The same cannot be said of John Paul II's first encyclical, *Redemptor Hominis* (officially dated 4 March, though it appeared, under an embargo that was astonishingly respected, on 15 March). It was a media event. But it left the media floundering. That was partly because of the erroneous presumption that an encyclical letter must condemn something; and what was being condemned here was not altogether clear. 'Did he condemn atheism?', a BBC radio interviewer asked Archbishop Derek Worlock of Liverpool. It was rather like asking whether he was for or against sin. Other instant commentators decided that the Pope was condemning intercommunion and aiming a blow at the then Anglican leader, Archbishop Donald Coggan of Canterbury (in section 20); the vigorous passage on the denial of human rights in Communist countries, where believers are treated as 'second-class citizens' (17), was taken by some to be the main point of the encyclical; while others stressed the complicated section 16, 'Progress or threat', and saw it as a plea for the third world, an attack on ideologies as well as on 'consumer attitudes uncontrolled by ethics'.

No doubt *Redemptor Hominis* had some of these implications. But in making 'condemnations' the starting point, commentators were barking up a whole forest of wrong trees. For the encyclical was above all, and explicitly, a positive statement of faith. The misunderstandings, however, were forgivable, for the document was formidably long. ('In these days of instant communication', said a *Tablet* editorial, 'it may be thought that the shorter specific message is likely to be more effective.') It was also written in a complex style derived in part from the Pope's philosophical studies. The best way into it is to pick out the key words and note the nuances.

One of the key words in John Paul II's vocabulary, perhaps *the* key word, is 'dimension'. He is not unaware of humanist attempts to explain the world and to define and defend man; but he regards them as inadequate and superficial. Humanism truncates man and frustrates his divine destiny. What happens in Christ is that man's true and full dimensions are revealed: 'Through the Incarnation God gave human life the dimension that he intended man to have from his first beginning' (1). One cannot say the last word on man unless one has recognized this dimension.

But the coming of Christ on earth is not a parachute drop to be followed by a rocket-like disappearance called the Ascension. Rather, it has permanently affected human history: 'God entered the history of humanity and, as a man, became an actor in that history . . .' (1). The opening sentence of the encyclical enshrines that truth. It can be taken as a conscious reply to the Communist Manifesto of Karl Marx, written 131 years before. Marx began bluntly: 'The history of all hitherto existing society is the history of class struggles.' John Paul II writes: 'The Redeemer of man, Jesus Christ, is the centre of the universe and of history.' The rest of the encyclical is a prolonged meditation on the consequences of that statement.

Christ, in the vision of John Paul II, opens up the extra dimensions of human history. But we can only lay hold of this truth, only 'appropriate it' (to use his own term in section 10), through awareness. This is another of his key concepts. Awareness means the personal assimilation of the truth and implications of the incarnation. Christian truth is not meant to loll about inert on the surface of the mind: it has to penetrate the whole human person. Newman talked about the need to move from 'notional assent' to 'real assent'. John Paul II's word for that is awareness. Awareness is already half-way to prayer. The task of the Church is to keep alive the awareness of the dimensions of human history.

It is not a new task. But – and here is the originality of *Redemptor Hominis* – it has to be realized afresh in the changed conditions of today, in the last fifth of the twentieth century, as spaceship earth speeds towards the year 2000. The year 2000 exercises a peculiar fascination for John Paul II. He referred to it in his first, programmatic speech. It commands the encyclical from the opening paragraph onwards. The exact shape of the future is unknown. But the Pope will be guided 'by unlimited trust and obedience to the Spirit that Christ promised and sent to his Church' (2). There is a certain openness in his approach. He does not want to prescribe or predict the future.

Yet John Paul II knows that the age-old and ever-renewed task of the Church must start from where the Church actually is and where the world actually is. This idea gives shape to the encyclical: the Pope deals with the present state of the Church (Part I, 'Inheritance') and with the state of contemporary man (Part III, 'Redeemed man and his situation in the modern world'); and linking the two is the person of Christ (Part II, 'The mystery of the redemption'). In the final section, the Church is seen in its intersection with the modern world (Part IV, 'The Church's mission and man's destiny'). French commentators, in particular, complained of unclearness, even of 'incoherence'. But Cartesian clarity is only one form of clarity. True to his phenomenological background, John Paul II prefers to 'unfold' his thoughts gradually.

How, then, does he see the Church in 1979? Since the Second Vatican Council there has been a new awareness of the nature of the Church. The Council changed the Church's self-understanding. It steered it in the direction of collegiality – the idea that the pope and the bishops form a team. John Paul II stresses that this is no abstract idea. There are the instruments of collegiality – the Roman Synod, episcopal conferences, diocesan synods, councils of priests – which all express and advance the Church's rediscovery of the importance of participation. In this way, he says in a striking phrase, the local Churches 'should pulsate in full awareness of their own identity and, at the same time, of their own originality within the universal unity of the Church' (5). The local Churches – in some contexts they could be called national Churches – have their own special contribution to make. True, this respect for the diversity of local Churches is qualified, though not destroyed, by the requirement of unity. Just how this balance will work out in practice remains to be seen. But one can say that John Paul II's address at Puebla was in illustration of the way he sees his own authority and the local bishops' meshing in together: he spoke at the beginning of their meeting, and then left them to work among themselves towards the solution of their own problems. He neither abdicated nor dictated.

Another vital aspect of the new self-understanding of the Church is ecumenism. It is not an optional extra. It is not a hobby for ecumaniacs. It is an essential dimension of the Church's mission. Some Catholics believe that the ecumenical movement is a Protestant Trojan horse. John Paul II puts two *num* questions, expecting the answer 'no', to such critics. 'To all who, for whatever motive, would wish to dissuade the Church from seeking the universal unity of all Christians, the questions must be put once again: Have we the right not to do it? Can we fail to have trust – in spite of all human weaknesses and all the faults of past centuries – in Our Lord's grace as revealed recently through what the Holy Spirit said and we heard during the Council?' (6). The recognition that the ecumenical movement was the work of the Holy Spirit was one of the most important achievements of the Council; it put an end to the idea, found in Pius XI's *Mortalium Annos* (1928), that ecumenism led to 'indifferentism' (the view that 'it doesn't matter what you believe').

But inter-Church ecumenism is only one of the dimensions that the Council opened up. John Paul II evokes also the wider ecumenism which seeks a dialogue with the other great world religions. They possess 'treasures of human spirituality' which Christians need, and they enshrine implicitly those 'seeds of the Gospel' of which the Fathers of the Church spoke. For these reasons the Pope concludes that there should be 'dialogue, contacts, prayer in common' (6). The mention of 'prayer in common' goes further than Vatican II, which spoke only of 'dialogue and contacts'. It could be of great importance in dealing with Judaism and Islam. The theological under-pinning of these statements is the conviction that the Holy Spirit can operate 'outside the visible confines of the Mystical Body' (6). Although the Church claims to be the privileged sacrament of the Spirit, the Spirit is unconfined and can blow where it wills.

John Paul II recognizes, however, that this developing self-awareness of the Church as collegial and in dialogue has not been without its growing pains. His attitude towards the 'crisis' in the Church is one of the most fascinating aspects of the encyclical. He does not deny its existence or its virulence. In section 4 he remarks on 'critical attitudes' which have become widespread and have assailed, from within, 'the Church, her institutions and structures, and ecclesiastics and their activities'. In the post-conciliar period, it has sometimes seemed as if Catholics, obliged to be polite towards other Christians, have transferred their stock of hostility to their fellow Catholics. The Pope does not analyse the phenomenon at any length. 'This growing criticism', he says, 'was certainly due to various causes and we are furthermore sure that it was not always without a sincere love for the Church' (4). That recognition of sincerity in the critics on what may be loosely termed the left is significant. John Paul II avoids Paul VI's tendency to attribute all criticism indiscriminately to ill will or incipient loss of faith. However, there is a limit beyond which criticism is better not carried: 'Otherwise it ceases to be constructive and does not reveal truth, love and thankfulness for the grace in which we become sharers principally and fully in and through the Church' (4).

The Pope also acknowledges that what was called at the Council triumphalism, an attitude combining arrogance with a strong sense of moral and doctrinal rectitude, needed denouncing (4). But the contrary of discredited triumphalism is not a lack of conviction, still less any kind of defeatism. It is not difficult to read between the lines here: in some parts of the Church the legitimate attack on triumphalism was being turned into an onslaught on all certainty in faith. John Paul II is anxious that this misunderstanding should be avoided. The Church has no need to be apologetic when it is faithful to its mission. It can be grateful for gifts and graces received without being arrogant.

But if John Paul II makes points which should give pause to critics on the left, he has a balancing word for those on the right who believe that the Church has 'sold out to ecumenism' or 'bartered its soul for a mess of ecumenical porridge' or 'fallen down to worship the golden calf of modernity' (all phrases gleaned from the right-wing press). The Pope recognizes the problem: 'Some even express the opinion that these (ecumenical) efforts are harmful to the cause of the Gospel, are leading to further division within the Church, are causing confusion of ideas in questions of faith and morals, and are leading in fact to indifferentism' (6; translation modified for clarity). The Pope understands these fears. Many people feel that the security of the fortress Church has been exchanged for the insecurity of the pilgrim Church, that they no longer know what the Church believes. Lefebvre is only one spokesman for such views.

Paul VI had denounced him. John Paul II merely remarks: 'It is perhaps a good thing that the spokesmen for these opinions should express their fears. However, in this respect, also, correct limits must be maintained' (6). In other words he does not favour repression: genuine anxieties should be expressed and brought out into the open, for if they go underground they can poison the inner life of the Church. It is noteworthy that John Paul II should recognize the sincerity of the left-wing critics and the fears of the right-wing critics. Though he regards them both as misguided, he has accurately diagnosed their dominant attitudes and motivations. In his analysis the Church is neither being undermined by ecumenism nor dependent for its future on the 'liberal agenda'.

This might suggest that John Paul II, like his predecessor Paul VI, is a moderate who picks his way nimbly down the middle, leaving his discomfited challengers to left and right. But it would be more accurate to call him a radical in the original meaning of the term: he goes to the root or essence of the Christian faith. That is his norm, his only norm. Indeed, far from claiming to be a 'moderate' (the common ambition of so many leaders in the late 1970s), he expressly says that he is glad to belong to the 'violent people of God' (11), where violence means the upsetting of staid calculations and comfortable pre-established ideas. Though he wants to reconcile the warring elements in the Church, the path ahead does not lie in compromise but in recalling everyone to the essential and prophetic mission of the Church.

After considering and putting in perspective the state of the Church in 1979, John Paul II turns to the present state of the world. Since this part of the encyclical was likely to be the most widely read, it provides a good test of his ideas. For although one might trust a man of God so long as he stays in the spiritual realm, doubt is cast on his spiritual insight if his account of the ordinary empirical world is patently false or distorted. Admittedly 'the present state of the world' sounds like an invitation to vagueness, and the description of it can only be in very general terms. But the Pope makes some effort to examine realities. He looks first at the 'map of the world' (11).

But it is a very special sort of map that he studies. It reveals first of all the large variety of religions found in the different continents. But there is a novel and disturbing feature: 'this map of the world's religions has superimposed on it, in previously unknown layers typical of our time, the phenomenon of atheism in its various forms, beginning with the atheism that is programmed, organized and structured as a political system' (11). The numbers game can be played endlessly, but it is a sobering fact that although the Roman Catholic Church, with over seven hundred million adherents, is the largest Christian body, it is still smaller than the population of China – where atheism remains, despite recent developments, 'programmed, organized and structured'. The Pope's Polish experience makes him aware that for religion to be regarded by certain governments as a threat, a relic of bourgeois attitudes, an obstacle to the emergence of the 'new man', is unprecedented in human history. Until the twentieth century atheism was sporadic, intermittent, and a dissident protest against prevailing conformity. Today the positions are reversed, and it is theism that represents protest and dissidence: 'Is it not often Jesus Christ himself that has made an appearance at the side of people judged for the sake of the truth?' (12). The Pope does not lament this new fact. It frees the Church (and the idea of Providence) from being merely the conservative prop of an unjust social order. It frees the Church, once more, for prophecy.

Against that general background, John Paul II asks (in section 15) an interesting question: What is modern man most afraid of? (Iris Murdoch remarks in *The Sovereignty of Good*: 'It is always a significant question to ask about any philosopher: what is he afraid of?'). Invited to write the answer on the back of a postcard, most of us would probably answer 'hunger' or 'nuclear war'. John Paul II's answer is that modern man is most afraid of 'alienation'. That is a philosophical concept, and it owes its modern development to Marx. The Pope knows this and puts the word in quotation-marks. Man is estranged, cut off from his true nature, robbed of the fruits of his work, and what should enable him to grow as a person is turned against him (like the car-worker in Wojtyla's poem). Alienation can take many forms, but they all involve a twisting out of the true, the loss of an expected good. It may throw light on his use of the term to quote his Corpus Christi sermon in June 1978: 'In the name of socialization people are herded into ever vaster industrial establishments and housed in multi-storey tower blocks where they are hermetically sealed off from each other. It is not only the walls that separate them, it is the whole atmosphere of distrust, indifference, and alienation. In such an atmosphere the human heart withers.'

But although John Paul II accepts this Marxist term as descriptively accurate, he does not accept the Marxist explanation of its causes (which Marxism traces to capitalism). Like Paul Tillich, he uses alienation or estrangement as the modern translation of the biblical idea of sin. He is very close to the ex-marxist Polish philosopher, Kolakowski, who has pointed out that man's alienation is much profounder than Marx imagined. It is not enough to change the economic organization of society in order to make the workers feel that they are genuinely participating in the fruits of their labour. What goes under the name of socialism has resulted in a form of state capitalism in which the worker feels just as alienated as before. And in the end, alienation exists on a much deeper level. It is part of the human condition. There are dimensions that economic organization and politics cannot touch: they have nothing to say to the handicapped or the bereaved or the broken-hearted. Alienation can be overcome only by spiritual progress.

Our notion of progress, John Paul II points out, is deeply ambivalent. We too uncritically accept the popular idea that progress can be measured in terms of the advance of science and technology, while ignoring the fact that there is loss as well as gain: the environment is polluted, the earth's scarce resources are used up heedlessly, and weapons of destruction absorb finance which could be used to make the earth fruitful. John Paul II sets himself resolutely against a purely utilitarian view of nature whereby man would 'see no other meaning in his natural environment than what serves for immediate use and consumption' (15). His own definition of progress is an echo of the themes of *The Acting Person*: the real question is whether 'man, as man, is becoming truly better, that is to say more mature spiritually, more aware of the dignity of his humanity, more responsible, more open to others, especially the neediest and the weakest, and readier to give and to aid all' (15). Progress, in other words, has human and not merely scientific criteria.

He then speaks of 'x-raying' progress, and the x-ray reveals that there are many modern forms of slavery: man can become 'the slave of things, the slave of economic systems, the slave of production, the slave of his own products' (16). The utilitarian work ethic – shared by both socialism and capitalism – can rob life of all joy and spontaneity. (One has the impression that John Paul II would be happier in a commune than as a nine-to-five commuter.) He also denounces, in the manner of Herbert Marcuse, the many types of 'manipulation . . . through the whole of the organization of community life, through the production system and through pressure from the means of social communication' (the media). Both the enslavement and the manipulation confirm that modern man has lost control over his own destiny. Nor is the Pope thinking merely of Communist societies. The consumer civilization of the West has its own forms of slavery and manipulation which, moreover, lead to a profound injustice, since the abuse of freedom by one group limits the freedom of others. The rich grow richer and the poor continue to grow poorer. One may conclude that John Paul II will be just as Third-World-minded as Paul VI. He is genuinely non-aligned. Both the power blocks in the world are tarred with the same utilitarian brush. One cannot make 'the greatest good of the greatest number' the criterion of morality, he had argued in *Love and Responsibility,* since optimum pleasure cannot be identified with optimum happiness. Happiness is a by-product, not directly attainable. It follows from the pursuit of the good, the true and the beautiful.

The rejection of utilitarianism which makes the Pope even-handed in his treatment of both East and West also makes him incline to the Western concept of human rights. His Polish experience has taught him that there is a marked contrast between official declarations on human rights and what actually happens. Section 17 of the encyclical is devoted to the contrast between the letter and the spirit. Governments cheerfully sign, for instance, the UNO Declaration on Human Rights or the Helsinki accords, but then these noble principles are regularly breached. The missing concept in all these discussions is that of the common good as an over-arching value to which everyone must be subject (17):

> The common good that authority in the State serves is brought to full realization only when all the citizens are

sure of their rights. The lack of this leads to the dissolution of society, opposition by citizens to authority, or a situation of oppression, intimidation, violence and terrorism, of which many examples have been provided by the totalitarianisms of this century.

Without the concept of the common good, there is an inevitable and dangerous tendency to absolutize the State or the Party. But that is a form of idolatry, in which the relative is made absolute. One could argue that 'God is the supreme dissident'; he makes the claims of State or party to dictate what is social morality appear paltry, secondary and – in the end – unjust. Among the fundamental and inalienable human rights is the right to freedom of religion. This claim is not based, says John Paul II, on revelation but on 'natural law'. The conclusion, learned the hard way in Poland, follows: 'The curtailment and violation of religious freedom are in contrast with man's dignity and his objective rights' (17). Political implications flow immediately from the assertion of the common good and objective human rights (17).

> The essential sense of the State, as a political community, consists in (the fact) that the society and people composing it are master and sovereign of their own destiny. This sense remains unrealized if, instead of the exercise of power with the moral participation of the society or people, what we see is the imposition of power by a certain group upon all the other members of the society.

John Paul II is a sound social democrat.

The really important feature of the encyclical is that it sees the drama of human history today as being played out against the backcloth of 'salvation-history' (*Heilsgeschichte*). This is another way in which John Paul II introduces an extra dimension into our thinking about world events. He may appear to be musing about human rights and other concepts which are the stuff of international political discourse; but he sees all these questions in the light of Christ, the Second Adam, the one in whom the human race sets off once more on its endless pilgrimage which is a journey towards the Father. Commentators on the encyclical would have made less heavy weather of it if they had noticed its literary form. In the final section (22) John Paul II writes: 'As I end this meditation . . .' In his mind it was not a set of directives or a call to order or a further development of traditional teaching. It was essentially a meditation on the human and the Christian vocation. And this, it may be added, revives a more ancient tradition of the encyclical letter: it is a profession of faith despatched by the Bishop of Rome so that other Churches may 'verify' their faith and see that they are in harmony with what he has to say. *Redemptor Hominis* has another feature which marks the start of an era: whereas the pontificate of Paul VI was backward-looking in the sense that its policies were entirely derived from the Council which ended in 1965, John Paul II is forward-looking. The reference and the commitment to the Council remain, of course, but he is more interested in the 'world in the making' and the 'threshold of the future'. He intends that the Church should contribute something as we advance towards the year 2000.

The third document of the pontificate which needs looking at in detail is the Letter to Priests. It would be a mistake to attribute to the Letter an importance it does not possess. It is clearly a less important document than the encyclical. However, the conclusion to the encyclical has observations on theological method which could usefully be applied to the priesthood and other controverted questions. The theological task has grown enormously, the encyclical says (19), because of advances in learning, in the exact and the human sciences as well as philosophy. It is here that John Paul II also concedes 'the virtues of a certain pluralism of methodology'. One of the reasons why the Letter to Priests was found disappointing was that it ignored those two principles: it was not influenced by 'the human sciences', and it made no concessions to 'pluralism of methodology'. Worse still, it seemed to brush aside collegiality. Before John Paul II had time to hear what the local Churches had to say on this highly controversial topic, he had rushed into print and pre-empted the ground.

Even so, the Letter is a moving document. The reader feels like an intruder on what is very much a private gathering. The Pope is a priest addressing his brother priests in a highly personal way. He speaks throughout of 'our priesthood', and tries to put himself on the same level as his fellow priests by adapting a famous remark of St Augustine's and saying: 'For you I am a bishop, with you I am a priest'. (In Augustine's version the last word was 'Christian'). The personal tone of the letter disposes of a silly Roman rumour that the document had been written towards the end of the pontificate of Paul VI, and that successive conclaves had imposed it first on John Paul I and then on John Paul II as a condition of election. This is nonsense, first because conclaves are not allowed to impose conditions on papal candidates and secondly because the Letter is authentically Wojtyla in style and even hardens some of the positions put forward in Paul VI's encyclical *Sacerdotalis Coelibatus* (1967). But the reason why the rumour arose is interesting: the Letter was seen as something of a setback, and since people wanted to continue to hope in John Paul II and the bright promise of the new pontificate the story was designed to let him off the hook. But he impaled himself, deliberately and with care, on it. His letter is uncompromisingly conservative.

It has its own explanation, for example, of why priestly identity has become a problem: 'Perhaps in these recent years – at least in certain quarters – there has been too much discussion about the priesthood, the priest's "identity", the value of his presence in the modern world, and so on, and on the other hand too little praying' (section 10). But the discussion took place because there was a problem: it was not the cause of the problem. It seems unlikely that, if there were less discussion and more prayer, the problem would tiptoe away. Moreover, the phrase 'in certain quarters' seems designed to discredit rare malcontents who have raised the problem. But this contradicts recent history: at the 1971 Synod a sizeable number of bishops wanted the ordination of married men and a complete review of the theology of the ministry. Archbishop Paul Grégoire of Montreal, who could not be described as irresponsible, had listed the reasons why there was a crisis of priestly identity, and he regarded them all as positive developments which could not be reversed. They were 'the emergence of a laity which has a greater awareness of its responsibility for the Church and for its prophetic and apostolic task; the stress laid by the Council on the common priesthood of all the faithful; the desire and need for presence to the world, and for the priest to be engaged in projects of culture and civilization, justice and peace; the resistance that priests meet with among the faithful towards any authority or teaching that is based on anything other than competence.' Grégoire offered these points as a stimulus to reflection on the ministry, a reflection which he believed had been made necessary by Vatican II. These factors undoubtedly existed. They could not be swept aside.

John Paul II ignores these differences of emphasis. He minimizes the second point (the Council's stress on a common priesthood), and everything else in his letter flows from that. True, he recalls (in section 3) 'the common priesthood of the faithful', but draws no conclusions from it, and prefers to dwell on the difference between this common priesthood and the 'hierarchical priesthood'. The two differ 'essentially and not only in degree'. He likes this phrase so much that he repeats it three times. The consequence is that although he refers to the necessary relationship between the (ordained) priest and his people, the relationship is only one-way: the priest 'serves' the faithful who are there as the 'object' of his action. The priesthood, John Paul II writes, does not 'take its origin from that community, as though it were the community that "called" or "delegated" '(4).

Except in Holland, few would quarrel with that statement as it stands. But many theologians would want to maintain that the needs of the people of God give rise to a demand for certain services which are then recognized and confirmed by the Church. Historically, that was how ministries grew up – in response to needs. And such thinking led to suggestions about new forms of ministry as well as to the ordination of married men and of women. Pope John Paul's starting-point leaves him with no room for manoeuvre on these fronts. He sees the priesthood as a state within the Church rather than as a function for the Church. And with this conception goes a sense of priestly superiority – 'You priests are expected to have a care and commitment which are far greater and different from those of any lay person' (5) – which is hard to reconcile with the language of Vatican II. It was often said at Vatican II that the unfortunate priest was ground between the upper millstone of the boosted bishop and the nether millstone of the emerging laity. There is no danger of that happening with John Paul II; but laypeople may well feel that the Church is being reclericalized and that they risk becoming, once again, second-class citizens in the Church.

It could perhaps be argued, in defence of the Letter, that its purpose is not to present a theological treatise on the ministry but to encourage, console and comfort priests in the front line. They remain, together with monks and nuns, the main professionals of the Church; and many of them have not had an easy time of it as the rug of comfortable securities has been pulled unceremoniously from under their feet. But they cannot have been much consoled by a return to a largely pre-conciliar theology of the ministry.

There is one category of priest which was most emphatically not consoled by the Letter: those who were wondering whether they were in the right place and were pondering the agonizing step of resignation. John Paul II is distinctly unsympathetic towards something that seems beyond his comprehension. Too bad, he says in effect, too late, you knew perfectly well what you were doing when you were ordained: 'It is a matter here of keeping one's word to Christ and the Church. Keeping one's word is, at one and the same time, a duty and a proof of the priest's inner maturity' (9). This recalls the doctrine of commitment found in *The Acting Person*. The priest in difficulties is exhorted to more fervent prayer. 'One must think of all these things', the Pope goes on, 'especially at moments of crisis, and not have recourse to a dispensation, understood as an "administrative intervention", as though in fact it were not, on the contrary, a matter of a profound question of conscience and a test of humanity' (9).

That is a baffling observation. John Paul II appears to be saying that some priests who resign (which means in practice who seek a 'dispensation' from the Vatican) do so in a light-hearted and cavalier manner, as though they were merely resigning from a club. It is difficult to think of any resigned priest who did not feel, profoundly, that the step he was taking was a matter of conscience and not merely of administrative routine. Consequently, the exhortation seems certain to fall on deaf ears, and all the more since it is linked with a warning about how priests may otherwise cease to be 'necessary and popular' (7). If the conclusion is that they ought to stay at their posts in order to remain 'necessary and popular', then some might be tempted to say that they prefer integrity to popularity – and they could make a good personalist case for saying so.

John Paul's practice has been entirely consistent with his

rigorist theory. Since he became Pope, dispensations, which were averaging sixty a month, have dwindled to a trickle. Priests wishing to marry have been bluntly told that they will not get a dispensation. The only ones allowed to slip through the net have been old men, approaching death, who wished to 'put their lives in order'. The effect of this change of policy, so different from that of Paul VI, will be that some priests, instead of leaving the priestly ministry quietly and without fuss, will be driven into conflict and – from a canonical point of view – irregularity and illegality. A priest who 'attempts marriage' without a dispensation is automatically excommunicated. His future relationship with the Church will be soured if not destroyed. Thus, instead of an orderly movement from one form of ministry in the Church to another, there will be an exodus accompanied by much bitterness. That does not seem a desirable result. And the alternative is even more catastrophic: that priests will stay put out of hyprocrisy.

Reactions to the Letter were unenthusiastic. Even those who claimed to be supporting it had to resort to vagueness. Koenig blandly explained that the Pope's main purpose was to lift the issues of ordination and celibacy above the level of 'mere administrative acts and to show that sacred promises and deep questions of conscience are involved'. But no one had ever doubted that. *The Tablet* printed the Letter almost in full (in the issue of 28 April), but with a commentary which spoke of 'the Pope's very simple approach'; it regretted that his concentration on the issue of celibacy had 'given the impression of a certain over-simplification'. The paper also put three sharp objections. The Pope had asserted that the Latin tradition of celibacy meant that the priest was more 'free' and therefore 'strictly ordered to the common priesthood of the faithful'. He was more available, in short. But where, asked the sober *Tablet*, 'does this leave the Orthodox and the Anglicans, let alone the Catholic priests of the Oriental discipline' (who are allowed to marry)? The paper also pointed out that the example given by the Pope of an 'abandoned shrine', where the Eucharist was no longer celebrated for lack of an ordained priest, 'is as powerful an argument for the ordination of married men as it is for the social value of a celibate priesthood'. And finally the paper argued that too many 'defections' had resulted 'from the despair of good men rather than simply from the infidelity of weak ones'.

Opposition to the papal Letter was particularly intense in France. A group of priests submitted a letter to the Pope through Cardinal Alexandre Renard of Lyons, who bears the proud title of 'Primate of the Gauls'. They began by saying that it was particularly difficult for the Pope to address a letter to all priests at once without being familiar with the different situations in which the ministry had to be exercised. The result was that the Pope's Letter appeared as 'a word from on high, too closely linked with a theology that had not assimilated the orientations of Vatican II'. What the Pope denounced as 'secularization' they saw rather as a form of presence to their people which gave new life to the ministry. On celibacy they observed that 'it is not fidelity to a state of life that has priority, but rather fidelity to the ministry that has been entrusted to them in the service of the community'. For this reason they rejected the parallel between the sacrament of marriage and the promise of celibacy made by a priest at ordination. 'It may be true', they argued, 'that marriage is the sacrament of love, but priestly ordination is not the sacrament of celibacy.'

There were Spaniards, too, who were upset. German theologians were even more severe. Hans Küng accused the Pope of 'violating the human right to marriage' within the Church, while posing as the defender of human rights outside. Küng had a point when he said that 'the Roman Catholic Church is paying a heavy price for imposing on all candidates for the priesthood something which should be adopted only by those to whom it is given as a free gift of grace'. That was the crucial point. The distinction between the call to priesthood and the charism of celibacy had become a commonplace of theological thinking since the Council. The Pope had chosen to ignore it.

An editorial in the *National Catholic Reporter* of Kansas City tried hard to put the Letter into perspective. In his lifetime, it said, the Pope has seen 'priests jailed, tortured and murdered; religious and civil rights denied; and a Church threatened with extinction unless it held firm. By contrast the qualms of priests who have left or who want to be laicized are as nothing to him' (20 April 1979). There is truth in this judgement, which coincides with that of the Pope himself. In Czechoslovakia, in Hungary more insidiously, in South Korea and El Salvador more dramatically, to be a priest is to be in the front line of a battle in which there can be no compromise; it is only the blinkered vision of Western intellectuals that permits a different belief. But if one accepts that, does it not follow that the Pope has transferred his own experience of being a priest in Poland to the universal Church, and has run the risk of misreading its needs in the process?

John Paul II's Letter to Priests was the first act of his pontificate in which he made absolutely clear his commitment to a conservative position. One cannot exactly say that it was his *Humanae Vitae*, since the Letter did not have the status of an encyclical, and its theme was not one calculated to arouse the immediate interest of the laity; but the comparison is valid in so far as both documents were meant to end controversy and inflamed it instead. The first doubts came creeping in. Would the Polish factor prevail? Were we in for a new era of reaction and toughness? There was no question about John Paul II's popularity and strength of personality, but to what ends would he devote them? Would he become a Spiro Agnew figure, appealing to the 'silent majority' over the heads of a handful of dissident theologians? His message to the world at large was, as this chapter has shown, important, opportune and fresh: but it would carry less weight if he had behind him a divided Church.

6

The Exile's Return

The visit to Poland, in early June 1979, was the explosion that never happened. The return of the exiled patriot could be expected to set off epic problems: congregations of unmanageable millions, appalling problems of feeding and sanitation, political demonstrations by dissident groups, and increased tension between a nervous Communist leadership and a confident episcopate under Wyszynski. None of that came about. Congregations at the open-air masses were for various reasons far smaller than expected, crowds and security forces behaved exemplarily, and dissenters held their fire. Relations between the State and the Church were manifestly better at the end of it all than they had been at the start.

Many things helped, including the good sense of Edward Gierek, the country's political boss. But the real key to the success of the visit lay in John Paul II himself and his determination to treat it as a religious event. That saved the country's Communist leaders from the humiliation of holding the ring for a demonstration of the power of the Church. At the same time it allowed the Pope steadily to re-assert his views on the importance of individual rights and beliefs. Above all there was the essential Polishness, the uninhibitedness, of his style. It explained how he could develop a rapport with a huge Polish crowd as easily as with any individual Pole, young or old; how one moment he could be bringing tears to the eyes of his listeners with the force of his humanity, and the next singing loudly and unselfconsciously with his congregation, even slightly out of tune. The Italian prelates in his entourage, at first bewildered, were eventually captivated. As an American television reporter put it, 'they went around looking like men who'd backed a winner'.

Despite 35 years of Communist effort, and in dramatic contrast to the situation everywhere else where Communists rule, the

Catholic Church in Poland has never been stronger than now. It is estimated that 90 per cent of the 35 million Poles are baptized Catholics, and at least 75 per cent are practising believers. The churches are packed to the doors every Sunday. Besides 8,000 monks and 32,000 nuns, the country has close on 20,000 priests (6000 more than after the Second World War); and there are nearly 5000 more in training. Poland is in fact an exporter of priests, mostly to the enormous Polish diaspora. In Britain today, for instance, there are 72 Polish parishes, in France 73, and in the United States over 1000.

The new Pope takes seriously his duties as Bishop of Rome. When he made an early series of visits to Roman parishes he began with La Rustica, because the church there happens to be dedicated to Our Lady of Czestochowa, in south-western Poland. It is at Czestochowa that the Black Madonna, in fact an ancient Byzantine ikon, is kept in its special chapel at the medieval monastery of Jasna Gora. Catholic Poles believe that in times of persecution or invasion the Black Madonna has saved them from disaster. Legend has it that at the time of the Mongol invasions she inspired national resistance, and that she was responsible for bringing down darkness on the invaders and throwing them back in confusion at a critical moment of the battle. Another legend asserts that in 1430, when a band of Hussites (Czechoslovak proto-Protestants) attacked the monastery at Jasna Gora and carried off the image, their horses froze in their tracks. The image was thrown to the ground, and a soldier struck at it twice with his sword; when he struck it a third time he fell dead. To this day two slash marks on the right cheek of the Madonna are said to have resisted all attempts by restorers to remove them. The Madonna is also credited with a hand in two seventeenth-century victories, over the Swedish invaders and then over the Turks besieging Vienna; and – even more recently than the 'miracle of the Vistula' in 1920 – with arranging, in 1956, Wyszynski's release from house arrest.

For dedicated Marxists all this was mere medievalism, an obstruction to the task in hand. A Polish pope increased its emotional force and presented Gierek and his colleagues with a new set of anxieties. At the time of the Pope's visit there was discontent among working people at the Government's failure to improve living standards, despite the huge programme of capital investment carried out during the early 1970s (which had created an accumulated Polish debt to the West of some sixteen billion dollars). Chronic shortages in the shops, notably of meat, did not help.

An additional irritant for the regime was the emerging sound of opposition voices, heard more loudly and persistently in Poland than anywhere else in Eastern Europe. It was first prompted by the brutalities of the militia (civil police with a paramilitary manner) in their repression of the strikes and riots which followed the food price rises of June 1976. It started with the formation by a small group of intellectuals of a committee which found lawyers for victimized workers and helped their families. From this small beginning developed a mass of uncensored publications, known by the Russian word *samizdat*, printed and distributed secretly and criticizing state censorship ceaselessly. Other opposition groups emerged, including one which revived an old feature of dissident life, the 'flying university' – programmes of lectures by academics in private on subjects not covered by the official university syllabus.

Remarkably, the groups worked, and still work, openly, keeping the Government informed of their policies and membership. The State's efforts to cow members by arresting them, beating them up, raiding their apartments or withholding their passports have failed. At the time of the Pope's visit the movement was estimated to be regularly involving some 40,000 people. It had had its successes, notably in securing the release of 98 workers from prison. The *samizdat* publications, more than forty of them, were being read by some 100,000 Poles inside the country.

The Church's relationship with this loose coalition of intellectuals, workers and students has been an informally sympathetic one: when the Pope was Archbishop of Krakow he sometimes allowed flying university classes to be held in Church property. But that was well short of full Church support for dissent. The process of 'normalization' required Wyszynski to sustain a dialogue with Gierek in pursuit of various objectives. They included permits to build new churches, especially on new urban housing-estates. The 365 permits granted during the previous five years had not met the need, and even after the granting of a formal permit the Church often found itself faced by a variety of bureaucratic delaying devices. (In the growing self-confidence of the Catholic community, country people sometimes went ahead and put up churches without waiting for formal permission.)

The bishops repeatedly called for an end to discrimination against Catholics in important civil service appointments, and to anti-Church propaganda. Another demand was that the State should acknowledge the Church's legal status; otherwise it could not claim its constitutionally granted rights before the courts. A further appeal was for an end to the banning of religious teaching in schools. Another Church complaint was against the State's making workers work on Sundays.

Probably the most pressing of the Church's demands was for an end to censorship. A month before he was elected pope, Cardinal Wojtyla signed a pastoral letter from the episcopate appealing to the Government to allow the Church access to the media, at least to the extent of broadcasting a Sunday Mass for the sick and aged and housebound. The letter complained that the media, which were the property of the whole human family, had been taken over by the State and made to serve an ideology which aimed at bringing up human beings without God. The letter went on:

> Things are not as they should be. The mass communi-cations media are abused in order to impose one kind of view only and one behaviour pattern only . . . To ignore our opinion, the opinion of the consumers, is to treat us as objects to be manipulated at will by those who have acquired power . . . We all know that the spirit of freedom is the proper climate for the full development of a person . . . State censorship has always been, and remains, a weapon of totalitarian systems. With the aid of censorship the aim is not only to influence the mental life of society, but even to paralyse the cultural and religious life of the whole people.

Up to the time of the papal visit the Polish bishops resented the absence of any return from the Government for the Church's work in helping to promote social stability, sobriety and hard work. True, the Church's position had improved since Gierek's access to power in 1970. The regime liked to point out that there were more churches in Poland in 1979 than in 1939, and that the ratio of priests to population was higher in Poland than in Italy. Nobody was prevented from going to church, and free speech reigned there. In addition, Polish Catholics have been able to hold huge public processions on feast days, especially Corpus Christi. When the 60th anniversary of Polish independence was celebrated in November 1978, upwards of 15,000 people filled Warsaw cathedral and stood hundreds deep around it. Most remarkable of all, perhaps, the Catholic university of Lublin survives and prospers in the face of continuous official obstruction.

Nevertheless, the Polish regime is still officially Marxist-Leninist and thus formally dedicated to the destruction of religious faith. The Church is harassed, sometimes savagely. There is severe censorship of religious publications, especially of the one independent Catholic weekly paper *Tygodnik Powszechny*. The allocation of newsprint to this paper, and for the printing of Bibles and other religious material, is ludicrously small in relation to the potential market. Schools time social and sporting events to conflict with church attendance on Sundays and feast days. Seminarians are often denied the national-service deferment granted to ordinary students.

Yet Church and State do share certain objectives. Both have in mind the importance of preserving a reasonable level of civic stability to discourage any possibility of Soviet intervention. Both want to see a high level of morality, thrift and industry. The Church strongly endorses the Government's policy of censoring pornography. By the time of the totally unexpected election of Wojtyla a remarkable degree of accommodation had been reached between the deeply respected and politically skilful Wyszynski and the moderate, pragmatic Gierek. No one – not the Pope, not the episcopate, not the Government, and presumably not the Soviet Union – wanted that accommodation disturbed by the papal visit. There was disagreement only about how best to keep the peace. Some of the Politburo's hardliners are believed to have recommended that the visit should not take place at all.

At the heart of these anxieties lay John Paul II's preoccupation with human rights. The Government was unhappy over the

Pope's expressed wish to be in Krakow in May at the time of the ceremonies to mark the death of St Stanislaw, killed 900 years before for criticizing a Polish king's licentious way of life. As archbishop, the Pope had borne a leading part in the seven-year preparations for the anniversary. The Church saw Stanislaw as a martyr; the Government favoured the view that he was a rebel bishop who intrigued against his ruler and was properly executed for the crime.

In its sensitivity over this issue, the Government blundered just before Christmas of 1978, when a State censor cut all references to Stanislaw out of a letter from John Paul II to his former archdiocese. The official was evidently uneasy about the Pope's description of Stanislaw as 'a magnificent example of concern about people, which we must compare with our own indifference, our negligence, our despondency and our concern with our own interests . . . .'

But in Poland today a censor cannot sub-edit papal messages with impunity. Jerzy Turowicz, the experienced and combative editor-in-chief of *Tygodnik Powszechny*, refused to publish a word of the mutilated version. As a storm of protest began to build up in the archdiocese, the Government's man in Rome was hastily told by Warsaw to go and explain to the Vatican why the cuts had been made. The fuss died down only after the Government gave special authorization for the message to be read in full in all the churches of the archdiocese. At the same time hints were dropped in Warsaw that a local censor had acted on his own authority. Few Poles believed them.

It had been the Government's first taste of the explosive power contained in the mere existence of a Polish Pope. Subsequently over two months of delicate negotiations were needed before officials of Church and State could compile an itinerary for the visit acceptable to both sides. Not until May did communiqués by each side appear. The episcopate's communiqué presented a detailed outline of the nine-day 'visit-pilgrimage'; it appeared in the daily *Slowo Powszechne* (published by a State-supported Catholic body named PAX) and in *Tygodnik Powszechny*. The Government's communiqué, issued by the Polish Press Agency PAP, gave a bare listing of the places the Pope would visit.

As early as 2 March the President, Henryk Jablonski, had

stated that 'the first son of the Polish nation in history to hold the highest office in the Church will be received cordially both by the authorities and the public'. A few weeks later a Government spokesman told a group of Western journalists that after being greeted at the airport by Jablonski the Pope would be driven to the Royal Castle for a meeting with Gierek. But the May communiqué left this item out. It said only that the Pope would be met by 'the highest authorities' in the State, with no names given.

It became clear that there had been difficult negotiations between Government and episcopate over whether the Pope should visit Silesia, a highly industrialized region of Poland which Gierek had managed as local Party secretary for many years before becoming first Party secretary. The Pope, it seemed, had been very keen to visit Piekary, about seven miles from the Silesian capital Katowice and site of an annual pilgrimage by Catholic men on the last Sunday in May. But it seemed that the Government was sensitive about Church influence among working people in the region, and strongly resisted the idea of a papal visit there. The communiqué revealed that a compromise had been reached: the Pope would celebrate a solemn Mass in Czestochowa on 5 June, and would preach there on that day and the next to workers brought from different parts of Silesia; but he would not go to Piekary. Similarly he would not conduct a Mass in the new church at Nowa Huta, a new steel town near Krakow. To do so would be to rub the Government's nose in the fact that it had opposed the building of any church there at all, and been overborne.

An admirable characteristic of Poles is their ability to extract last-minute order out of confusion. A month before the pontiff was due to set foot in Poland, the casual visitor would never have imagined an event of such magnitude was imminent. Once the papal itinerary had been agreed, though, a sense of national pride obliged the Polish Government to spend large sums on improving the appearance of some of the shabby-looking places the Pope would be visiting – Gniezno, the original Polish capital; Czestochowa, the country's most important religious shrine; Wadowice, the Wojtyla birthplace. The sudden appearance of wooden scaffolding in these places, turning each of them into ants' nests of feverishly working plasterers, carpenters and painters, was for the benefit not so much of the Pope (who knew all about the decades of neglect along Polish streets) as of the world's television crews. By the beginning of June the streets on the Pope's route had been spruced up, the walls with attractive pink, beige or white coats of paint, the woodwork picked out in white gloss, and plaster mouldings restored and repainted.

In Nowa Huta, the month before, an explosion had blown a leg off the huge statue of Lenin and broken hundreds of windows in the apartment-blocks surrounding it. Now the damage was cleared up almost overnight. The authorities never traced the people responsible, or at any rate never said they had. Many Poles suspected that the explosion was the work of the authorities themselves, to give them grounds for an extensive security sweep among dissident groups before the papal visit. When the security men were questioning steel workers who customarily handled explosives, the suspects laughed and said 'You can be quite sure that if we had done the job Lenin would be smashed into small pieces by now.'

The Polish press, apart from its tiny religious section, remained oddly silent about the visit; and the silence seemed the more unreal against the fact that the visit had become virtually the main topic of conversation in the country. There was endless speculation about whether people would be let off work or school, what transport there would be, how many people would gather, whether they could be fed and watered, how the militia would behave, what likelihood there was of people being crushed to death.

The daily arrival of aircraft from abroad at Okecie airport outside Warsaw continued to bring a steady flow of tourists, mostly of Polish origin but settled in the West. The silence in the non-religious domestic press continued. The first mention of the Pope for weeks was an eight-line paragraph in the main Government paper, *Zycie Warszawy*, only five days before the Pope was due to arrive.

The following day, in a longer report, the paper did write of 'great foreign interest' in the Pope's visit, pointing to the accreditation of nine hundred overseas journalists. (Whether because the visit now promised to be orderly, or because covering it promised to be expensive, that figure was less than a third of the numbers earlier expected.) There was still not a word on the obsessive home interest. But the most ludicrous example of the Government's determination to give minimum press publicity to the event was the listing in *Zycie Warszawy* for 28 May, on the back page, of extensive traffic restrictions that would be in force in central Warsaw from 31 May to 3 June. Not a line indicated that the reason for the restrictions was the presence of the Pope. The Warsaw populace had to learn the details of the Pope's itinerary from the religious papers and from large notices outside the main churches.

The city was alive with rumours – hospitals to be cleared for casualties, bars to be closed – and jokes. ('Karol Wojtyla's a fine example of how a non-Communist can make good in Poland.' 'Why isn't there any yellow paint in the shops? – It's all been bought up by the militia to paint their truncheons to look like candles.' 'Why can't you buy white or black material? – The militia have taken it all so they can dress up as monks or priests, for security purposes.')

On the night of Thursday 31 May came what for many people would remain the most dramatic visual recollection of the entire papal visit. At about half past ten a large low-loader lorry arrived at Victory Square and drove up to a spacious steel and wood platform, carpeted with hessian to look like solid stone, which had been built during the few days before. On the lorry was a huge cross, some thirty feet in length, consisting of solid oak planks fixed to a framework of tubular steel. Under television lights, a mobile crane slowly lifted the cross until it hung over the platform. The four steel spigots at its foot were lowered into the steel sockets prepared for them; within a few minutes the cross was planted in the platform, the lorry and crane were away, and the people of Warsaw – of the world – were aware of a kind of miracle.

For the next two days this towering cross, embellished with a large red stole as a symbol of the resurrection, dominated Victory Square. On Friday, the day before the Pope's arrival and the first open-air Mass, inhabitants of Warsaw came on foot in their hundreds just to stand under a blazing sun and gaze at this symbol of the indestructibility of the Roman Catholic Church in Poland. Those 35 years of Communist hostility seemed to have their answer. It is true that by midnight on Saturday an army of workmen had swept away all trace of the cross to make a take-off pad for the papal helicopters; but for 48 hours it had dominated Warsaw.

Friday 1 June was notable for the spate of rumours sweeping the city about the illness of the prime minister, Piotr Jaroszewicz. He was known to have had a heart-attack; many people were now convinced that he had died, and that the Government was concealing the news until the end of the Pope's visit. In fact Jaroszewicz was well enough to have asked his doctors if he could get up for the reception ceremony at the Belvedere Palace; but press reticence encouraged credulousness.

That same day appeared a bland but firm article in the weekly *Polityka* by its editor Mieczyslaw Rakowski, generally regarded as the voice of Gierek and an internationally known member of the moderate group in the Party's central committee. Making clear that it was still the Marxists who managed Poland, despite any pretensions the Church might nourish, Rakowski stressed the common interest of Church and State in achieving international peace and co-operation.

Rakowski's article pointed to the elimination of hunger, poverty, war and oppression as aims to which every religious and social movement could contribute. Different sources of inspiration were accepted, he said, and the Pope cared about social and economic problems as well as religious matters. Emphasizing the national aspect of the visit, Rakowski wrote: 'He is a Pole coming to his home country. We will welcome him as a Pole, a great satisfaction to all Poles, believers and non-believers.' Rakowski rejected suggestions that the State was embarrassed by the election of a Polish pope; on the contrary, he said, they shared common goals, and the Pope had experience of encounters between Catholicism and existing socialism. 'The Pope says Governments cannot forbid citizens to believe; similarly, the Church cannot force people to her faith. We believe the visit will strengthen the unity of Poland in realizing goals underlying our national identity.' There was a warm tribute to Wyszynski, who had 'led the Roman Church in Poland in sometimes difficult situations, making decisions worthy of a great statesman'; and the article ended with what could be interpreted as official though conditional readiness to meet some at least of the Church's demands. 'If the leaders of the Catholic church in Poland will continue the policy of the past few years in a policy of co-operation as opposed to confrontation, and if they will take an active part in building our socialist fatherland, then the Marxists will certainly be ready to help settle problems which still exist today . . . Conditions between Church and State cannot be static.'

It was becoming evident that the Government was seeking, by a number of measures, to restrict as far as possible the attendance at the scheduled open-air Masses. Students in Lublin, it was said, had at first been refused special coaches for trains to Czestochowa, but eventually the local *wojewod* (regional governor) intervened personally under student pressure. In Warsaw itself, in addition to the ban on the sale of alcohol (which had turned from rumour into fact) and the restrictions on traffic, there were reports of the closure of main roads into the capital. Other official discouragement of advance excitement was tight restraint on the amount of public decoration of churches and other religious buildings, though in fact there was a reasonably generous show of banners in blue and white (for Mary), yellow and white (for the Vatican), and red and white (for the nation); and pictures of the Black Madonna and John Paul II himself were liberally displayed. The authorities seemed particularly worried about Warsaw students, for whom the Pope was to hold a special Mass on the morning of Sunday 3 June. The young people of the university parish had asked permission to issue 100,000 tickets for the occasion, which was to take place in front of St Anne's church in the rebuilt Old City. They were told they could only print 30,000; but with the tacit approval of Wyszynski they went ahead and printed 100,000 all the same. Attempted restraints of this kind suggested that, whatever agreements Gierek might have reached with the episcopate, at lower levels of the political hierarchy (as well as in the Politburo itself) there was much less support for the conciliatory approach. In army circles, and among Party ideologists, there was evident disapproval of the visit.

Proof of the ruling Party's anxiety about the effect the visit might have abroad came to hand afterwards in an astonishing document entitled 'Principles of accreditation for Polish journalists and of press coverage of the papal visit to Poland'; it had been prepared by the central committee's press department, and was issued during May for departmental use. A copy of it leaked to the foreign press towards the end of June and was published in *Time*. Early in July the Polish research section of Radio Free Europe (the American-funded station in Munich) published the document in full.

It set out arrangements by which the foreign press accredited to the papal visit would be under continual surveillance and guidance from Polish journalists. There were to be organized into a number of pools, one of which would include journalists of the secular press who 'in consideration of their ideological and political experience and knowledge of foreign languages will make sure that foreign journalists are efficiently provided with satisfactory information on problems of present-day Poland and current religious problems, and will counter-balance certain foreign journalists predisposed to be hostile to us'. The memorandum went on to say that this particular group of journalists would in principle have no duties connected with news coverage for their own agencies and offices. Polish lay journalists who did cover the visit would be informed immediately before the Pope's arrival of the ideological and propaganda assignments they would be expected to perform throughout.

The document anticipated that 'the centralized system for approving all press and news material connected both directly or indirectly with the visit will be strictly observed throughout its duration'. The document went on to lay down precisely what the different types of Polish publication would be allowed to print before, during and after the visit. On the first day, 2 June, for instance, the morning and afternoon papers would publish one picture of the Pope, a story on the start of the visit, a biography, and a commentary from PAP. It was laid down that PAP was to have exclusive rights to provide information on the visit (except to the Catholic press, which would be subject to normal censorship procedures). Weekly papers due to appear on the news-stands at the start of the visit would publish no material about it.

These, and a welter of other detailed instructions to the Polish media, were not known to the foreign press or other observers while the visit was in progress. Clearly the orders were modified in the light of experience as the visit proceeded. (The representative of *The Sunday Times* accredited to the visit, it should be recorded, never became aware that he was the target of the kind of Polish journalistic surveillance and ideological guidance specified, unless a generally friendly and helpful attitude on the part of his Polish colleagues could be interpreted as such.) In retrospect the main interest of the document lay in its demonstration of the way the ruling Party sought to control what was written, heard and seen of so historic and politically sensitive an occasion, and also of the way information is customarily managed behind the scenes in Poland.

The question of Polish television coverage of the visit had been hotly argued between Church and State authorities, with the Church naturally seeking extensive nationwide coverage of all the events and the State wanting the minimum.

The State finally yielded to the extent that the Pope's arrival, his reception by the country's political leaders at the Belvedere Palace, his first open-air Mass in Victory Square and his open-air Mass at Auschwitz-Birkenau (Oswiecim-Brezinka) would be broadcast nationwide, while all other events would get local coverage. The regime's dislike of nationwide television coverage was due in part to the fact that audiences in neighbouring Communist-ruled states – Soviet Lithuania, the Ukraine, Byelorussia, East Germany and Czechoslovakia – might pick up the transmissions. When the question was raised at an eve-of-visit press conference attended by Kazimierz Kakol and others, members of the platform party appeared not to understand, no matter what language was used. There was a murmured dismissal of 'useless speculations'.

The day of the Pope's arrival, Saturday 2 June, was cloudless; the heatwave of the previous fortnight continued, and was to last (with one short break for rain) until after his departure eight days later. Ahead of him, as the Alitalia Boeing 727 took off from Rome, were visits to the capital and four other major towns, and eight open-air Masses; and in his bag were 32 sermons or speeches, every one written by himself.

The actual arrival ceremonies at Warsaw's military airport were slightly anticlimactic, because invitations had been given to only 500 people to enter the grounds of the airport; and that included diplomats. Tight security, combined with a general sense of restraint disseminated by officials of both Church and State, kept the atmosphere subdued. But in the capital itself, and along the seven-mile route from the airport, things were noticeably livelier. Even at seven in the morning, three hours before the scheduled landing time, a thin line of people had already taken up position. It was estimated that about a million extra people had entered Warsaw during the previous two or three days, despite the road blocks. The city centre around Victory Square, scene of the open-air Mass to be held that afternoon, was alive with people, many with small children.

For once the daily newspapers were being snatched up at the kiosks – even *Tribuna Ludu*, the Party daily; at last they carried reports and commentaries on the papal visit. *Tribuna Ludu* had increased its daily print from one million to one and a half.

At the airport, tension grew. Suddenly Wyszynski was there, in black habit, taller than any of his assembled fellow clergy, thin, erect, unsmiling, watchful – a totem pole of a man. The State contingent arrived, with Jablonski, a smallish, white-haired, benevolent, professional-looking figure at its centre. Next marched in a military band, accompanying the three-service guard of honour; the guard's immaculate performance won a burst of clapping from official guests and even journalists as it snapped to attention and total immobility.

Alitalia's 'Città di Bergamo' was on time; the steps were in place; Wyszynski was up and inside. The reunion of the two men remained private. At last the Pope emerged, his arms widespread and waving up and down as though to embrace not only those before him but the whole of Poland and its people. There followed the expected moment: as John Paul II reached Polish tarmac he fell to his knees and kissed it. Then he walked across to the guard of honour and bowed deeply in front of the army standard before starting his inspection of the guard, with Jablonski at his side, and his greetings to the dignitaries.

Next came a ritual trio of speeches, from Primate, President and Pope. As Wyszynski put on gold-rimmed spectacles to read his short speech, in which he said with evident emotion 'In your hands, Holy Father, you hold our jubilant hearts, and before you rises the noble spirit of "Poland ever faithful" ', the Pope folded his arms, revealing a glittering steel wrist-watch. On his feet could be seen a pair of neat, maroon-coloured, soft leather slippers.

The warmth of Jablonski's speech came as a surprise, as he spoke of the 'exceptional character of the grand moment and its meaning'. So did his repeated use of the term 'Your Holiness'. The tone was strongly nationalist: 'Our satisfaction is the greater', he said, 'that our nation will be host to its son who after his promotion to the post of highest dignity in the Church has formulated the memorable words that he is "with all his heart with beloved Poland, motherland of all Poles".' He offered the hope that the visit would bring joy to the Pope and instruction to all the participants.

The Pope's changing facial expression showed clearly how touched he was. In expressing his gratitude he repeated what he had said before coming, that his visit had been dictated by strictly religious motives. But he went on to voice the desire 'that the fruit of this visit may be the internal unity of my fellow-countrymen, and also a further favourable development of the relations between the State and the Church in my beloved motherland'. He continued:

> I have kissed the ground of Poland on which I grew up – the land from which, through the inscrutable design of providence, God called me to the chair of Peter in Rome – the land to which I am coming today as a pilgrim . . . I greet each and every one of you with the same words I used on October the 16th last year to greet those present in St Peter's Square: Praised be Jesus Christ!

From Wyszynski and the Polish Church he extended his greetings to 'every human being living in the land of Poland', to guests from other countries, and particularly to 'those who represent the Polish emigrants throughout the world'. Then off he drove, in a yellow and white six-wheeler popemobile very like the Mexican model, into Warsaw.

After a brief visit to the cathedral, and then a pause for breath at the Primate's residence in the old city, the Pope presented himself at a second reception ceremony – one presided over by Gierek at Jablonski's official residence, the Belvedere Palace.

(The Pope was twenty minutes late, as if in gentle reprisal for all the times that Polish officials had kept churchmen waiting.) Here the world got its first taste of the Pope's skilful technique of making apparently innocuous, indeed quite acceptable, observations which could nevertheless be read as criticism by anyone so disposed.

The two groups faced each other across the Belvedere conference hall – a symbolic confrontation. As Gierek spoke – at some length, and in a deep and asthmatic monotone – the Pope contemplated him expressionlessly. Gierek concentrated on aspects of the visit stressed by earlier Government communiqués, such as its service to world peace. He spoke of the coming celebration in Poland of the 35th anniversary of the 're-birth of the motherland'; and at that point his speech became almost provocative. He cited the alliance with the Soviet Union as a main factor in solving national problems. 'Basic social transformations, industrialization and urbanization have brought civilizational and cultural advantages to the widest circles of the population, to the entire nation, as well as new, decent living conditions opening broad development prospects', claimed Gierek.

The Pope's reply remained conciliatory. Picking up Gierek's comments on the 35th-anniversary celebrations, the Pope said that peace and the drawing together of the peoples could only be achieved on the principle of respect for the objective rights of the nation – the right to existence, to freedom, to social and political activity, to the formation of its own culture and civilization. His speech acquired political point as he stressed that the Church wished to serve people also in the temporal dimension of their life (a concept which Poland's Marxist rulers reject vigorously):

> Given that this dimension is realized through people's membership of various communities, national and State, and is therefore at the same time political, economic and cultural, the Church continually rediscovers its own mission in relationship to these sectors of human life and activity . . . By establishing a religious relationship with man, the Church consolidates him in his natural social bonds.

He defined the fundamental mission of the Church as being to make man better, more conscious of his dignity, more devoted in his life to his family, social, professional and patriotic commitments; to make man more confident courageous, conscious of his rights and duties, socially responsible, creative and useful. 'For this activity,' he said, 'the Church does not desire privileges, but only and exclusively what is essential for the accomplishment of its mission'. Agreement on these lines with the State auth rities had been sought for thirty years. Pointing out that the vast majority of the nation's sons and daughters were members of the Catholic Church, the Pope went on: 'We see such an agreement as one of the elements in the ethical and international order in Europe and the modern world, an order that flows from respect for the rights of the nation and for human rights.'

These speeches were accompanied by an exchange of gifts, and followed by informal conversation. The political score at this stage was one-all, with no hard feelings on either side.

During the morning and afternoon the population was pouring steadily into Victory Square for the open-air Mass. There was a festive air everywhere. People converged on the centre carrying refreshments and sometimes folding chairs; lorries loaded with food and non-alcoholic drinks were parked in side streets; water points and public lavatories were clearly marked; fo d and drink kiosks had been set up; all was admirably organized.

Ticket-holders were being directed to their sections, marked out like pens with crush barriers. An army of men, young and middle-aged, had been appointed by the parishes to act as Marshals; they wore cotton forage-caps in yellow, blue or green according to their sectors. The vast crowd, estimated at about 300,000, took their cue from their spiritual leaders and behaved impeccably. The marshals' orders about keeping gangways clear were obeyed without argument, a singularly un-Polish spectacle; there was a minimum of jostling, few voices were raised.

Before the Mass, the Pope paid tribute to the grave of the Unknown Soldier on the far side of the square, praying before the flickering flame for several minutes, and kissing the tombstone. Accompanied by a throng of clergy with Wyszynski at their head, the Pope walked some two hundred yards to the raised altar, giving the huge crowd their first clear sight of him. When his burly and slightly stooping figure appeared on the platform he was greeted with prolonged clapping, but no shouting; the attitude of the crowd seemed a compound of delight, possessive affection, a touch of local-boy-makes-good admiration, excited expectation and above all a deep respect.

As Wyszynski welcomed him it was difficult not to be struck by the utter strangeness of the scene. It was in this square that occupying Russians in the nineteenth century had built an Orthodox church; that Tsar Alexander I had laid out a parade-ground where he watched Polish cadets pass out into the Russian army; that the Germans had constructed a V-shaped monument to their 1939 conquest. Wyszynski recalled Warsaw's wartime sufferings, and Pius XII's references to it as a city transformed by its own sons into a fiery place of execution. Wyszynski said they should rather think of it as a melting pot in which gold was refined to the highest purity.

And now the Pope's rich, strong voice began reading his first papal homily on Polish soil from beneath the oak cross, reminding the throng that it was Paul VI who had first wanted to come to Poland, and whose desire to do so had been so strong that it had transcended one pontificate and had been fufilled today. 'The Pope could no longer remain a prisoner of the Vatican; he had to become Peter the pilgrim once more.'

He asked whether his pilgrimage to his homeland was not a special symbol of their Polish pilgrimage through the whole history of the Church, which traversed not only Poland but Europe and the world. 'Should we not claim that Poland has in our times become the land of particularly responsible witness – that it is from here that the word of Christ must be spread with particular humility and firm faith? . . . If all that I have ventured to say is accepted, what enormous tasks and duties are implied.'

The Church brought Christ to Poland, he went on, and that showed a way to the understanding of that great and fundamental reality which was man: man could not be finally understood without Christ, or rather, man could not ultimately understand himself without Christ. 'He can understand neither who he is, nor what his proper dignity is, nor his vocation, nor his final destiny; he can understand nothing of this without Christ. That is why

Christ cannot be excluded from man's history anywhere in the world.'

At intervals during the homily there were outbreaks of clapping in recognition of political allusions, and sometimes bursts of religious song. When singing began, the Pope stayed silent, listening attentively and with obvious pleasure.

Before the administration of the sacrament by a small army of concelebrant priests, the congregation heard a psalm performed by a choir and string orchestra placed behind the platform. Many people came up to the platform to receive Communion from the Pope himself; some had evidently been chosen for the distinction, but matters began to get out of hand as others came crowding up the steps and had to be turned away and re-directed to the priests circulating in the huge crowd.

At last a semblance of order was restored, the Mass came to an end with the Pope embracing each of the priests who had assisted him, and he departed to Wyszynski's residence for the night. As dusk began to fall, lorry-loads of workmen came rolling up to Victory Square and started dismantling the steel crush barriers and compounds. Another group attacked the platform, tearing apart the heavy wooden timbers and loading them on to lorries. Towards midnight there was little left save the cross. The low-loader lorry and the large mobile crane which had brought and erected the cross on Thursday night now reversed the procedure, and by midnight the cross too had disappeared. The place was clear for the papal helicopters. A convoy of coaches had carried off some 600 reporters, photographers and broadcasting technicians to the central station to take the special sleeper trains to Gniezno, the Pope's next destination. Interpress, the Government agency for guiding foreign journalists, was working smoothly. The first day had gone without a hitch, and several hundred Polish functionaries, from Gierek down to the humblest Interpress interpreter, could heave a sigh of relief.

Whit Sunday, 3 June, began with the Pope's second open-air Mass in the capital. At seven in the morning an enormous crowd of students and other young people, mostly in jeans and T-shirts, with a plentiful sprinkling of older people on the periphery, stood in front of St Anne's church. Some of them had set off on foot for Warsaw from as far as twelve miles outside the town, marching through the night and early morning, often with small birch crosses in their hands. Poland's student population is regarded by the Polish security authorities as an unpredictable sector of society; hence the unsuccessful attempt to limit tickets.

This Mass for the first time gave an idea of the extraordinary rapport John Paul II has with Polish youth. His sermon focused on the question all students ask themselves: who am I? His answer was that man must be measured by the yardstick of heart, the deeps of personality. The Pope said he wished to pray with the students for the gifts of wisdom, reason, knowledge, courage, piety, human dignity and finally the fear of the Lord – 'the beginning of wisdom'. His words were repeatedly interrupted by applause and songs.

In Victory Square the helicopters were waiting. An hour later the Pope was two hundred miles away to the west, descending on to a huge dusty meadow outside Gniezno with half a million people in it.

The Gniezno meadows at Gebarzewo, the nearest village, serve as an artillery and rifle practice range for the Polish army. They could accommodate a couple of million people without difficulty, but the size of the crowd had been deliberately kept to about a quarter of that with road blocks and a limit on the number of official tickets. Even so the turnout was impressive. There was a large proportion of farming people in the crowd – women in headscarves, men with ruddy bucolic faces; it produced a perceptibly more devout atmosphere than in the comparatively middle-class Warsaw gathering.

By 11 o'clock, when the Mass was due to start, the sun was scorching. Swarms of tiny black flying beetles (irritating rather than stinging) crawled over faces, necks and bare arms, while the fine dust kicked up from the dry earth descended everywhere on perspiring skin, on cameras and binoculars, on food and drink. The congregation, spread over an area about a quarter of a mile square, was again penned into numbered and lettered sections marked out by steel crush barriers. The perimeter of the concourse was defined by tall banners in the familiar red-and-white, blue-and-white and yellow-and-white colours. At the edge of the gathering, near where the Pope's helicopter and his three escort machines were due to land, stood a large platform with an altar at its apex. A white canopy protected the altar from the sun.

The problem of feeding and watering this great mass of humanity – there was 'much grass in the place' and little else – had been solved by setting up a small lorry-borne township half a mile away on the edge of the meadow. About three hundred lorries had driven out and been marshalled into rows; their tailboards were lowered, crates of soft drinks and foodstuffs were brought forward, and there was the temporary Gebarzewo shopping-centre, arranged into five 'streets'.

The popemobile was parked beside the helicopter landing pad; it had been driven over from Warsaw during the night. As the minutes passed towards eleven o'clock, a priest was talking to the crowd over the powerful public address system. 'You must remember this is a most solemn occasion; this is not a sensational encounter. This is a holy place, the Holy Father is head of our Church, there must be no commotion, no pushing. Please behave with dignity.'

At last the four helicopters began coming in on a very low trajectory, the three escorting craft in the lead. They discharged favoured journalists and cameramen, State and Church functionaries, and a doctor carrying a first-aid case with a large red cross painted on it – sudden reminder of the vulnerability of the central figure in the spectacle. (It was persistently rumoured that Gierek, during his private conversation with John Paul II the previous day, had persuaded him to wear a bullet-proof waistcoat under his white soutane.)

When the Pope finally emerged from the fourth helicopter there was a great burst of sustained clapping and cheering. The reaction was more excited and lively than in Warsaw the previous day. Here it was possible to feel the country atmosphere, well short of hysteria, but nevertheless overwhelmingly enthusiastic and affectionate. The Pope rejected the offer of a wheeled vehicle and walked the three hundred yards to the platform, waving his greetings to the people lining the way as others flocked round to kiss his ring.

Up on the platform the Pope walked slowly round the altar, his arms spread out in a comprehensive embrace to each point of the compass in turn, so that everyone could see him clearly. His homily here was fairly short; it was punctuated by clapping and by sudden outbreaks of song from different parts of the crowd, in the manner that was gradually becoming familiar to reporters following the tour.

The main point of his address was the importance of the task of catechesis; much depended on the common effort of parents, family, parish and priests. The huge crowd listened in deep silence as the loudspeakers sent the Pope's words booming across the vast open space. For the listeners it was an astounding experience. The Pope – hitherto distant, inapprehensible, almost disembodied – was actually here, before their eyes, a big, strong, vigorous Pole speaking to them in their own tongue and in simple, loving, direct terms. Small wonder that so many people in the crowd had tears running down their cheeks as they listened. And at the end of the Mass, following his practice of ensuring that as many people as possible saw him at close range and he as many of them, he set off to criss-cross the crowd in the popemobile along lanes kept clear by marshals for the purpose.

His next appearance was in the town of Gniezno itself. He went to the ancient cathedral where Poland's earliest kings were crowned; here he prayed at the tomb of St Adalbert, who came from Czechoslovakia in the tenth century at the invitation of King Boleslaw the Brave as a missionary to the Baltic tribes, and died at the hands of Prussian pagans. St Adalbert's Czech origin explained why the Pope, preaching at the open-air Mass outside the cathedral, dwelt on his own Polish and Slavonic background. He traced the origins of Christianity in Poland, recalling that Mieszko I had married the daughter of a Czech prince who was a Christian before him.

The Pope had noticed in the crowd a banner which said: 'Let us not forget the Czechs either'. Acutely aware of the misery suffered by Roman Catholics in Czechoslovakia, the Pope called out: 'Remember, Father, all your Czech children.' This pope, he continued, who carried in him the Adalbert heritage, could not forget them. Perhaps, he suggested, Christ had chosen him, the first Slav pope in the history of the Church, to bring into the community of the Church a special understanding of all those Slav words and languages which still sounded alien to ears accustomed to Romance, Germanic, Anglo-Saxon and Celtic languages. 'Does not Christ wish to hear . . . with special understanding, special sensitivity, those sounds of human speech which are interlinked in a common root, a common etymology, and which (despite well-known differences, including spelling) sound close to each other and familiar? Is not the Holy Ghost disposed to see that this Polish Pope, this Slav Pope, should at this very moment reveal the spiritual unity of Christian Europe?'

Continuing his historical survey of Christianity among the Slavs, he spoke of their Lithuanian brothers, who had always respected the traditions of the East – the Orthodox Church – during the Polish millennium of Christianity, while the Poles had elected to be part of the Western tradition. He would like to ask those who respected the Eastern tradition to join in the search for a new Christian unity, the era of a new ecumenism. They should remember the conversion to Christianity of the Slavs, Croats and Slovenes; of the Bulgarians, whose Prince Boris was baptized a hundred years earlier than any Pole; of the Moravians, the Slovaks, the Czechs, the Ruthenians. With great earnestness John Paul II continued:

> The Pope has come to speak to the whole Church, to Europe, and the world, to speak about the nations and peoples so often forgotten . . . He has come to gather all these nations and peoples, together with his own, to the heart of the Church. I do hope that they can hear us. I hope they can hear me, because I cannot imagine that any Polish or Slav ear, in any part of the world, would be unable to hear words spoken by a Polish Pope, a Slav. I hope they can hear me, because we live in an epoch where the freedom to exchange information is so precisely defined, as is the exchange of cultural values.

The veiled attack on Soviet repressiveness drew a roar of understanding.

But the Gniezno visit became especially memorable because of the open-air Mass for young people a few hours later, as late afternoon slipped slowly into dusk. On this occasion the Pope let himself go for the first time, singing with a gusto that astounded the throng of journalists at the Interpress centre nearly a mile away when they heard his fruity baritone voice loudspeaker-borne to them across the lake.

He conducted the gathering from the first-floor balcony of the archbishop's palace, immediately opposite the cathedral. Beside him for much of the time stood Wyszynski, Archbishop of Gniezno as well as Warsaw. He played the part of stern-faced foil to the jesting Pope; four other bishops stood with Pope and Primate on the balcony, obviously enjoying every minute. This meeting, like the one at St Anne's in Warsaw at the start of that day, took the form of a dialogue between the Pope and his young listeners. Among them were groups of singers and musicians, playing guitars and other instruments. They would erupt quite unpredictably into accompanied song; and the Pope would at once join in, usually harmonizing the song by singing the bass line. If it was a new and unfamiliar 'sacro-song' he would feel his way with it, humming gently.

Sometimes it was the Pope himself who started the singing. He invited the crowd to sing 'The Red Belt' ('*Czerwony Pas*'), a song very popular in Eastern Europe and Russia, in honour of the Primate, who was wearing a red belt or sash over his black soutane; and the Pope sang the first two lines himself at the top of his voice. A feature of these youth meetings, with their family-gathering atmosphere, was his frequent affectionate references to Wyszynski, who behind his forbidding facade did seem touched. 'Long Live the Primate' was a cry that frequently went up from the crowd, repeated over and over again like an incantation. Wyszynski made several attempts to bring the dialogue to a close (though at one point he himself proposed the singing of the 'Mountaineer' song). But both the Pope and his youthful audience seemed reluctant to make an end, though dusk had fallen, and the special trains were waiting at the station to carry the pilgrims home to neighbouring regions. Just when it seemed to be all over, a voice was raised to lead yet another sacro-song, this time sung by a very good close harmony group. The Pope listened attentively, and pronounced it delightful. Then a tiny child sang, accompanied by a guitarist. 'That was lovely', said the Pope. But at last even he realized that it must end. 'The time has come to shorten things', he declared. 'We must light the camp fires.'

The fourteenth-century Pauline monastery at Czestochowa stands on the low hill of Jasna Gora at the western edge of the town. Czestochowa itself is a steel and textile centre, with a population of nearly a quarter of a million: the panorama seen from the top of Jasna Gora takes in factory chimneys and high-rise blocks. But the grass slopes below the monastery's high walls are bounded by tree-lined streets, and the general impression there is almost rural.

By the time the Pope arrived from Gniezno by helicopter for his three-day stay in the monastery, about 300,000 people had been marshalled into their places by the small army of orderlies. Earlier that morning the image of the Black Madonna had been brought out from its chapel and placed on the altar; many in the crowd wept at the sight of it. In the subsequent hour or so a priest, in the manner of a compère warming up an audience for the main attraction, had read prayers, snatches of verse, messages and instructions and led the singing of sacro-songs, conducting the enormous crowd with a yard-long baton painted bright red.

To accommodate the large numbers of priests, nuns and special guests who would be seated close to the Pope during the following three days of religious observances, a platform had been built which reached out over the ramparts. On the platform had been built an altar; over the altar and over the Pope's throne was a large red and gold canopy. The whole construction made a wonderful polychrome picture, with Vatican banners, glittering chandeliers, panels of white, yellow, red and blue, and five deep blue cloth panels bearing the Marian crown and double fleur-de-lis. High on the church wall behind had been fixed the figure 600, signifying the six hundredth anniversary of the Black Madonna's arrival, to be celebrated in 1982. Red and white roses and carnations in large vases stood beside the Papal throne. The deluge of colour contrasted strikingly with the black and white habits of hundreds of priests and nuns.

The Pope was to spend two nights and three days in Czestochowa. Predictions of the size of crowds made a month earlier proved greatly exaggerated, though if there had not been strict limits on the number of tickets issued to parishes, and severe traffic restraint at road blocks outside the town, the total number of pilgrims might have passed the million mark. There were also signs of a campaign of discouraging rumour. A restaurant manager at the press centre in Czestochowa said he had heard that over eighty people had been crushed by the crowds during the Pope's visit to Mexico, and he was not going to risk that by going to see the Pope himself; he preferred to watch the proceedings on television. The untrue story about scores of people being crushed to death in Mexico kept recurring, and evidently did act as a deterrent for some people. Another crowd-shrinker was the refusal of factories or schools to grant workers any holiday for the period of the Pope's stay, though in the event there was a tremendous amount of absenteeism.

Czestochowa has as much experience in coping with enormous concentrations of pilgrims as any shrine in Europe. During the papal visit the area in the vicinity of the monastery was well provided with sanitary facilities and water points. Food was obtainable (at temporarily inflated prices) at stalls served by batteries of old-fashioned field kitchens, something like portable Aga cookers; rows of them were steaming away all day cooking sausages, *bigos* (steamed white cabbage with meat and seasoning) and other Polish specialities. Large numbers of kiosks were selling light refreshments, ice cream and soft drinks; and innumerable stalls at the foor of the ramparts and the main entrance to the monastery offered devotional wares – rosaries, miniature coloured photographs of the Pope made up into badges.

From his helicopter the Pope was driven to Jasna Gora in a large black limousine with a sunshine roof in which he stood gesticulating happily to the clapping and cheering throng. He made his way up to the platform, with Wyszynski behind him, and walked slowly from corner to corner of it, leaning over the balustrade, his arms outspread in his customary wide embrace, giving everyone a good sight of him; thousands of tiny paper flags were waved by the people below. When silence fell at last, the Pope's first words, spoken in a deep voice, were 'I am here.' The response was an electrifying explosion of cheering.

Though his voice and manner were more serious than in Gniezno the previous evening, he made jokes, hummed and sang when sacro-songs were sung by the crowd, and gave his papal Mass a flavour somewhere between a revivalist meeting and a large family reunion. The Polish crowds repeatedly broke out into the song '*Sto lat, sto lat* (literally 'A hundred years, a hundred years, may he live a hundred years', and approximately equivalent to the

English 'For he's a jolly good fellow'); and there was frequent rhythmic shouting of the phrase '*Niech zyje Papiez, niech zyje Papiez*' ('Long live the Pope'). The Pope always appeared touched by these signs of affection. At Gniezno, after a burst of '*Sto lat*', he had called back: 'If this Pope lives all those years your grand-children will be coming to see him, and what can be done with such an old Pope? I can see only one solution: he'll have to run away and live in a monastery.'

One of his endearing practices throughout his tour was to break off from the prepared text of his sermons when some new thought crossed his mind. He also had a habit of addressing personal greetings to individual cardinals and other senior prelates on the platform or in the congregation, usually managing to inject a humorous or warm note into his words. At the start of the first pontifical Mass at Czestochowa, for instance, he went through a list of names of people he wanted especially to welcome. Because of the intensely hot sun, many of the senior clergy had put up umbrellas or sunshades; so he said 'You must forgive me if I have left out any important names, but it's difficult to see exactly who is here under those umbrellas'.

So often did he interrupt his own sermons, or allow them to be interrupted by singing, that he frequently felt obliged to offer disarming apologies. Referring to those responsible for the organizing and timing of the programmes, he would say: 'They will be cross with me for lengthening the service like this. I prom-ise to go back to my sermon, but I can't help sharing these happy moments with the people. What can you expect from a Slav pope?' And the crowd would laugh happily with him.

He knew that both Church and State authorities had worked hard. When he left Gniezno for Czestochowa that morning he had said: 'I should be ungrateful if I did not at this point thank all the organizers of my stay in Gniezno, and before that in Warsaw. As far as the administrative authorities are concerned, a lot of care has been put into these preparations, and at the same time so much discretion has been shown . . . Finally, since I became Pope I have been surrounded all the time by police escorts – such is my fate. That is how it is in Rome, that is how it was in Mexico. When the Pope says he wants to move somewhere out of the Vatican, even if it is only a hundred yards, a problem at once arises

about how many security men and police are needed. I should like
to thank the Polish security service and the Polish militia for the
fact that they are carrying out their duties so carefully and so
discreetly.'

The Pope's occasional friendly and appreciative references to
the militia, a body on the whole very unpopular with the Polish
masses, were always extremely well received by the militiamen, as
could be judged from overhearing their comments to each other.
They were encouraged in their comparative unobtrusiveness during the tour: they tended to leave crowd control to the Church
marshals.

It was a small but characteristic example of the Pope's ability to
captivate people who came in contact with him. The large
numbers of reporters who went round with him were forever
discussing and seeking to analyse the phenomenon of his personality. How was it that with a few words he could bring tears to
totally unsentimental and non-religious eyes?

To begin with he is a big man, well built, obviously in excellent
health, exuding energy and vigour and a love of life itself. His
features are regular and strong, markedly Polish in the deep-set
eyes, long nose, strong square chin, high cheekbones and fresh
complexion. His voice is exceptionally flexible and wide-ranging,
capable both of deep, vibrant baritone notes and of the gentlest
tones. Though his acting experience will have fostered his sense of
timing, he never gives an impression that he is hamming his lines;
his delivery is the most natural imaginable.

As for the less overt elements of his personality, it is evident
that although he is highly intelligent he is primarily a man with a
big heart. People living in his old archdiocese of Krakow say it
was his deep concern with each individual which made him such
an outstandingly good pastor there: every second person knew
him. When he preached, they remember, he would look deep into
the eyes of a particular member of the congregation as though his
words were intended for that member alone; and his attentive
gaze would pass from person to person as he spoke, as if
penetrating each heart. His expression in general is kindly and
friendly; while he rarely laughs out loud, he smiles a great deal.
During his tour a woman reporter was asked by a friend whether
she had been introduced to the Pope. 'No', she said, 'but I never

felt I need d to be; after being with him at a Mass I felt I had already met him.'

Poles have a distinct advantage in appreciating him. His compatriots say that not only is his writing a model of clarity and construction, totally free of clichés, but also that his diction and way of speaking their language is a delight to hear.

These gifts were kept at full stretch during his three crowded days at Czestochowa. His first sermon there, lasting almost an hour, was largely devoted to Mary's role in Polish history and life. 'She is present here in some strange way,' he said. 'Poles have become used to bringing all their problems to Jasna Gora, to tell their Mother everything.' Jasna Gora, he said, was the internal cementing agent of Polish life.

The best musical moments came at the very end of the first day, when the Pope attended the evening invocation to Mary. It started as a serious occasion, with the Pope at first quite alone on the platform, looking taller than usual in his long scarlet robes, standing in the strange radiance of the fading daylight and the television lights. There was a deep silence as the final blessing was given. A large brass band played softly; a final hymn was sung, well harmonized, with organ accompaniment. Then came a series of musical offerings, among them a number of sacro-songs specially composed by a young woman, Alicja Golaszewska, a musician working at the monastery. She herself had a strong, sweet voice, and was accompanied by an accordionist. At the end of her recital the Pope said 'I had to come to Poland to learn to sing again.' He embraced her at some length, and later said jokingly to the people: 'You were certainly wondering what I was saying to her. I was saying that I was terribly greedy for songs and music.'

One of the features of each Mass was the presentation of gifts – pictures, carvings, needlework, books, bread, flowers. They were carried up to the Pope by representatives of every kind of organization. Each man, woman and child kissed his hands; each was in turn warmly embraced, especially the youngest children. After one of the Masses, two middle-aged Polish women were overheard discussing the Pope's special affinity with children. One said: 'This Pope would have been such a good father if he'd had a wife and family.'

During his visit to St Sigismund's church in Czestochowa the Pope spoke of the importance of the family, 'the foundation of the human life in any dimension'. He went on to tell his audience how much importance he attached to the travels throughout Poland of a copy of the Black Madonna ikon consecrated by Pius XII in 1957 and on the road ever since. This visitation had been a special presence:

> Mary appeared as our Mother in a particular fashion. For a mother not only waits for her children in her own house, but follows them everywhere where they set up their own homes – everywhere they live, work, have their own families, are confined to a bed of suffering; even where they are led astray, where they forget God, where their consciences are weighed down by sin. To all these places . . . Mary brings hope in the form of her image.

These devout references intensified speculation that John Paul II's next visit to Poland might be in 1982, six hundredth anniversary of the arrival from Hungary of the original portrait.

During the same service the Pope had welcomed Cardinal Laszlo Lekai, the Primate of Hungary. 'An old Polish proverb says "Hungarians and Poles are like brothers" – but I shan't quote the rest.' (His audience knew that it ended: ' – whether they are fighting or drinking'.) He went on to recall that it was from Hungary that Queen Jadwiga had come to Poland. He loved these links between the Eastern European faithful.

Tuesday (fourth day of the tour, and second in Czestochowa) began with a Mass for nuns. At least fifty thousand of them had converged on Jasna Gora, and a great phalanx sat on the platform, some in white habits, some in black. The service started with a strident brass fanfare. Then came a long procession of white-habited priests from a door at the foot of a monastery tower; a storm of clapping from the nuns greeted the appearance of John Paul II bringing up the rear, his mitre glittering in the bright sun. Once again the polychrome picture was stunning, with the church orderlies' yellow armbands on black sleeves, the red-edged canopy over the altar, the white-covered balustrade round the platform, pale yellow candles, red and white carnations in masses, red carpeting, the purple skull caps of the clergy, the white overalls of the medical orderlies – and the bright blue peaked caps of the ABC television team from the United States.

To the nuns the Pope said that the living witness of each of them was without price.

> Embracing with faith, hope and charity your divine spouse, you embrace in him the sick, the aged, the crippled, the handicapped. They cannot be looked after by anyone else. It calls for truly heroic devotion.
>
> I have still before my eyes all the homes for handicapped children: the one I visited in Wadowice, for instance . . . Let the most fervent enemy of God go there for a while and watch and see. If there is even a speck of humanity in him he is bound to leave that home in a state of shock – shocked to the depths of his soul – shocked by the picture he has seen of man, even of small children, and at the same time shocked by the quantity of devotion to them.

Near the press benches a row of a dozen nuns knelt as the Pope prayed. A photographer suddenly noticed them, moved to within three or four feet of one young nun who wore a look of special rapture, and began taking pictures. In a moment the man's colleagues and competitors spotted him, and fearful of being outdone they too moved in on other nuns in the row. For about five minutes the row of nuns submitted to a flurry of circling, clicking men shooting faces at a range of two feet or less. Some nuns began to cry. Finally four priests drove the photographers off.

The Polish bishops had taken occasion to meet in the monastery in conference; and the Pope, addressing them, used the opportunity to state his views on relations between Church and State in Poland. In one of the longest, most thoughtful and most important addresses of the entire pilgrimage, the Pope recalled his own work of many years with the Polish episcopate, and said he had realized what a special and responsible place Poland, and especially the Church in Poland, occupied on the map of the modern world. The Church's hierarchical system had played a decisive part in the nation's history, and at the same time the nation's history had in some providential way been incorporated into the structure of the Church in Poland, giving it firm foundations.

> We can correctly define the importance of a problem which has been a topical one for several years in Poland, that is, the problem of normalizing relations between Church and State. In our age, insight into the fundamental rights of man – among which the right of religious freedom has undoubted, central importance – speaks in favour of the process. Normalization is proof of practical respect for that right.

The Pope's address was in essence a justification of the Church's inescapable involvement in political affairs, domestic and international. He recalled his own words in January 1979 to the diplomats accredited to the Holy See, when he rejoiced at the presence of so many and said he would be happy to see many others. The Apostolic see, he had said, wished to be at the centre of this brotherly rapprochement now developing.

The Pope then went straight to the heart of the matter in Poland. In the key paragraph of his address he recalled that the Polish episcopate had worked out a series of documents and pastoral attitudes confirming a readiness for dialogue.

> They clearly show that authentic dialogue must respect the convictions of believers. It must ensure all the rights of citizens, and normal conditions for the activity of the Church as a religious community to which the vast majority of Poles belong. We are aware that this dialogue cannot be easy, because it takes place between two concepts of the world which are diametrically opposed. But it must be made possible and effective if the good of individuals and the nation demands it. The Polish episcopate must not cease to undertake, with solicitude, initiatives which are important for the present-day Church.

The Church must keep its principles clear, he emphasized. He went on to indicate that he was thinking of moral issues such as the sin against nascent life, in other words abortion, and sins of sexual immorality and alcoholic abuse, which bore within them the lowering of human dignity: 'inner insensitivity easily takes root in human hearts'. The Polish episcopate, he pursued, must add to its present mission and ministry a particular solicitude for the whole Polish cultural heritage. 'It is well known that it is precisely culture that is the first and fundamental proof of the nation's identity', he added.

Bishops from many other countries besides Poland were in the Pope's train. When he emerged from the conference to say the Angelus at noon, he told the crowd: 'We will pronounce the blessing in Latin, because there are various episcopates represented here, and the one language that all bishops can still speak is Latin – for the time being!'

It was late that afternoon that he preached to the tens of thousands of pilgrims who had travelled specially from Lower Silesia. The numbers on the slopes below the ramparts were the biggest yet seen at Czestochowa, possibly in the region of half a million. It appeared that the militia had been less strict about allowing private cars into the town on the second day, probably in the light of the previous day's calm behaviour and the good discipline of the crowds under the Church marshals. But Polish television viewers got little notion from their screens of the size of the gathering, since Polish cameramen were limiting their shots to close-ups of the Pope and small groups of those present, mainly priests and nuns and older people, even though the great majority present were younger people. Sermons were cut about, too. The policy moved Vatican Radio, in its Croat service, to high indignation in defence of free speech.

The word to the people of Lower Silesia was the importance of family unity, founded in the sacrament of marriage and finding fruition and reward in the love and trust of children. A parallel political message, for those who had ears to hear it, emerged in his development of the theme on the national level.

Although it is difficult to liken our nation, this multi-million society, to a family, yet in the nation too unity depends on the satisfaction of the needs and problems and tasks of every member of the nation in such a way as not to cause dissonance or contrasts or differences which bring privileges to some and wrongs to others. We

know from the history of our homeland how difficult
this is, and yet one must never give up the enormous
effort to construct a just unity amongst the sons and
daughters of the same homeland.

Poland was unexceptionably merged with the rest of the world in
the Pope's plea for human rights:

They include, first of all, the right to exist and the right
to self-determination, then the right to one's own
culture and to multi-directional development. We know
how much the violation of these essential rights has cost
us; and that is why we repeat the call for reconciliation
among the nations of Europe and the world. Injustices
have to be made good, and the wounds have to be healed.
Permanent reconciliation among the nations of Europe
and the world will be the fruit of true respect for the
rights of every nation . . . May this Pope be able to work
successfully in the cause of unity and reconciliation in
the contemporary world.

Always observant, he had noticed a banner held up in the crowd
with the device: '*Berlin grüsst den heilige Vater*'. He took the
point for his peroration. 'I can also see right in front of me a banner in German with greetings to the Pope from the Catholics of
Berlin. And it is in this spirit of unity and reconciliation that we
greet our brothers and sisters who have come here to pray with us
for peace among the nations of Europe and the world.'

On the third and last day at Czestochowa the vexed question of
the ministry was to the fore. Wednesday 6 June dawned bright
and warm as ever. Crowds had kept their usual all-night vigil on
the Jasna Gora slopes, and before the Pope emerged on to the
terrace of the monastery a young priest had conducted sacro-
songs and said prayers. The long red carpet laid out from the
tower door up to the altar had been duly vacuum-cleaned by
nuns. The first event was a Mass for seminarists, novices and
those newly called to a vocation in the Church. The Pope reminded
his audience that he rejoiced for every priestly and religious vocation as a particular gift of Christ the Lord for the Church and
the people of God, as a singular witness to the Christian vitality of
their dioceses, parishes and families. The ceremony was as usual

punctuated with sacro-songs, choruses of '*Sto lat*' and 'Long live the Pope', and as usual the Pope joined in as the songs began.

(He would occasionally offer some such mild protest as 'Don't think we're going to stop with that one song, but for the moment one is enough.' At one point he said: 'That's not a very liturgical song. I think we had better stop singing or I'll never get on to the next point of my sermon'; and there were roars of laughter.)

With the next event, a meeting with diocesan and monastic clergy in Czestochowa cathedral, the mood changed. There was no mass singing here. The Pope started his 40-minute sermon on a light-hearted note enough, asking that instead of wishing him a hundred years of life the congregation should pray for him not to lose his voice before Sunday, the last day of his visit. 'Each of you is well aware of the saying, "A priest is a man who exists for other people". The French sometimes say he is "*un homme devoré*", so you will be aware that, *mutatis mutandis*, the same applies to the Pope. People simply want to eat him. But if they are going to eat him, let them eat a Pope who can still speak rather than one who has gone completely hoarse and lost his voice.

'But now *ad rem*', he pursued; and the matter in hand turned out to be the Letter to Priests of two months before. Despite the criticism, his hearers learned that there was no question of second thoughts. It did not even appear that the critics had had much of his attention:

> Here and there it has been suggested that the Pope was trying to impose the Polish model of priesthood on the whole world. But these were isolated voices, looking for something that was not there. For the most part the letter was received with satisfaction as a very simple, clear and at the same time brotherly statement of affairs which are of fundamental importance for our co-operation in the universal Church. There can be no conceptual gaps, no imprecision. We need to know from the very start where we stand, what it is we rely on.
>
> Occasionally concerned voices were raised, concerned about whether the Church could survive this vision of priesthood in today's secularized world. But I left Poland in the deep conviction that it was only with this vision of priesthood that the Church would survive.

Some were concerned that it was this very vision, this image of priesthood linked with celibacy – the priesthood to which a man dedicates himself completely – that frightens people away, discourages the recruitment of candidates, slows down the process of vocation. I came away from Poland with the conviction that the opposite was the case: that it was this vision of priesthood that could reopen a wave of vocations throughout the Church, because young people everywhere want to know where they are going, what they are dedicating themselves to . . .

And it seems that in general the Letter to Priests was interpreted like that by bishops and priests. It is free of what may be described as clericalism, although attempts have been made here and there in press comment to suggest that it was a vision of a clerical Church, that it was a clerical vision of priesthood, that we ought to move towards a greater secularization of the office of priesthood.

The Pope ended with a discussion of the very great demand for Polish missionary priests and nuns throughout the world. He recalled that when he was Archbishop of Krakow he used to receive visitors from all over the world in search of priests for pastoral work. He would tell them that there had to be a system of allocation if the needs of the whole Church were to be met. 'I used to explain that we too were a country of missions, that we found ourselves in a special situation, a front-line situation, in which there must be no lack of priestly power, and in which priestly work was truly difficult, truly missionary.'

Nevertheless, the Pope now went on, he did realize that as far as quantity was concerned they were in a better position in Poland than other missionary countries, even Latin American countries. In Cuba, for instance, there were forty thousand souls per priest. 'In comparison with that we enjoy a privileged position', he said. 'We give as much as we can, and we are very sought after, thanks to the personal make-up of the Polish pastor. It does not raise objections or anxieties; whereas bishops are frequently afraid that priests arriving from other countries and other milieux may do more harm than good . . . I am glad that the Church in Poland is increasingly becoming a missionary Church and that there are more and more Polish missionaries in the world.'

That afternoon he talked about the role of a university to academics and students from Lublin. A university, he said, existed mainly to help the student, who had 'wings hidden in his head and his heart'. Just producing more and more scholars solved no problems. The aim was to develop real human beings, and the university must help in that – or at least not hinder it. (He voiced in passing, to explain that comment, the gloomy fear that universities all over the world were undergoing 'some kind of deformation'.)

Because the Lubliners knew his intellectual background, he could carry his political point further than usual. He had explained in *The Acting Person* that real human beings need to feel both solidarity and opposition: they must belong to society, yet they must think for themselves. The danger, the Pope now argued, was that the first would overwhelm the second. That would in fact be bad for whatever ideology appeared to profit from it:

> Any man who chooses his ideology honestly and through his own conviction deserves respect. The real danger for both sides – for the Church and for the other side, call it what you will – is the man who does not take a risk and accept a challenge, who does not listen to his deepest convictions, to his inner truth, but who only wants to fit in somehow, to float in conformity, moving from left to right as the wind blows.

In Poland, at any rate, the implication was clear. There (whatever might happen, for example, in Ireland) the instinct for conformity could only push you towards the collectivist or Communist side. The function of a Polish university, therefore, was to foster the kind of independent thought which prompted Christian opposition.

The Pope's last appearance on the terrace of Jasna Gora came late that afternoon when he addressed hundreds of thousands of the faithful who had travelled from Upper Silesia and the Dabrowa basin, the great coal-producing region of Poland, where despite the intense Party activity the Catholicism is deep and intense. Miners, technicians, engineers, managers – the crowd, the biggest of all throughout the three days at Czestochowa, was a striking cross-section of the populace.

The first lesson was read by a young miner, wearing the traditional white-plumed pill-box hat; the second by a young mine manager; and the Pope talked about work, its ethical as well as its technical importance, in terms of the human dignity and self-fulfilment he steadily stressed. 'Work must help man to become better, spiritually more mature, more responsible, so that he can fulfil his human mission on this earth, fulfil himself as a person in his own right and in community with others.'

The Pope's final act was to take a formal, dedicatory farewell of the Madonna of Jasna Gora.

> I surrender myself to your maternal servitude of love, I surrender to you the Church as a whole . . . mankind and all my brother human beings, all peoples and nations . . . I surrender to you Europe and all the continents; I surrender to you Rome and Poland united with a new link of love.

During his three days in Czestochowa, the estimated total of pilgrims he had addressed was three and a half million. (In Poland as a whole he was seen by some twelve million, roughly a third of the country's population.) In the process he had nearly lost his voice.

Almost as if directed by a higher power, the rain stopped in Krakow just twenty minutes before the Pope's arrival from Czestochowa, giving the waiting crowd a chance to put away their umbrellas and dry off. The three accompanying choppers came in first, whirling across the vast Krakow *blonia* or meadows over the heads of the tens of thousands of people. Two minutes later the Pope's helicopter came to a stop only fifty yards from the specially erected platform. The gust from the spinning blades neatly re-rolled the length of red carpeting that had been unrolled up to the steps of the platform; two men struggled gallantly against the blast to unroll it once more.

Wearing his broad-brimmed scarlet hat and long crimson cloak, the Pope came out of the helicopter door and stood at the top of the ramp, his arms spread wide, the crowd applauding. At the foot of the ramp, waiting to greet him, was a group of Church and State functionaries, led by Cardinal Franciszek Macharski, his tall, ascetic-looking, bespectacled successor as archbishop. On the platform the Pope spoke softly into the microphone, nursing his tired throat, showing signs of the emotion he felt at this return to his own city as a pilgrim from the Holy See. 'I have discovered in Rome', he said, 'that it is not easy to leave Krakow behind.'

He went on: 'My heart has not ceased to be united with you, with this city, with this patrimony, with this "Polish Rome" '. But he had travelled a great distance since then. 'I see there are some Mexicans in the crowd', he suddenly called out, 'who have come to spy on how the Krakovians receive me. How did it go?' '*Bonito, bonito, Papa!*' shouted the Mexicans. The Pope responded, 'I remember that Mexican cry, "*El Papa, El papa, ra, ra, ra!*" '

He drove away as dusk fell, standing up at the front of his popemobile – it had arrived from Czestochowa during the afternoon – down the long road beside the meadows leading to the town, every yard of the way covered with flowers. At the Wawel cathedral he reminded a congregation of bishops and priests how they and he had long prepared the observances for St Stanislaw, and planned that visits should be made with the saint's relics to all the parishes in the archdiocese. 'Through my visit here', said the Pope, 'I am indirectly visiting every parish.'

At the Archbishop's palace, a sixteenth-century building in Franciszkanska Street, his old room had been prepared for him. Huge crowds gathered in the street below the palace windows, singing and applauding and calling for him. Despite his evident tiredness and his sore throat, the Pope could not resist responding to this manifestation of love. He did it in the form of a dialogue. From the central first-floor window of the palace he called out: 'May I ask you a question?' 'Yes!' was the roared-out response.

'Right', said the Pope; 'I will ask you this question. Do you think it right that a citizen should disappear from a town for eight months without anybody going to look for him and bring him back?' This was greeted with delighted laughter, and a voice shouted 'We will come and look for you'.

'Very well, I'll ask you another question. Do you intend to go to sleep tonight?' 'No!' came the answer, as if with one voice. The Pope replied, 'Well, I'm going to bed, because tomorrow I've got to walk on my feet, not my eyelashes.'

Still the crowd stayed on below the window. Finally the Pope said, 'Listen, we shall say the Angelus together, and a prayer for the dead, and then you do what you like. As for me, I'm going to bed.' And he went through his programme, said goodnight and closed the window firmly.

He had a long day ahead. It was Thursday, the sixth day of his visit; and it encompassed both his own birthplace at Wadowice and the vaults of death at Auschwitz. After breakfast he helicoptered first to a Bernardine monastery at Kalwaria Zebrzydowska. He told the fathers how often he had visited that place and walked along its paths, as a child, as a young man and as an archbishop. 'Most frequently I came here alone', he said, 'so that no one might know, not even the cloister guardian. The thing about Kalwaria is that it is easy to hide from the cloister guardian.'

In the small square at Wadowice, where most of the town's fifteen thousand inhabitants seemed to have squeezed themselves, a battle of banners had been joined. 'Blessed is he who comes in the name of the Lord' competed with 'Celebration of 35 years of the Polish People's Republic – the pride of all Poles'. But scarcely a window in the square was without its religious tribute – a portrait of the Pope, candles, blue-and-white or yellow-and-white favours, a picture of the Black Madonna of Jasna Gora. Faces, too, were at every window, and there were young people balanced precariously on roofs. The parish church, where Karol Wojtyla was baptized, had been freshly painted for the visit, its walls a delicate beige, its scrolls and mouldings white. Across its facade a large platform had been built for local dignitaries.

Young Father Fidelius, the Wadowice warm-up man, was equipped with a walkie-talkie link to colleagues at the helicopter landing-pad in the nearby stadium. Suddenly he became excited. 'The Pope's landed!' he cried, to loud cheers. More information came crackling in to his little receiver. 'Now he's walking over to the edge of the stadium! He's walking along the lane towards the square!' The crowd followed the movements of the still invisible Pope with excitement. Suddenly he was there, smiling, waving, climbing up on to the platform, while the church bells crashed out, the brass band gave everything it had, and Father Fidelius urged decorum.

The encounter everyone wanted to see duly took place. Father Edward Zacher, the Pope's old teacher of religion and still parish priest at 78, was waiting on the platform. The two men embraced. The crowd sang '*Sto lat*' over and over again. Father Zacher made a short formal speech of welcome. In quiet tones the Pope expressed thanks all round, to the civil authorities, to the nuns and priests, even to the journalists for making his birthplace so famous. He praised the band, too. 'When it comes to bands', he said, 'Wadowice has a particularly fine one.'

With the sun beating down, the swallows cutting sharp arcs round the church towers, the rooks soaring over the crowds, it was a happy morning for the Pope, a kind of armour against an afternoon that was to be filled with tears, with painful memories, with the recollected stench of death.

After a buffet lunch in the parish priest's house, the Pope flew on to Auschwitz – Oswiecim, by its Polish name. The camp has been preserved as a museum. The papal visit to this awful place, and to the even more horrible Brzezinka (in German Birkenau) not far away, was one of the few events the Polish Government had agreed should be televised live to the whole country. Three Government ministers were in attendance. It has been consistent Polish policy not to allow the nation's memory to fade; neither forgiveness nor forgetfulness has been permitted.

No pope before him had walked through that main gate, under the wrought-iron lettering of that savagely ironic slogan '*Arbeit macht frei*'. It was the route taken by most of the victims who died in the gas-ovens of the two camps. Two and a half million of them were Jewish. According to Polish statistics, the Auschwitz-Birkenau complex was the deathplace of some four million people all told, of 50 nationalities and from 28 countries. It was the main site for the intended extermination of the Polish nation, with about six thousand German SS-men carrying it out. Among the victims had been Polish priests: 416 priests and nuns were imprisoned in Auschwitz, and 166 of them lost their lives.

The name that has lived on is that of Father Maximilian Kolbe, whose decision to offer himself for death in place of a fellow Pole with a family of ten children led to his being beatified by the Catholic church in 1971. Kolbe was a well-known Franciscan monk who came to Auschwitz in May 1941. He worked at forced labour for 78 days, until he put himself forward in exchange for Franciszek Gajowniczek, one of ten men sentenced at random to die of starvation. Kolbe sustained the other nine in their extremity, and was himself among the last to die, on 14 August 1941, his end hastened by an injection of phenol.

The Pope had been to Kolbe's cell many times during his Krakow years. He went straight to block 11, the 'death block', and to cell 18, where Kolbe died. He prayed alone in the cell for several minutes. Outside it stood Gajowniczek, now 78 years old.

Gajowniczek had remained in German camps until the end of the war. Within earshot of a group of visiting German church dignitaries, reporters asked him whether he had forgiven the Germans. 'As a Catholic', he replied, after a moment's hesitation, 'it is my sacred duty to forgive. But as a Pole and as a human being, I should have to think very long about that question.'

From Kolbe's cell the Pope walked to an adjacent block to pray at the place where thousands of prisoners were shot, known then and now as the wall of death. Afterwards he was silent as he left with his entourage to drive to his helicopter and fly to Brzezinka.

He landed close to the international monument to the victims of fascism, where nineteen stone plaques are inscribed in nineteen languages. Close by, along the rotting railway tracks which carried the death transports to the gas-ovens, on the very platform where the condemned left the train, an enormous dais and altar had been constructed for this one occasion. It was a massive piece of carpentry in unpainted pine. The wooden canopy was supported by four squared wooden pillars, stained dark brown in contrast with the white wood of the rest. A soaring cross, with its stem passing right through the canopy, carried a large coil of barbed wire, symbolizing both the crown of thorns and the fact of imprisonment. From it streamed a striped flag bearing the letter P (for prisoner) and the number 16670. It was Kolbe's camp number.

The symbolism was very bold. The striped flag drew an overt parallel between Kolbe's death and Christ's: the world's intolerable evil was overcome wherever a Christ-like death was died.

The chaplet of barbed wire implied an even bolder claim: that all the dead of Auschwitz died for humanity. (Professor Ulrich Simon of King's College, London, whose own father died in the camp, suggested in *A Theology of Auschwitz* in 1967 that not just the few who died 'with meek obedience and serenity' but the many 'died also for the sins of others, for in as much as they died there they took the place of all who could have died there, being morally culpable of the many causes which brought the horror into being. Their voices plead the cause of the unity of the whole human race. Not one life given there can cease to speak to the world as an accusation and as a warning.')

The Pope robed in a single-storey wooden hutment which had served as the administrative offices where SS guards decided which prisoners were to die. During the Mass that followed, he was assisted by 150 priests who had survived imprisonment at Auschwitz. The survivor priests marched solemnly and very slowly on to the platform, wearing bright red vestments splashed with irregular white patterns. They were mostly elderly men, of course; one leant heavily on a stick, some were grey-bearded, some very tired and lined; yet some were erect and showed pride in their survival and their work. Many carried cameras, to take snapshots of the enormous gathering against the background of watch-towers and high barbed-wire fences. Thousands in the throng had chosen to wear the pyjama-like suits, in blue and white vertical stripes, that were worn by prisoners.

The Pope started his sermon with the story of Maximilian Kolbe and his victory won through faith and love 'in this place of terrible holocaust'. John Paul II wondered how many more such victories had been won in that place, how many other instances of humanity there had been which were the very opposite of the systematic denial of humanity practised there. He went on:

> Can anyone on this earth be surprised that a Pope born and brought up in this land, a Pope who came from the archdiocese in whose territory the camp of Oswiecim is located, began the first encyclical of his pontificate with the words '*Redemptor Hominis*'? Can anyone be surprised that he devoted that encyclical in its entirety to the dignity of man, man's human rights and the threat to

those rights, which can be trampled on so easily and annihilated by man?

It is enough to dress him in another uniform, to equip him with the apparatus of violence and the means of destruction. It is enough to foist on him an ideology in which human rights are arbitrarily subordinated to the requirements of the system.

Was the Pope referring to Nazism? Or was this an attack of Communism? It was another of his messages to any who chose to receive them.

He had come to Oswiecim, he said, to kneel down 'on this Golgotha of our times, on these graves which are mostly nameless, like a gigantic tomb of the Unknown Soldier'. He spoke of the nineteen plaques:

Let me pause with you for a moment at the plaque bearing the sign in Hebrew. This inscription brings memories of a nation whose sons and daughters were destined for complete extermination. This people has its origin in Abraham, 'the father of us all', as St Paul called him. This people, who were given by Yahweh the commandment 'You shall not kill', have experienced killing themselves in special measure. Nobody should pass this tablet with indifference.

I have chosen another tablet, with the inscription in Russian. I make no further comment. I know what contribution this people made during the last terrible war to the cause of freedom. We must not pass this tablet, either, with indifference.

Finally I must pause at the tablet in the Polish language. Six million Poles perished during the last war, one fifth of our people. It was another stage of the struggle of this people, my people, for its basic rights among the people of Europe – one more loud cry for the right to its own place on the map of Europe, one more painful settling of accounts with the conscience of contemporary humanity.

Any meditation at Auschwitz is a wrestling with the problem of evil. The place was a symptom of war, the Pope said. It was war that brought a disproportionate growth of hate, destruction and cruelty. Yet it could not be denied that war also gave opportunities for human courage, heroism and patriotism.

> Nevertheless on balance the losses predominate – increasingly so, the more war becomes a contest between calculated techniques of destruction. Responsibility for war rests not only with those who directly cause the war, but also with those who do not do everything in their power to prevent it.

His final appeal began with a phrase quoted from a speech of Paul VI's at the United Nations in 1965:

> Never again war – peace and only peace should guide the fate of nations and the whole of humanity . . . One nation can never develop at the expense of another, of its subordination, conquest and oppression, of its exploitation and death . . . I am speaking not only on behalf of the four million victims who perished on this huge field. I speak on behalf of all whose rights are infringed and violated anywhere in the world. I speak because I am committed, we are all committed, to the truth – committed to speak for man's welfare.

Having earlier spoken of the Russians generously, he drew back now from mentioning them in blame; but the double application of his words, to the Soviet Union as well as to Nazi Germany, was audibly caught by his listeners.

As the Pope ended his sermon there were tears on hundreds of cheeks. A distant factory chimney threw a black line of smoke lazily across the horizon, evoking the incinerator chimneys of nearly forty years ago. A woman in the crowd said: 'Every time I see a bird flying here I am reminded of the dead. The birds were the only living things which could touch the camp fence wires without being electrocuted. We used to watch them with envy and longing.'

That night there was yet another encounter with the adoring crowd of mainly young people more or less permanently packed into Franciszkanska Street under the window of the archbishop's palace. It happened on each of the four nights the Pope slept there. Each night he came to the open window to conduct an affectionate dialogue with them, in between the flow of songs they kept up. 'Stay with us, stay with us', they would shout, 'we need you so much, you know it.' Or half jokingly, half serious, 'Don't abandon us, hear our cry for help, our SOS . . .' And the Pope would wave to them, his smile conveying his own special blend of love, concern, wistfulness and seriousness. When he could get a word in edgeways, he once said to the crowd 'You know, it's hard to be a Pope in Rome, but in Krakow it's impossible – there's no time to read, no time to write, and I have the whole world on my head. Now will you please go to bed. Goodnight!' And he would join in a final song, and in the end – reluctantly, it seemed – close the window and disappear within.

Next morning, Friday, was his morning in his beloved mountains. Nowy Targ, on a high plateau with immense meadows round it, is a market and tourist town in the foothills of the massive Tatra range. All night, long files of people had been advancing on the meadows from the surrounding valleys. To the ordinary dissuasions – rumour, traffic restrictions, refusal of a holiday – had been added drenching rain; so there were perhaps half a million people in a space that could have held two million.

But at ten o'clock the sun picked out the bright white lines of the quartet of helicopters. The altar to which the Pope made his way had been gracefully constructed in the style of a mountain chalet or chapel. Beside it stood a gilded wooden carving of yet another of Poland's famous Madonnas, this one Our Lady of Ludzmierz, a fourteenth-century artefact brought specially to the Pope from the village of Ludzmierz three miles away.

Thousands of the mountain people in the crowd wore their traditional dress. The women were in bright multi-coloured striped skirts, the men even more gorgeously attired in embroidered jackets and white felt trousers with fifteen-inch-wide leather belts like vast external corsets, heavily decorated with brass whorls, buttons and lozenge-shaped knobs in a multiplicity of symmetrical patterns.

Only thirty miles away were the passes into Czechoslovakia,

where Catholics undergo intense repression. The Pope began his sermon with a reference to that southern frontier; but his tone was studiously uninflammatory. 'I wish to welcome warmly', he said, 'our kinsmen from the south. This open and friendly border, not only from our side but also on their side, should today make it possible for them to be here. I do not know if they are here. But if they are not here, please tell them, when they come, that we remembered them and prayed for them specially, as they are dear to us.'

He knew perfectly well that some 3,500 Czechoslovak Catholics had tried to cross into Poland to see him, but the border guards had not allowed them in on the pretext that the supply of Polish zlotys for them to buy had run out. In the end a mere couple of hundred managed to enter. Cardinal Frantisek Tomasek was only allowed to leave Prague the next day, for Krakow.

The sweet green of the meadow was ringed with dense pine woods; in the middle distance were the mountains. The Pope used the land, in his sermon, as a link to themes nearer his heart – notably the inadmissibility of abortion. The Creator had given land to man; on man's conquest of soil he based man's right to life; and that was closely connected with the family. The nation depended on what the family was:

> I desire that man should develop completely with the support of indissoluble bonds between husband and wife in a family atmosphere which cannot be replaced by anything else. And I desire that the Polish family should give life, that it should be faithful to the sacred right to life. If the right of man to live is transgressed at the very moment when he starts to become a human being, in his mother's womb, then the entire moral order – which indirectly serves to protect the inalienable welfare of man – is jeopardized.

After the Mass the rain came down again.

In Krakow that day the Pope had meetings with old academic and clerical friends; and his final appointment was to address a huge concourse of students in the large enclosed space beside the church of the Pauline fathers on Skalka (the very place where, according to legend, St Stanislaw had been killed).

In an atmosphere of general good humour, the students had begun assembling hours before the Pope was due. The trees overlooking the open space were packed with small boys, perched like birds along the boughs. The Pope was delayed for well over an hour; but the students entertained themselves with excellent music from a string orchestra and with the usual sacro-songs, which every Pole in the country seems to know by heart. When the Pope did at last appear the welcome was tumultuous. Flowers were thrown to him in their thousands; those that fell short were sent on their way by students at the front, so that a single flower could describe four or five arcs before it finally landed at the Pope's feet, like a leaping salmon making its way upstream.

Greatly moved, John Paul II laid aside his prepared text and spoke direct. 'I was formed by my work with young people', he said. 'I hear it said that the youth of today is materialistic and seduced by the consumer society. Well, it's simply not true!'

The cheerful interruptions and general commotion reached such a level at one point that the Pope jokingly pretended to abandon the dialogue, and sat down on a step of the altar. But he was entreated to speak again. When silence fell, he stood up and read the very last paragraph of his prepared text:

> You are the future of the world, of the nation, of the Church. You must carry into the future the whole of the experience of history that is called 'Poland'. It is a difficult experience, perhaps one of the most difficult in the world, or in Europe, or in the Church. Do not be afraid of the toil. Be afraid only of thoughtlessness and pusillanimity. From the difficult experience that we call 'Poland' a better future can be drawn; but only on condition that you are honourable, temperate, believing, free in spirit and strong in your convictions.

And so finally back through the crowded streets of Krakow to Franciszkanska Street, where the usual throng was singing and waiting under his window to bid him goodnight. 'All's well that ends well' were the Pope's parting words to them. 'Tomorrow is another day. Goodnight!'

The penultimate morning of the papal tour, Saturday 9 June,

brought another abrupt change of scene and mood. The Pope found himself breathing the acrid atmosphere of Nowa Huta (which means New Steelworks). It was here that in the 1950s the State's planners had deliberately founded a town without a church. Only a small wooden church on the edge of the complex had remained. But the workers and the clergy made this their temporary religious base while they fought a prolonged battle to build a large new downtown church on subscription and by voluntary labour.

The completion of the building was not only the Church's greatest post-war triumph in Poland; it was also something of a personal victory for Karol Wojtyla, local bishop from 1958 on. He consecrated the church in 1977. Three months before his return to Poland as Pope, when details were being argued between Rome and Warsaw, he asked to conduct a Mass in Nowa Huta church. It would have savoured of gloating; and as a compromise it was agreed that he should celebrate instead at the Franciscan church at Mogila, the village still existing on the rim of Nowa Huta. And so it was that on this Saturday morning he helicoptered the few miles from Krakow to a field at Mogila and conducted yet another of his cheerful open-air Masses, with the now familiar pattern of singing, joking, cheering, praying, with moments grave and gay, with carnations and poppies and chrysanthemums spread on the ground every yard of the Pope's route from aircraft to altar, with a dozen cardinals and many more bishops providing splashes of colour on the raised platform, with two young guitarists and a fiddler at the altar beside him, and his dignified yet delighted presence dominating it all, a burly, benevolent, smiling, waving figure, never losing his authority, switching quickly from laughter to prayer. During his sermon, in which he kept interrupting himself to react to something sung or seen in the crowd (perhaps an unexpected poster waved by a group from Chicago), he laughed at himself and said 'Just imagine what the world must think about me – a man who starts a sermon and can't finish it. What a Pope!'

With the smoke of Nowa Huta blast furnaces in his nostrils, he applied his humanistic calculus to yet another problem: industrial relations. Christianity and the Church had no fear of the world of work, he declared:

The problems being raised today about human labour do not come down in the last analysis either to technology or even to economics but to a fundamental category, the category of the dignity of work, that is to say, of the dignity of man . . . Remember this one thing: Christ will never approve that man be considered, or that man consider himself, merely as a means of production, or that he be appreciated, esteemed and valued in accordance with that principle.

And so back to Krakow for a number of lesser encounters before his last goodnight in Franciszkanska Street.

'It is not easy to leave Krakow behind.' Those words were even more apt on Sunday 10 June. John Paul II left Poland from Krakow airport; and in his farewell speech he said 'Although this parting cannot possibly break the strong spiritual and emotional bonds which link me with my city, my homeland and its inhabitants, nevertheless this is a painful moment for me. But my see is now in Rome, and I must return to Rome . . .'

The pain of parting hung over the whole city all the previous night and the whole of Sunday. Two days earlier, it was learnt, the Pope had wandered out into the streets and squares of Krakow incognito at about four in the morning to feel again their special associations for him. Now as the dark gave way to dawn on this warm Sunday morning one could make out the shadowy shapes of humanity converging on the flat, triangular, two-hundred-acre *blonie* at the edge of central Krakow. For something like twelve hours before the start of the 10 a.m. Mass that movement had been under way – quietly flowing streams of peasants and workers from outside the town at first, many families with their small children, then the citizens of Krakow itself, all pressing on through its ancient streets, forming a river at the entrance to the meadow, and gradually filling it with a lake of people. Many spent the night in churches. By five it seemed there were already half a million people gathered. By ten, when the Pope arrived on his special vehicle with Wyszynski, criss-crossing the avenues kept clear in the endless concourse, it was estimated that two million people were there. (It could be seen then how big the crowds might have been at Gniezno and Czestochowa without official deterrence.) The focal point that Sunday morning was the largest open-air platform and altar that had been constructed anywhere for the visit, about a hundred yards wide and twenty deep, with a white backcloth stretched across a huge wooden framework.

The Mass followed the familiar pattern, but the usual bantering rapport between Polish pontiff and Polish people was replaced by an almost palpable intensity of emotion and love. In the distance could be heard the deep tones of Zygmunt, the enormous cathedral bell rung only at moments of high solemnity. The Pope could not hide his underlying sadness. He read his sermon, over an hour in length, without unduly interrupting himself, only waiting from time to time as sacro-songs broke into his words. 'Never abandon your faith' was its burden. The only overt political reference in it was an addition to the prepared text prompted by the sight of a banner in the crowd right in front of the altar which read 'Peter, revive us in Czechoslovakia', when he renewed his gentle reproach that Catholics from neighbouring countries of the Eastern bloc – 'our other brothers in language and historical destiny' – were not there in any numbers.

Just before leaving the Archbishop's palace for the airport, the Pope spent half an hour on a courtyard balcony greeting members of his press retinue. Speaking by turns in Italian, English, French and Polish, he praised the work of journalists in terms which were as much an appeal to conscience as a compliment. 'They devote their whole lives to an ideal, the ideal of serving the truth. As long as they are faithful to that ideal they deserve respect and gratitude from everyone.'

The six miles of road to the airport were lined with people waving goodbye – and with militiamen at thirty-yard intervals. On the tarmac at the airport stood the shining white Soviet-built TU-134A airliner from LOT, the Polish Airline. The return to Rome in a Polish aircraft was the *quid pro quo* for the arrival in an Alitalia plane nine days earlier. The inside of the plane had been completely stripped and rebuilt; there was a saloon at the front with a couch and armchairs, and behind it comfortable quarters for the entourage and the secretarial staff. The food and drink had been provided by Blikle (Warsaw's smartest catering establishment, still surviving from pre-war years); but the Pope was so tired and drained that he ate nothing on the flight, and drank one glass of champagne.

The speeches at the little airport reduced practically every Pole who heard them to tears, to say nothing of the Pope himself. Jablonski was on hand again, and Wyszynski, and a couple of ministers. Jablonski's speech was politically flavoured, dwelling on the State's concern with many of the issues that the Pope had raised in his sermons. Wyszynski was less inhibited. He thanked the Pope for his open arms; he spoke of the Slav face that inspired trust. 'Everything about you is dear to us and fraternal . . . We promise you, Holy Father, that we will not leave you in peace in the Vatican either, because we know you are glad to see us in your home. Before Polish wings carry you to Rome, look once again at your children and at your fellow countrymen, and bless the dear homeland.'

The Pope's voice was unsteady as he said his goodbyes and spoke of the painful moment of farewell. He expressed thanks to the President for his kindness and to the civil authorities for their hospitality. He realized, he said, how much effort was concealed under the pleasant word 'visit'. He went on to thank Wyszynski and all the Polish clergy for their welcome and prayers. 'Back there beyond the Alps I shall hear in my soul the sound of bells calling to prayer . . . the heartbeat of my compatriots.'

It was a last hint that the Church was the essential reality in Poland, not the State. Yet he made clear in his next breath his continuing interest in accommodation rather than challenge:

> No doubt this unprecedented event represented an act of some courage on both sides; but such an act of courage was required by our time. That is why we must have the courage to move sometimes in a direction which no one has followed before. Our age very much needs this kind of token which proclaims the will to come together, the will for rapprochement between people and systems, as a necessary condition for peace in the world. The requirement of our age is that we should not confine ourselves within rigid frontiers when the good of man is involved.

Three moments of high drama followed. As the Pope said 'I bid farewell to Poland, my homeland . . .' he knelt swiftly and kissed the tarmac, the hood of his cape covering his head as he did so.

He stood up, tears on his cheeks, and continued in strained tones: 'On my departure I kiss this soil from which my heart can never be separated.'

As he approached the aircraft the Pope shook the hands of each of the personalities there. But there was a gasp as he went up to a short, bulkily-built man who had been in charge of the plain-clothes security ring round him. John Paul II shook the man's hand warmly and spoke to him for several moments. Three hard-faced security men on the press platform, who had already shown signs of emotion at the Pope's farewell words, were now over-whelmed. 'What a man', one of them was overheard to mutter. 'What on earth's happening? Nobody normally ever thanks *us* for anything . . .'

The third incident was the most dramatic of all. Shaking Jablonski's hand for the last time, John Paul II suddenly leaned forward and embraced him on both cheeks, a gesture reciprocated with clear and deep emotion by Jablonski in bending to kiss the Pope's hands. The moment was captured by the photographers, and the next day the picture was on the front page of practically every newspaper in the country.

A few moments later the Pope had mounted the ramp, and with a final wave disappeared inside the plane, the Primate stand-ing below with raised hand. The last sight of John Paul II was his face at a porthole. The plane taxied off without delay, and was quickly airborne and soon out of sight over the Tatra peaks. Sud-denly, Poland felt very empty.

The day after John Paul II left Poland, the chief spokesman at the Polish Foreign Ministry declared his Government 'deeply satisfied with the course of the Holy Father's visit', and even looked forward to formal diplomatic relations with the Holy See. The newspapers fell cheerfully in behind. A Warsaw radio bulletin on 11 June, summing up domestic press reaction, said that 'all reports continue to stress the discipline of the faithful in Poland, the dignified, warm and sincere atmosphere surrounding the Pope throughout his stay in his native land, and the good co-operation between the State and Church authorities'.

It was clear that the ruling party had decided to continue the pre-visit policy of dialogue with the Church authorities; yet what would that amount to in practice? How many of the Church's demands would be met? Would there be specific concessions, and when? Or would the State negotiators revert to their old tactic of filibustering through their meetings with the episcopate?

The visit raised a number of questions to which there could be no answer for some time. What damage to Party morale was done by the full revelation of the strength of Catholicism in Poland? How upset were the middle and lower ranks of the Party, as distinct from the Politburo, by the spontaneous demonstration of the true views of so many millions of Poles – not least the generation under 35, who had lived all their lives under Marxism and yet not been converted to it? Would Party men concede that in practice the Communists could only rule Poland with the consent of the Church?

And the Kremlin – was it sorry that the Poles had not stopped the Pope coming (as they did Paul VI when he thought of helping celebrate the millennium of Polish Christianity in 1966)? Did the amicable co-operation between Church and State over the visit comfort Soviet Party leaders or alarm them? What would be their response if the visit bred demands for a liberalized treatment of Catholics not just in Poland but in neighbouring States of the Eastern bloc?

Yet a number of things were clear to observers who were in Poland before, during and after the papal visit. Chief of these was the boost to the morale of the Polish Catholic people, in other words most of the country. In a sense, the Pope did for the Poles what General de Gaulle did for the French during the Second World War: he reminded them of their identity, restored their self-confidence, renewed their faded hopes for a better future. They were left with a comforting feeling that someone of importance in world affairs cared for them, understood them, identified with them, and would not let them be overlooked or forgotten.

At the same time, the Pope raised few false hopes. A middle-aged man in Warsaw was heard to say; 'It was moving to see Wojtyla and Jablonski embracing, with tears on their cheeks, but in our situation things can't change all that quickly or easily.' Yet a waitress in a Krakow restaurant, shown a front-page picture of the embrace, was astounded. 'Heavens', she said, 'times *are* changing.' There was truth in both reactions.

Catholic intellectuals in Poland hoped that the Party would show a better understanding than before of people's real feelings. Yet the hope was not lively. On previous occasions when the regime had been in trouble, as for example during the rioting over food prices in 1970 and 1976, it had sought the episcopate's help in bringing calm; but very little was conceded to the Church's requests once the crisis of control had been overcome.

For the moment, both sides profited. While the Church was strengthened, the Party certainly gained its own share of advantage. The spectacle on national television of the country's political leaders in apparently affable association with the Pope and the episcopal hierarchy, culminating in an emotional embrace between the Pontiff and the head of State, must certainly have enhanced Gierek's personal authority, while the visit as a whole equally enhanced Poland's standing in the world. And the Pope never directly criticized the country's rulers. At all times he seemed to be making it plain that he accepted the political realities of Poland – that while he ardently hoped Poland's branch of socialism would take on a human face, the Church he led was in no way preaching rebellion.

To extreme anti-Communist campaigners, indeed, the Pope's posture looked dangerously like the offer of an unholy alliance between two authoritarian systems of thought – Christian Catholicism and atheistic Marxist-Leninism. But the relationship between Catholicism and Communism in Poland, as Rakowski had written, could not have remained static. The central question was whether the two were to advance on a collision course, or whether the Pope had succeeded in starting a process of parallel progress towards a society in which commonsense co-operation made built-in ideological conflict tolerable to live with. If that happened, the eventual impact on Eastern Europe and on Marxist attitudes in general could be of immense importance.

7

Keep True to the Faith

He was not back at base for long. On 29 September John Paul II
left Rome for two days in Ireland and a week in the United States.
The journey did more than round off his opening year in office. It
was his first encounter as pope with the developed West. It gave
him opportunity to show that his prescriptions for moral health
were the same in societies which knew about personal freedom as
in countries where the Catholic Church faced secular totali-
tarianism. Indeed, his sense of the special temptations of wealth
persuaded him to sharpen his Western message. As a predictable
consequence, reasoned criticism of his papacy could for the first
time be distinctly heard. It became possible to suspect that this
Irish-American voyage would mark the point from which his
reputation began to decline.

Putting its distresses aside for a few weeks, Ireland prepared for
the Pope's passage in high good humour. Seventy-six prisoners
thought unlikely to be dangerous to the public were chosen for
early release from gaol. The rest of the prison population was
allowed extra television time. An elderly woman in Drogheda
wanted to hang her yellow-and-white flag from an inaccessibly
high point on the old people's home where she lived: the mayor
called out the fire brigade to do it for her. The Dublin newspapers, a world away from the reticence of Warsaw, filled page
after page with the honour done to Ireland by the Holy Father,
the blend of Irish and would-be Polish food he would be given
to eat, the life history of everyone who would come within a
hundred feet of him, the colour of the blanket on his bed in the
Aer Lingus jumbo that would bring him from Rome, and the
whereabouts of the first patch of Irish turf he would glimpse from
it. A colonel of the Irish Air Corps let it be known that the Corps
would shoot down any unauthorized planes which strayed into

the jumbo's airspace: but warning shots, the colonel felt sure, would be enough to frighten them off. Against the ultimate disaster, blood supplies belonging to the papal blood group would be on tap at every papal stop.

Even traditional ogres broke into a frosty smile. The British Army sent tents down from Northern Ireland for 2500 children to sleep in before the Drogheda rally. A middle-rank British Minister from Belfast who was also a Catholic, Hugh Rossi, decided to be there too – in a private capacity, his office carefully explained. Protestant churchmen in the North declared that they welcomed the visit. Certain Presbyterians among them were only sorry that their own leaders' encounter with the Pope in Dublin would be short: they would have no proper chance to convert him. The Reverend Ian Paisley, leader of the Free Presbyterians and of Protestant irreconcilables generally, did characterize the Pope as 'that Antichrist, that man of sin and son of perdition'; but since these were scriptural phrases applied to the Pope by the Westminster Confession, a statement of the Presbyterian faith drawn up in 1647, the stern words dwindled into a literary allusion.

The visit was undeniably good for the economy. Squads of carpenters hammered away at gigantic open-air platforms on which acres of carpet from Irish mills were then nailed down. Presents for the Pope were commissioned from tapestry-weavers, glass-engravers, sculptors, jewellers. Likenesses of him – bas-reliefs sandblasted on to Connemara marble, or simple coloured photographs in little gilt frames – were offered at every price. Singers made records with titles like 'Welcome John Paul' and 'Viva el Papa'. Camp stools to sit on during the open-air services, and photocopying paper to reproduce the Pope's plentiful utterances for visiting journalists in four languages, were consumed by the truckload. The fillip to the tourist trade at the end of an indifferent season was colossal: in Limerick alone it was valued at a million pounds. At Knock, featureless County Mayo village where the Pope was to visit a Marian shrine on its centenary, this boost was expected to be permanent: a local businessman who had barely finished building half a dozen identical souvenir shops was now planning a 200-bedroom hotel. The two main Irish banks were heartened enough by all this circulation of wealth to contribute £100,000 each to the Catholic Church's considerable costs. Even strikes, a passion the Irish had caught of late years from the English, were held to an innocuous minimum. The Irish Army swept away the last traces of a Dublin dustmen's dispute with unprecedented zeal. The worst that happened was that the sale of gold and silver papal medallions was held up by a go-slow among the Assay Office men who stamped the hallmarks on them.

The word was that the visit was to be purely pastoral: it was to address the moral, not the political, problems which beset Irish believers. The Pope was a pastor, not a politician: repeated in various forms, it was the only observation of substance heard from the Holy Father during a disorderly press conference over the Irish Sea on the way in to Dublin, when journalists swarmed towards his suddenly appearing figure with such eagerness that the jumbo dipped its port wing, and *The Sunday Times* representative was knocked to the floor by a cameraman while the Pope still had hold of her hand. (The cabin crew was at least as anxious to get near him. Even if they were stationed in the rear of the plane, all the green-suited Aer Lingus hostesses contrived an excuse to peep through the green tweed curtain which separated them from the forward, papal compartment; and one of them – a few minutes after he had been issued with an Irish breakfast of four sausages, four rashers of bacon, a length of white pudding and a length of black pudding – burst back through the curtain to announce with shining eyes: 'He's cleaned up his plate!'.) At the airports at either end, too, he carefully deployed the term 'pastoral visit'; and at Dublin it was echoed by Cardinal Tomas O Fiaich, Archbishop of Armagh and Primate of All Ireland.

O Fiaich and his brother bishops hoped for nothing less from the visit than that it would recall Irish Catholics – whom they equated with the Irish nation – to old patterns of morality. 'The Pope's visit', said Archbishop Joseph Cunnane of Tuam, 'will be the greatest spiritual experience in the history of Ireland.' He meant that Ireland would be brought back from what he called 'the eat-drink-and-be-merry pagan attitude' to a sober and assiduous faith. A pastoral letter from the whole hierarchy spelt out the point:

Pope John Paul's visit is an invitation to the lapsed and the careless to come to God's pardon and peace. We bishops, with our priests, wish to speak now to all who have drifted away from the Church and from Mass and the sacraments. We hope you are listening. We say to you: come back. We have missed you. We need you. The Church is your Mother. She wants you back. You will never find happiness anywhere else. The Church's door is open and she is waiting to welcome you home. Christ is there.

Until the Pope himself corrected the balance, the implication seemed to be that there was nothing the matter with Ireland which regular church-going would not put right.

Even by that test it was true that all was not well. As the economic necessity for emigration had diminished, and young couples were bringing up their families at home, Ireland had become a young country. A 1977 Government survey found that a third of the country's three-million-odd people were under fifteen, and nearly half under twenty-five. The problem for the bishops was that this new generation was not staying within the fold. The proportion of young adults who were not practising Catholics was twice as high, at twenty percent, as in the population at large. At least as serious for the Church, the number of young people coming forward to be priests, monks and nuns was dropping fast. A Galway convent of nuns which ten years before took in nine or ten novices a year had received in the past three years a total of three. Over the same period the diocese of Killala had registered no vocations at all. 'If this trend continues', said the Bishop, Thomas McDonnell, 'there will be no Church in the Killala diocese in twenty years' time.'

The culprit, in the hierarchy's view, was the change brought about by the affluence of the 1970s. Membership of the European Economic Community had made Irish farms more prosperous, better equipped and less labour-intensive than before: foreign investment provided work in the towns, and particularly in the region round Dublin. It was the Irish industrial revolution, nearly two centuries after the English. The result was that young Irish adults were exposed as never before to the perils – as the bishops considered them – of ordinary urban life.

To a point, the Pope accepted this diagnosis. Looking out over a sunlit crowd of more than a million people in Phoenix Park on the edge of Dublin, with the wind ruffling his short silver hair and bringing back a multiple echo of his words from distant loudspeakers, he played cunningly on the endemic Irish sense of persecution. Alien scourges like Oliver Cromwell, he implied, or the penal code which the British applied to Catholics in the eighteenth century, had been succeeded by the new menaces of modernity:

> Yes, Ireland, that has overcome so many difficult moments in her history, is being challenged in a new way today, for she is not immune from the influence of ideologies and trends which present-day civilization and progress carry with them. The very capability of mass media to bring the whole world into your homes produces a new kind of confrontation with values and trends that up until now have been alien to Irish society. Pervading materialism imposes its dominion on man today in many different forms and with an aggressiveness that spares no one. The most sacred principles, which were sure guides for the behaviour of individuals and society, are being hollowed out by false pretences concerning freedom, the sacredness of life, the indissolubility of marriage, the true sense of human sexuality, the right attitude towards the material goods that progress has to offer. Many people now are tempted to self-indulgence and consumerism, and human identity is often defined by what one owns. Prosperity and affluence, even when they are only beginning to be available to larger strata of society, tend to make people assume that they have a right to all that prosperity can bring, and thus they can become more selfish in their demands. Everybody wants a full freedom in all the areas of human behaviour, and new models of morality are being imposed in the name of would-be freedom. When the moral fibre of a nation is weakened, when the sense of personal reponsibility is diminished, then the door is open for the justification of injustices, for violence in all

its forms, and for the manipulation of the many by the few.

He seemed almost to be saying that 'consumerism' – which his translators used in the sense of excessive, rather than informed, consumption – had prepared the ground for the IRA. The antidote he proposed was regular attendance at the Eucharist, preceded by confession: that would generate Christian lives. He even drew the parallel which the Bishops had been busy suggesting in the days of preparation for the visit – between the gathering in front of him and the huge eucharistic congress held in the same place in 1932. (A Polish contingent had been brought there by Wyszynski's predecessor as primate, Cardinal August Hlond.) The congress had in fact been designed to register a demand that the constitution of the new State of Ireland should explicitly acknowledge the central place of the Catholic Church and its social teaching: and five years later the demand was met.

John Paul II said the same thing at his 'Mass for youth' under an Irish mist on Galway racecourse the following day, aiming his words specifically at young people gathered from all over the island:

> I know, I understand, young people; and I know that you, like other young people of your age in other countries, are affected by what is happening in society around you. Although you still live in an atmosphere where true religious and moral principles are held in honour, you have to realize that your fidelity to these principles will be tested in many ways. The religious and moral traditions of Ireland, the very soul of Ireland, will be challenged by the temptations that spare no society in our age.

He was at particular pains to warn them against 'the lure of pleasure', notably in the sexual domain.

At Knock, that afternoon, standing beside the church gable end where Mary was believed to have appeared a hundred years before, and taking as his reiterated text her instruction to the servants at Cana to do whatever Jesus told them, he warned the crowd:

So many different voices assail the Christian in today's wonderful but complicated and demanding world. So many false voices are heard that conflict with the word of the Lord. They are the voices that tell you that truth is less important than personal gain; that comfort, wealth and pleasure are the true aims of life; that the refusal of new life is better than generosity of spirit and the taking up of responsibility; that justice must be achieved, but without any personal involvement by the Christian; that violence can be a means to a good end; that unity can be built without giving up hate.

May prosperity, he concluded, never cause Irish men and women to forget God or abandon their faith.

On the boggy racecourse at Limerick, finally, he warned Ireland that it was 'living again the temptations of Christ': it was being asked to prefer 'the kingdoms of the world' to the kingdom of God. Satan would be using 'all of his might and all his deceptions to win Ireland for the way of the world'. A few Dublin sophisticates wondered whether the Devil would have time to concentrate so exclusively on Ireland, and traced this demonological approach to the bookish and conservative hand of Jeremiah Newman, Limerick's bishop; yet even in Dublin two women were heard under the hairdriers at Brown Thomas's agreeing that it was time the Devil was brought back to the pulpit. For Limerick, and with the Bishop's help, the Pope had restyled his message to touch the kind of godly, rural Ireland which he acknowledged to be in decline. In Ireland in the past, he said, life was in a sense organized around religious events. Now modern industry and urban life must be transformed by the same Gospel spirit.

Today you must keep the city and the factory for God as you have always kept the farm and the village community for him in the past . . . To those who have gone to the cities, here or abroad, I say: keep in contact with your roots in the soil of Ireland, with your families and your culture. Keep true to the faith, to the prayers and the values you learned here, and pass on that heritage to your children, for it is rich and good.

And in this sermon, his last before he left, he went into greater detail than before about exactly how his listeners were to keep true to the faith. The primary field of Christian action for the Irish laity, he told them, was the family.

The article of the 1937 Constitution stating that 'The State recognizes the special position of the Holy Catholic Apostolic and Roman Church as the guardian of the Faith professed by the great majority of the citizens' was deleted by referendum, in a spasm of tact towards the Protestant North, in 1972; but an article baldly laying down that 'No law shall be enacted providing for the grant of a dissolution of marriage' survived. The Pope was all for that.

> Divorce, for whatever reason it is introduced, inevitably becomes easier and easier to obtain, and it gradually comes to be accepted as a normal part of life. The very possibility of divorce in the sphere of civil law makes stable and permanent marriages more difficult for everyone. May Ireland always continue to give witness before the modern world to her traditional commitment to the sanctity and the indissolubility of the marriage bond. May the Irish always support marriage, through personal commitment and through positive social and legal action.

Politicians, in government and opposition, bridled a little at the implication that legal action was within the competence of the Church. Given the influence exercised by bishops and parish priests on constituents, and thence by constituents on politicians, it was a little too true to be welcome. But it was not to be thought a mark against the Holy Father: 'some bishop overstepping his position', said an Opposition frontbencher.

The Pope had more yet to say about marriage. It was not to become 'a self-centred relationship of two individuals'. It must include 'openness to the gift of children': there should be no interference in the course of nature either before or after conception.

> Respect the God-given cycle of life, for this respect is part of our respect for God himself, who created male and female, who created them in his own image, reflect-

ing his own life-giving love in the patterns of their sexual being.

And so I say to all, have an absolute and holy respect for the sacredness of human life from the first moment of its conception. Abortion, as the Vatican Council stated, is one of the 'abominable crimes' (*Gaudium et Spes*, 51). To attack unborn life at any moment from its conception is to undermine the whole moral order which is the true guardian of the well-being of man. The defence of the absolute inviolability of unborn life is part of the defence of human rights and human dignity.

And he concluded with a passing swipe at women's emancipation – 'May Irish mothers, young women and girls not listen to those who tell them that working in a secular job, succeeding in a secular profession, is more important than the vocation of giving life and caring for this life as a mother' – and a plea for the renewal of family prayer. It would encourage those needed vocations to the priesthood and the monastic life.

For Bishop Newman, at any rate, it had all been exactly what was wanted. 'The Pope's coming', he said afterwards, 'was like the visit of a good parish priest to the family home.'

Clearly the Pope achieved some of his purposes merely by his coming. The ideas advocated could not but gain in circulation, at any rate, through being put forward by a man so widely found winning. Virtually the whole country saw him on television: a third of it saw him in the flesh, sometimes going to considerable lengths for the purpose. (At Limerick, favoured places were reserved in advance for the handicapped. 'It has been astonishing', said a Limerick diocesan cleric, apparently without irony, 'to discover that so many people need care in our society.') The Pope appeared to recover the missing young people at a stroke. They were very evident in the crowds which his popemobiles traversed (on the pattern set in Poland). At Galway in particular the crowd was alight with the brilliant reds and yellows and blues of young people's anoraks, hoods up against the soft rain. Faces shining, hands joined aloft, bands of young men and girls swayed in great waves as they sang 'Rivers of Babylon' or 'This is the day that the Lord has made'. When a company of priests fanned out across the racecourse carrying the Communion in bowls, their escorts were an equal number of schoolchildren carrying black and white umbrellas.

In a tour which was capably organized everywhere, Galway was the prime success; and its stage-manager was the rumbustious Bishop of Galway, Eamonn Casey. After the service the Pope struck him on the chest with a clenched fist and said: 'You are the strong one.' The main rally outside Dublin might have been expected to be at Cork, Ireland's second and disproportionately successful city: there was a certain glee elsewhere when Casey won the occasion for Galway – partly on the ground that it was more central for bus loads of children, especially from the North, and partly because it would draw off crowds from Knock and keep the village from being swamped. Casey ran everything, and delighted in it. His volume of advice to the public was the size of a phone book. Before dawn on the great day he walked from his palace up on to the racecourse, uttering comfortable words about first-aid posts to women who said: 'Asha Bishop maybe we're foolish to bring the little ones, but sure as long as they live they'll be able to say "We were on Galway racecourse the day the Pope came".' After the papal lunch at the palace, when the Pope – already late for Knock – wanted one more *bain de foule*, Casey twice physically objected. He recalled afterwards: 'I said, "Holy Father, I'm in charge here." I again put my hands on his shoulders and turned him towards the helicopter. He just looked at me and went inside. Like a bold child, he knows exactly when he's been bold.'

Casey said of the Pope and his young hearers: 'They saw him as a man who lives the values behind the words.' The observation was just; and it might have been carried further. The values outweighed the words. The persona had more impact than the actual message. The best effects were non-verbal. In Phoenix Park there was nothing to touch the moment when the green-and-blue-and-white jumbo floated across the crowd on its way in to land, with tiny red-and-silver fighters at each corner like the four evangelists, a million faces upturned to the sky, and innumerable hands and pennants raised in greeting. Whatever his verbal skill in his native land and tongue, outside Poland John Paul II is at his best as a communicator without words. Clasping a young head to him with as confident an affection as if he had been the child's real father; pursing his lips to retain his self-control as he looked out over a sea of cheering devotees; scrutinizing a young woman reading an address to him at Galway – 'We stand by you who stand for him who is the way, the truth and the life' – as intently as if he were in the process of discovering not just what it was like to be young and intelligent in the west of Ireland but what it was like to be that young woman; listening, rapt, to a choir singing, the crucifix on his crozier held against his cheek; hugging a boy blinded by a rubber bullet in an encounter with the British Army in Derry – in much that he did he showed beyond argument, whatever the counter-implications of his sterner sayings, that his interest in human lives was universal; and it was universal because it started from the particular. Television, itself needing precisely these visual rather than verbal evidences of character, abetted him in turning them into an unspoken language. The best remembered sentence he spoke in Ireland was also the simplest. The anorak wearers on Galway racecourse applauded his moral exhortations civilly; but they erupted into twelve minutes of sustained cheering and singing when he said at the very end of his sermon, with slow and equal emphasis on the last three words, 'Young people of Ireland, I love you.' The assurance was believed because he had already demonstrated its truth without words.

'He hasn't the English that good, you know', an admirer was heard explaining while the Pope was at Knock; and it was true enough. A crowd of *soi-disant* journalists (a high proportion of them wearing clerical collars) serenaded him at a Dublin monastery with 'For he's a jolly good fellow'. After a pause he replied with great deliberation: 'It was very pleased to me of hearing that I am greeted as a good fellow.' It was the one occasion when he asked his hearers to take his already-issued speech – a thoroughly sensible admonition to journalists to show their love for their neighbour by telling him the truth – as read; and without his prepared texts he was largely at a loss.

Yet even with them he was nothing like as effective as he might have been. He had written the originals himself – with a certain input of information from Irish bishops, both in their recent reports to the Congregation of Bishops and on visits to Rome. The bulk of the Irish and American material was composed during August and September at Castelgandolfo, the papal summer residence, between eight and eleven each morning. Interruptions were forbidden. Through the open windows the Pope could sometimes be heard singing, which the household took as evidence that he judged things to be going well. He wrote in longhand, and in Polish. Among Poles he has the reputation of writing Polish with grace and freshness. But his words had to be translated first into Italian and then into English – and then they were checked by the English-language desk of the Secretariat of State; and somewhere along the way the freshness was squeezed out. Spoken Polish, to judge from the Pope's own speeches in Poland, can stand long sentences. Good spoken English demands at least a modicum of short ones. It also asks the use of short words where they fit. In an accent where 'love' becomes 'laugh', and 'praise' is 'press', and 'intolerable' rhymes with 'table', and 'presence' has the stress on the second syllable, and so does 'irreplaceable', and rhymes with 'feeble', mere intelligibility counsels the use of the plainest words possible. A phrase like 'traditional commitment to the sanctity and the indissolubility of the marriage bond' shows that the translators were at no pains to supply them. Certainly it was remarkable that the Pope could manage English at all, among so many other foreign languages; but the complexity of his scripts put him in a false position. And not merely were the words often long, and the sentences long, but the sermons as a whole were long – three-quarters of an hour and more, which is above the tolerance of modern Western congregations. So for great parts of these encounters, so valued on either side, the Pope stood with his nose in his script, only partly understanding and only partly understood. Such rapport as there was between him and his audiences was in the astonishing fact of his presence there rather than in the words he spoke.

The reflection may comfort those who were uneasy at the kind of Ireland which, by his speeches, John Paul II sought to preserve or revive. Their concern was this. His words, as distinct from his visible attitudes, seemed to undergird an Ireland where compassion was extended to people in general but not to the suffering individual. Outlawing divorce may well redound to the general good by encouraging stability in marriage; but it bears hardly on particular cases – the country's 15,000 abandoned wives, victims of 'divorce Irish-style', where there is very little legal basis on which the husband can be obliged either to fulfil his duties or renounce his rights. Ten days after the Pope's visit, the European Court of Human Rights in Strasbourg found that Irish immobilism about divorce was in fact a breach of the right to a properly protected family life, since for most people there was no means whereby a potentially violent husband could be excluded from the broken home. (The case had been brought by the wife of a Cork truck-driver.) Certain Irish bishops half acknowledged the sad facts by permitting annulments more open-handedly than before, to the number of several hundred a year in total. But the bishops gave no encouragement to politicians who might introduce a secular divorce law to give those annulments practical force.

The hand of the bishops in social legislation is all on the side of general rather than particular compassion. There is no provision for legal abortion in Ireland – even after rape, or where the health or sanity of the mother is threatened: the bishops regard deliberate abortion as 'always gravely sinful', in the words of a pastoral letter of May 1975. The same ban is extended to contraception: its availability 'will only spread further the mentality and style of life which produce the demand for abortion'. Parents should trust in Providence instead. Accordingly, the law in Ireland permits the sale of contraceptives only on prescription; and though family-planning clinics dispense them without interference, supply is difficult for the unmarried and the incompetent – precisely the people who most need help. It may well be that the general level of reverence for life in Ireland, and of chastity, is in consequence high; but thousands of particular lives pay for it. The bishops themselves acknowledge that 'at present more than 2200 Irish girls are officially registered as having abortions in Britain each year'. The true figure is commonly reckoned to be much higher. And for lack of the contraceptive provision which might have helped prevent that, an incalculable number of unintended children arrive in the world at the risk of their own and their parents' self-fulfilment. This was the Ireland which the Pope's Limerick sermon sought to keep in being.

Senior Irish clerics have taken the same unbending *pour-encourager-les autres* line about the indissolubility of ordination. The parallel between the priesthood and marriage, as used in the

Pope's Letter to Priests, was a favourite one. To some extent it reflected Irish popular piety: a priest was married to his vocation, and it was a good match. Irish parents have traditionally been proud to have a priest in the family, embarrassed if he abandons his orders or even his ordination studies (to the point where they prefer him not to return to their own neighbourhood), and uneasy if a daughter marries such a defector. At Maynooth, the theological seminary outside Dublin which is also part of the nominally secular National University, teachers even of secular subjects who so much as tried to give up their orders have been dismissed: the example was too dangerous. Failure to wear a clerical collar gave special offence. John Paul II, on his own visit to Maynooth early on a foggy morning, underwrote that whole approach. To a gathering which included a thousand seminarians from all over the country, together with great numbers of priests, missionaries, monks and nuns, he said:

> What the people expect from you, more than anything else, is faithfulness to the priesthood. This is what speaks to them of the faithfulness of God. This is what strengthens them to be faithful to Christ through all the difficulties of their lives, of their marriages. In a world so marked by instability as our world today, we need more signs and witnesses to God's fidelity to us, and to the fidelity we owe to him. This is what causes such great sadness to the Church, such great but often silent anguish among the people of God, when priests fail in their fidelity to their priestly commitment. That counter-sign, that counter-witness, has been one of the setbacks to the great hopes for renewal aroused throughout the Church by the Second Vatican Council.

Hence all those appeals for laicization sitting blocked at the Vatican.

The Maynooth crowd was a little puzzled by an address aimed so exclusively at the professionals in its midst; but it clapped approvingly when the Pope urged them to stick to their uniforms as well as their vocations:

> Rejoice to be witnesses to Christ in the modern world.
> Do not hesitate to be recognizable, identifiable, in the

streets as men and women who have consecrated their
lives to God and have given up everything worldly to
follow Christ. Believe in the value for contemporary
men and women of the visible signs of your consecrated
lives. People need signs and reminders of God in the
modern secular city, which has few reminders of God
left. Do not help the trend towards 'taking God off the
streets' by adopting secular modes of dress and
behaviour yourselves.

And to his bishops in Ireland the night before he had indicated
that there was to be no weakening on another priestly commitment:

Our priests have made many sacrifices, including the
renunciation of marriage for the sake of the kingdom
of heaven; and they must be firmly encouraged to
persevere.

It was renewed notice that, in order to strengthen the many in
their vows, the comparatively few priests who wished to change
their state and marry would have to suffer instead.

The Ireland which John Paul II sought to leave in place behind
him was uncompromisingly Catholic. There was to be no practical
quarter for rival denominations. 'Let no one ever doubt', he told
a Dublin gathering of Irish Protestant leaders, 'the commitment
of the Catholic Church and of the Apostolic See of Rome to the
pursuit of the unity of Christians.' His encyclical had witnessed to
the same aim. Yet there was still room for doubt – unless unity
was taken as meaning the universal acknowledgement that Rome
was right. Catholic bishops and priests in Ireland refused to treat
Protestant Christianity as being of equal worth with Catholic.
The children of inter-Church marriages were in practice still
required to be brought up as Catholics, despite a softening of the
rules in 1970 by Paul VI which had been taken advantage of by
other European hierarchies. No countenance was given to the
notion that Catholic children might sometimes, as an experiment
in neighbourliness, be educated with Protestant children: one of
the most potent, grave and reverend of Irish bishops, Cahal Daly
of Ardagh and Clonmacnois, had lately declared that the Catholic

position on that was 'not open to negotiation'. Time could not be found for the Pope to visit an ecumenical vigil being held in St Patrick's Anglican cathedral in Dublin while he was there; and his meeting with Protestant leaders, brief and late at night, could not have occupied a lower place on his schedule. Small wonder that the Presbyterians, in their prepared address to the Pope for that meeting, said of their long ecumenical labours to that point:

> Sadly it must be said that many of those who participated enthusiastically now feel that much of this is getting nowhere: that fine words and exhortations are not matched by actions, nor by movement from entrenched positions of ecclesiastical power and influence. Our ecumenical scene, like our political, is at a standstill if it is not in retreat.

The Pope said and did nothing in Ireland to change that melancholy conclusion.

Ireland was to be confirmed not merely in a rigid but in a credulous Catholicism. The nub of the visit was Knock. 'The centenary of the sanctuary of the Mother of God at Knock constitutes, this year, a providential occasion for the Pope's visit to Ireland', he said in Phoenix Park; and at the start of his sermon at Knock itself, 'Here I am at the goal of my journey to Ireland'. And yet Knock was a point of special doubt within a disputable area of the faith.

During a period of about two hours on the evening of 21 August, 1879, some 22 villagers saw three illuminated figures whom they took to be Mary, Joseph and John the Evangelist against the south gable wall of Knock church. That much is reasonably well attested; but from then on, oddities crowd in. No special sanctity or religious gifts seem to have attached to the people favoured with the apparition – unlike, for example, that seen by Bernadette of Lourdes. If it was an exercise in exalting the humble and meek (the light it is sometimes presented in), it was slightly miscalculated: Knock was by no means the poorest or most hunger-stricken of the County Mayo villages where Michael Davitt's successful movement for land reform was then striking root. The figures themselves were generally said by the witnesses to have looked like statues or images and to have remained motionless as well as speechless throughout their two-hour stay: supernatural beings might have been expected to make better use of their time. The witnesses themselves did not seem much impressed with what they saw: they left before the apparition ended, and one of them, the parish priest's housekeeper, did not think it worth while to call her employer. The incident was followed by a flurry of similar sightings at Knock and elsewhere in Ireland; some were found to have been set up with magic lanterns, then much in vogue. A magic lantern remains much the likeliest source of the Knock manifestations: there is some evidence that a religious slide-show was being rehearsed at the time by a local policeman (who happened to be a Protestant). The difficulties about some such explanation are certainly no greater than those of the received account.

For all those reasons, the Catholic Church's habitual caution towards such claims was for 50 years nearer frank scepticism about Knock. It was not till 1929 that the place was visited by the local archbishop, Thomas Gilmartin of Tuam. After that the business of pilgrimage, not least from the United States, attained its own momentum; and from 1954, after Mary's assumption to heaven had become a dogma, Rome made successive gestures which amounted to recognition. Pius XII blessed a Knock banner, John XXIII presented the shrine with a candle, Paul VI allowed pilgrims there to have Communion twice in a day. By the centenary year, O Fiaich felt able to claim in so many words that Mary had revealed herself there; and the approved centenary prayer began with the words: 'Our Lady of Knock, Queen of Ireland, Mother of the Church, a hundred years ago you came to Knock.' John Paul II did not go quite so far in what he said there; but his mere presence, and his formally conferring the status of basilica on the new church across the asphalt from the old, was an authentication beyond price.

Attempts to demonstrate that something special happened at Knock in 1879 have concentrated on cures effected there since. Here the argument is easier to respect. The telling pictures from Knock are not the endless imaginings of the apparition on sale in the lines of souvenir shops – even including those tableaux under a tiny glass dome which you shake to produce a snowstorm. They are the smudged old photographs showing crutches and sticks left against the gable wall by people who felt they no longer needed them. Monsignor James Horan, a man who has done much for the Knock cult as parish priest there since 1963, prefers to contemplate 'the spiritual miracles – the return of seemingly lost souls to God'. Even the return of seemingly crippled bodies to health does not necessarily posit miraculous agency. What the pictures and the case histories do suggest is that Knock has created in many invalids that disposition to be cured which can sometimes do more than doctors.

It was present, certainly, when the Pope came. Some 2500 of the seriously afflicted were gathered, with their attendants, in the twelve-sided basilica; and they believed with a fearful intensity in the possibility of cure. To attract the papal glance, the papal blessing, the papal touch in this place was life and death to them. They held out bunch after bunch of flowers, mysterious little packages, even a gold-wrapped box later discovered to contain boiled sweets. Of those whom the Pope touched in rapid succession, a man crossed himself fervently, as if to seal in the good effect; a woman gave a tight little nod to herself, as who should say 'That's got it'; a child was passionately kissed by the father who held him.

And in case nothing happened, the Pope still left these people with a metaphysical sense of purpose beyond themselves, if they could bear to accept it. In a very short address he said to them:

> By his suffering and death Jesus took on himself all human suffering, and he gave it a new value. As a matter of fact, he calls upon the sick, upon everyone who suffers, to collaborate with him in the salvation of the world. Because of this, pain and sorrow are not endured alone or in vain. Although it remains difficult to understand suffering, Jesus has made it clear that its value is linked to his own suffering and death, to his own sacrifice. In other words, by your suffering you help Jesus in his work of salvation.

Yet his hearers were not there for that. In the basilica and outside, they were there because they believed in miracles. As his little red helicopter landed, thousands of rosary beads were held up to it to increase their efficacy. He himself lent his influence to exactly the same kind of piety: he left a bunch of gilt metal roses as his personal present to the shrine, he prayed earnestly at the glassed-in gable end, he lit a candle beside the wall.

For a long time it refused to light, while the security men and the helicopter pilot looked agonizedly at their watches and the darkening sky, knowing that they needed at least a little daylight to land in Dublin by. The Pope persisted: the flame was to call the nation back to family prayer. At length the ever-present Marcinkus whisked the candle from its stick and performed an operation on it. When the Pope tried again, a tall bright flame shot up. 'It was quite simple', Marcinkus explained afterwards. 'I was the only one there carrying a penknife.'

But by now the helicopter men were adamant. There was no time left to drive along the avenues of matting specially laid through the crowd. Casey's efforts to get his man away from Galway in time had not after all been enough. Many of the four hundred thousand people at Knock had been there since dawn, often in the rain, and had seen their spiritual chief only as a distant speck. The disappointment went deep. All they could do now was sing a forlorn strain of 'Will ye no' come back again?' as the helicopter lifted off. It was a pity: older and more unquestioningly devout than the crowds that met him elsewhere, they represented exactly the Ireland he had come to save. But the modern world was too much for him in spite of himself.

The faith to which the Pope called Ireland home was not merely a matter of keeping Mother Church's rules. His bishops may have implied that negligence in that department was all that was wrong with Ireland; but the Pope's vision went a little wider. Lifting up his eyes to the North, he gave his hearers a dose of Christian pacifism.

It followed logically enough from his Message for World Peace Day of nine months before. The surprise was that it withstood the counter-influences. Fighting in the North continued because the Provisional IRA wanted the British Army out, and successive United Kingdom Governments would not withdraw it until an agreed local administration in the North could keep the peace in the Army's absence. Historically, the British were an occupying power: they were in this predicament now because in the sixteenth and seventeenth centuries they had established Protestant colonists on a Catholic island to secure it against Britain's foreign enemies. The descendants of those Protestants were the people who now chiefly opposed a devolved and shared administration for the Northern enclave which had been left behind when the rest of Ireland withdrew from the United Kingdom in 1921.

The Pope himself was disposed by his Polish origins to dislike occupying powers, and especially where religious differences were in question. The advice open to him about Ireland fed that predisposition. Archbishop Gaetano Alibrandi, his nuncio in Dublin, was a man whose diplomatic self-command would give way to a Sicilian vindictiveness when he spoke of the Protestants in the North. O Fiaich, Alibrandi's nominee, was a nationalist Northerner a good deal more zealous in his anti-Britishness than most Southerners. (He had not been entirely accepted in the South as the Primate of All Ireland; and the Pope, by twice using that title with the stress on the 'All', and by allowing O Fiaich to ride everywhere with him and share the plaudits, seemed to be shoring up the Primate's national position.) These two men were the chief planners of the papal visit.

O Fiaich almost led the Pope into folly. He wanted him to cross the Border into the North. North and South are one ecclesiastically, and O Fiaich's see-town of Armagh is in the North, and a papal visit there would in Church terms have been an unexceptionable move; but politically it would have been crass. Because Irish Catholicism and all-Ireland nationalism are more or less conterminous, a papal journey to Armagh would have appeared to many Protestants in the North the staking of a territorial claim; and they would have become even less ready to trust the local minority of Catholics than before.

When the Pope's journey to Ireland was first announced, at the end of July, that point seemed understood at the Vatican. At any rate, no foray to the North was planned. The British Minister to the Holy See, Geoffrey Crossley, was told as much.

But the Irish bishops had not till then expected the Pope to go anywhere but Knock at the most. They were 'thunderstruck', one of them said afterwards, by the discovery that he proposed to visit several other centres of the faith as well. Why not, in that case, in the North? Though a few brother bishops counselled caution, O

Fiaich in particular was 'bursting for him to visit Armagh'. The Primate went determinedly to work in Rome, sped by kindly Anglican sounds of welcome from bishops of the Church of Ireland; and a detour to Armagh was duly planned. The Pope believed in the Vatican's powers of mediation: since January it had been broker between Argentina and Chile in a territorial dispute over three islands in the Beagle channel off the southern tip of South America, and those negotiations were just approaching the stage of talks under an Italian cardinal's chairmanship in Rome. The same influence might work in Northern Ireland. But then at the end of August the Provisional IRA took twenty two lives on the same day: Lord Mountbatten – elderly relative of the British royal family – and three others on his boat off County Sligo; eighteen British soldiers in an ambush in County Down, just inside Northern Ireland. (The Pope's man in London, Archbishop Bruno Heim, was at the massive Mountbatten funeral there; but no Catholic bishops came from Ireland.) Protestant indignation in the North was recognized as being for the moment beyond calming: in Rome the Secretariat of State was worried about the Pope's physical safety if he ventured there. The detour was called off again. For a while there was thought of missing out the whole Irish visit.

In the event the Pope delivered the speech written for Armagh, the word to the North, from Drogheda: still in the South, but near enough the Border to be within the archbishopric of Armagh, and a town of special significance as having particularly suffered from random English reprisals against Catholics during the changing fortunes of the seventeenth century. The Pope prayed in front of relics of an Archbishop of Armagh martyred at that time and lately canonized, Oliver Plunkett; but nothing more was made of the unhappy past. A great many Northerners were in the crowd; and the tone of the assembly was set when John Hume, the most patient and imaginative of the North's Catholic politicians, read the passage from the third chapter of 1 Peter about not returning evil for evil. The Pope developed the point.

Christianity forbad, he said, seeking solutions to 'unjust social or international situations' by the methods of terrorism. 'The command "Thou shalt not kill" must be binding on the conscience of humanity.' Violence was evil, unworthy of man, a lie, destructive of what it claimed to defend, a crime against humanity. Murder should never be called by any other name than murder. In the central passage he said he wished to speak to all men and women engaged in violence:

> I appeal to you, in language of passionate pleading. On my knees I beg you to turn away from the paths of violence and to return to the ways of peace. You may claim to seek justice. I too believe in justice and seek justice. But violence only delays the day of justice. Violence destroys the work of justice. Further violence in Ireland will only drag down to ruin the land you claim to love and the values you claim to cherish. In the name of God I beg you: return to Christ, who died so that men might live in forgiveness and peace. He is waiting for you, longing for each one of you to come to him so that he may say to each of you: your sins are forgiven; go in peace.

As a Provisional spokesman unkindly pointed out a little later, the Pope was not in fact on his knees. He was standing at a microphone, reading in flat and sometimes obscure tones – 'pleading' came out as 'playding' – without taking his eyes off his script. But the 'On my knees' sentence was greeted with prolonged applause: and it was the least equivocal and most authoritative dissuasion which the Catholic Church had ever put to its Provisional members.

He gave a similar message to his young hearers at Galway, asking them to decide where they stood on the matter, and reminding them of the call to love their enemies.

> The command of Jesus does not mean that we are not bound by love for our native land; they do not mean that we can remain indifferent before injustice in its various temporal and historical aspects. These words of Jesus take away only hate. I beg you to reflect deeply: what would human life be if Jesus had never spoken such words?

And at Knock he ended his sermon by praying to Mary: 'Mother, protect all of us and especially the youth of Ireland from being overcome by hostility and hatred. Teach us to distinguish clearly what proceeds from love for our country from what bears the mark of destruction and the brand of Cain. Teach us that evil means can never lead to a good end; that all human life is sacred; that murder is murder no matter what the motive or end.'

Both the British and the Irish Governments professed themselves delighted with the Pope's condemnation of violence. There was even a little holding of breath in case the Provisionals did see the light. The tension did not last long. The very next day the word from them was 'The war goes on'. The day after that, two British soldiers were hurt when the Provisionals machine-gunned their Land Rover on a motorway on the edge of Belfast. Business was soon as usual again. A man delivering vegetables to a Catholic primary school in County Fermanagh was shot dead in front of the schoolchildren because he belonged to the British Army's part-time wing, the Ulster Defence Regiment. A Provisional spokesman told two reporters from *Paris-Match* that peace would not result from an IRA surrender, because the cause of the conflict would persist: the British presence. It remained to be seen whether the Pope's appeal would have any effect at the margin on the IRA's recruitment or its refuges.

The failure of the papal plea ought to have been no more surprising than the pacifist form in which it was cast. The denunciation of violence was by no means as unequivocal as it had at first seemed. The formulation the Pope used at Knock implied that there were after all forms of hostility which patriotism excused. At Galway he told the young listeners not to 'remain indifferent before injustice'; and they applauded him for it. At Drogheda, in particular, he implied a belief that there were injustices in the North at least as grave as those in Mexico or Poland. He went on:

> Each human community – ethnic, historical, cultural or religious – has rights which must be respected. Peace is threatened every time one of these rights is violated. The moral law, guardian of human rights, protector of the dignity of man, cannot be set aside by any person or group, or by the State itself, for any cause, not even for security or in the interests of law and order.

As long as injustices existed, he pursued, true peace would not.

There was no point in saying that kind of thing in Drogheda unless he thought it had a lesson for the British, and the Protestants, in the North. And of course no army fights a war in total observance of the rights of communities or the moral law; and although discrimination by Protestants against Catholics in the North had been comprehensively outlawed and considerably reduced, instances of it could certainly be still found (notably in the private sector of employment, where the law took a long time to reach). The Provisionals were therefore comforted with the assurance that there was an abuse here needing remedy; direct rule of the North from Westminster, the compromise which held the ring between the Protestant wish to run a Protestant State and the Catholic wish to join the Catholic republic to the South, was pontifically declared unacceptable; and the Provisionals needed only to discard the pacifist part of the Pope's argument – as every Western Government, including the British, had done within living memory – to feel justified in resorting to the remedy of force.

The Pope would claim that what he was urging (at the instance of the Irish bishops and notably Cahal Daly) was reform by British politicians: they must 'act for just change'. They tried to, within a month, when Humphrey Atkins announced a conference with the four main political parties in the North. He was Northern Ireland Secretary in Mrs Thatcher's Government, and he was acting more on her prompting than his own. His hesitation was borne out. It was three months before the conference had any prospect of life; and even then Protestant politicians were busy confining its scope in ways which severely limited its usefulness. Again, the Provisionals could draw the conclusion that no human devices were worth so much as explosive ones.

The Catholic Church had fired its biggest gun, and the Irish battlefield had not fallen silent. That itself was dispiriting: one more possible recourse had been shown to be unavailing, and the quantum of accessible hope was by that much diminished. Yet the disappointment by itself was no reason not to make the attempt. There was another respect, though, in which the Pope's visit made the Northern Irish problem perceptibly worse, even without his setting foot across the Border. It was a consideration which many people foresaw the moment the visit was mooted, and yet which no Catholic adviser could have put before him.

The Northern Irish problem existed because two people of different loyalties and traditions occupied the same patch of land. That had been the fact for the best part of four hundred years, and could not now be altered. But it was conceivable that the two groups could arrive at a secure system of living side by side; and then the British Army would be able to go home, and the Provisionals in consequence to hang up their rifles. It was analytically clear that such a system would be one with which the Republic to the South, as well as Britain, was associated: then the Catholics in the North, as well as the locally dominant Protestants, would have their protector, their part in a respectable wider loyalty. Such a system might for example be a federation of the whole British Isles in which Northern Ireland would be one separate unit; or it might be a federation of the island of Ireland, with special dual-citizenship arrangements for Northern Protestants, and the protection of an external court (perhaps the Human Rights Court at Strasbourg). Historically, Northern Protestants had always opposed any kind of association with the Catholic South, because they feared that their distinct Protestant tradition – which included greater liberty of belief and conduct than most Catholics allowed themselves – would be swamped by the ethos of their more numerous rivals; and fear made them behave obstinately and unfairly. Before they could rescind those fears, and set about discussing the new federated arrangements which would release the whole of the British Isles from a shaming burden, they needed to be assured that Catholicism in the South was changing: that either it was moving in the direction of greater liberty of conduct, or at the least it was becoming less certain that its views and ways were the only right ones. The Pope hit both those hopes hard on the head. He copper-fastened a theocratic polity where clerics applied rigid rules to moral dilemmas of infinite complexity; and by gathering Southern Catholics into enormous crowds, as he was bound to do, he made them feel and look confident and uncompromising. Northern Protestants took note and put up the shutters. The day when they themselves would be ready to compromise was put back by years.

It was clear that neither John Paul II nor any of the Irishmen advising him had any notion that compromise was a virtue. You knew what was right: you cleaved to it. They might disclaim triumphalism in words, but their every decision spoke of it. A telling example concerned the use of the Irish language. A persistent fear among Northern Protestants had been that in any association with the South they would be forced to use Irish, a language they found difficult and unlovable, and be discriminated against if they did not. With some justice, they regarded Irish as a symbol of all-Ireland nationalism. At O Fiaich's insistence, the papal services in the South – all extensively televised – made far more use of the Irish language than almost any ordinary Catholic services in the South would have done; to the point where in some places the pronunciation of it was as haphazard as the Pope's own.

Whether or not the bishops knew what effect all this would have in the north, the politicians certainly did. Jack Lynch, the Prime Minister, sent a directive to his Cabinet colleagues in advance of the visit to say that when they met the Pope at Dublin airport they might bow, but they were not to kiss his ring. Lynch perfectly understood what that single image of the subservience of the secular to the spiritual power might otherwise do in the North. Yet the spiritual power, of its nature, could not share that kind of knowledge. So the visit remained a proud celebration of what Catholicism had done for Ireland and what Ireland had done for Catholicism; but towards solving Ireland's most burning problem it could do little.

8

Whistling for Rain
at a Clear Blue Sky

John Paul II's week in America was epitomized on a Friday in Chicago. In the morning, in the auditorium of a 'preparatory seminary' built in the confidence of the late 1950s to guide Catholic schoolboys towards the priesthood, he read out to three hundred and fifty American bishops a headmaster's list of activities which had come to his notice among American Catholics and which were to stop. There was to be no argument and no appeal. In the afternoon, in Grant Park, between the skyscrapers and Lake Michigan, several hundred thousand people – mostly Catholics – turned out in admiring affection to worship with him. Whatever the fate of the message, the man was for the most part delightedly received. But there was a tension there, a puzzle, which in the end was unresolved.

The list of things which the Pope cast his vote against in the course of the week was formidable. Some of them would find few overt defenders. At the United Nations in New York, the body whose invitation was the occasion for his coming, he denounced torture, oppression, war, the arms race, materialism, the unfair distribution of wealth, violations of human rights, and denials of religious freedom. (At Yankee Stadium, that evening, he pointed his denunciation of disproportionately high living straight at wealthy Americans, whom he thought the world's chief culprits. 'The poor of the United States and of the world are your brothers and sisters in Christ. You must never be content to leave them just the crumbs from the feast. You must take of your substance, and not just of your abundance, in order to help them. And you must treat them like guests at your family table.' And again: 'We must find a simple way of living.' He continued in the same vein for twenty-five minutes before there was the first flicker of applause.

But it was a sermon he had wanted to get off his chest for months.)

Some of the items on his blacklist were things which most people might well be happy to see disappear if the world, the flesh and the Devil permitted – drugs; divorce; sex outside marriage; active homosexuality; abortion; euthanasia. Some of them were activities where the case against, and the majority against, was by no means clear. One such was contraception. There were others in the world of Church life. They included intercommunion; the laicization or the marriage of priests; the ordination of women; self-assertion among Ukrainian-American Catholics; and theological freethinking.

This callover of crimes was received at the time with little audible protest. It was after all standard teaching. Much of it was put forward positively enough, as respect for human dignity or the Church's mission. Much of it represented a standard of conduct which many people were happy to see restressed as an ideal – and one which not a few, especially among Church members in late middle age and beyond, found little difficulty in abiding by. And for the time being, John Paul II's followers in the United States seemed more concerned with what he was than what he said. His human appeal had gone before him, stilling doubts. The effect was noticeable even on his most sceptical audience, at the United Nations. During his long address the delegates sat on their hands, and applauded only perfunctorily afterwards; but that afternoon they stood in an interminable line to shake his hand. Next morning, when he stood up to speak to teenage schoolchildren in Madison Square Garden, they kept their desultory cheering alive as children do who mean to shorten the time allotted for lecturing them in; but the Pope seemed perfectly happy with the wordless contact, responding with a strange high-pitched mooing sound (dutifully translated afterwards by his entourage as the Polish for 'wow!'). He identified the incident as a 'charismatic moment'. In Philadelphia, early that evening, on the balconies of an elegant apartment block on Logan Circle, there were champagne parties to view the Pope at Mass. Maids in cap and apron handed platters and pushed trolleys. The partygoers had no interest in listening to the Pope, but they wanted to be there to see him. The national atmosphere was of hero-worship;

and although scepticism was sometimes near the surface, it could not easily find expression for the time being.

The major document of the trip was that Chicago seminary speech to the bishops. He came to them as a brother bishop, he said. He spoke of the divine mandate they shared to proclaim the duties of the Christian law, and to guard and teach the sacred deposit of Christian doctrine. He reminded them that they had upheld the inherent demands of the word of God in statements and pastoral letters; and they had done this 'in a very special way' in a 1976 pastoral letter called 'To live in Christ Jesus'. ('In a special way' was a catch-phrase of his English-language translators, imparting a nursery cosiness to a locution which seems in the original to have meant nothing more than 'especially'.) John Paul II cast his message to America in the form of an extended quotation to the gratified bishops of their own pastoral letter, beginning with his United Nations themes, but soon moving into more difficult territory:

> You spoke explicitly of the Church's duty to be faithful to the mission entrusted to her. And precisely for this reason you spoke of certain issues that needed a clear reaffirmation, because Catholic teaching in their regard had been challenged, denied, or in practice violated. You repeatedly proclaimed human rights and human dignity and the incomparable worth of people of every racial and ethnic origin, declaring that 'racial antagonism and discrimination are among the most persistent and destructive evils of our nation'. You forcefully rejected the oppression of the weak, the manipulation of the vulnerable, the waste of goods and resources, the ceaseless preparations for war, unjust social structures and policies, and all crimes by and against individuals and against creation.
>
> With the candour of the Gospels, the compassion of pastors and the charity of Christ, you faced the question of the indissolubility of marriage, rightly stating: 'The covenant between a man and a woman joined in Christian marriage is as indissoluble and irrevocable as God's love for his people and Christ's love for his Church.'

In exalting the beauty of marriage you rightly spoke against both the ideology of contraception and contraceptive acts, as did the encyclical *Humanae Vitae*. And I myself today, with the same conviction of Paul VI, ratify the teaching of this encyclical, which was put forth by my predecessor 'by virtue of the mandate entrusted to us by Christ'.

In portraying the sexual union between husband and wife as a special expression of their covenanted love, you rightly stated: 'Sexual intercourse is a moral and human good only within marriage, outside marriage it is wrong.'

As 'men with the message of truth and the power of God' (2 Cor.6.7), as authentic teachers of God's law and as compassionate pastors, you also rightly stated: 'Homosexual activity . . . , as distinguished from homosexual orientation, is morally wrong.' In the clarity of this truth, you exemplified the real charity of Christ; you did not betray those people who, because of homosexuality, are confronted with difficult moral problems, as would have happened if, in the name of understanding and compassion, or for any other reason, you had held out false hope to any brother or sister. Rather, by your witness to the truth of humanity in God's plan, you effectively manifested fraternal love, upholding the true dignity, the true human dignity, of those who look to Christ's Church for the guidance which comes from the light of God's word.

You also gave witness to the truth, thereby serving all humanity, when, echoing the teaching of the Council – 'From the moment of conception life must be guarded with the greatest care' (*Gaudium et Spes*, 51) – you reaffirmed the right to life and the inviolability of every human life, including the life of unborn children. You clearly said: 'To destroy these innocent unborn children is an unspeakable crime . . . Their right to life must be recognized and fully protected by the law.'

And just as you defended the unborn in the truth of their being, so also you clearly spoke up for the aged, asserting: 'Euthanasia or mercy killing . . . is a grave moral evil . . . Such killing is incompatible with respect for human dignity and reverence for life.'

One of the greatest rights of the faithful, he concluded, was to receive the word of God in its purity and integrity as guaranteed by the authentic magisterium of the bishops of the Catholic Church teaching in union with the Pope. The faithful had their own insights, true: the Holy Spirit was active among them. 'But these insights of faith and this *sensus fidelium* are not independent of the magisterium of the Church, which is an instrument of the same Holy Spirit and is assisted by him. It is only when the faithful have been nourished by the word of God, faithfully transmitted in its purity and integrity, that their own charisms are fully operative and fruitful.' One of the greatest truths of which bishops and Pope were humble custodians was the doctrine of the Church's unity, 'which subsists indestructibly in the Catholic Church'. Only the unity of perfect faith was acceptable. 'We must pray and study together, knowing however that intercommunion between divided Christians is not the answer to Christ's appeal for perfect unity.' And John Paul II quoted the testament of Paul VI: 'Let the work of drawing near to our separated brethren go on, with much understanding, with much patience, with great love; but without deviating from the true Catholic doctrine.'

The clear implication of that message was that unity with other Churches was on offer only on the Catholic Church's own terms; and ordinary Catholics were not to suppose that – for example – they and their Protestant spouses might anticipate that distant day by simply taking Communion at one another's altars.

(In Washington at the end of the week, at an ecumenical meeting in the chapel of a women's college, it was the orthodox prelates of the Orthodox Church that the Pope seemed chiefly to smile on. Theological dialogue between his Church and theirs would soon begin 'on a worldwide basis', he promised. Conversations with Protestant denominations were mentioned only secondarily; and a further cloud was cast over them when he said: 'In this context, recognition must be given to the deep division which still exists over moral and ethical matters. The moral life and the life of faith are so deeply united that it is impossible to divide them.')

The whole of that Chicago passage was harder, more specific, less easy to back away from afterwards, than anything he had said at Galway or Limerick. The gaps in the code were filled in at his other American stops. In the dark and the rain on Boston Common, on the evening of his arrival (Monday 1 October), he had added drugs to the list of delusive escapes which might tempt young people. ('Faced with problems and disappointments, many people will try to escape from their responsibility: escape in selfishness, escape in sexual pleasure, escape in drugs, escape in violence, escape in indifference and cynical attitudes. But today I propose to you the option of love, which is the opposite of escape.') His double denunciation of materialism, both in nations and individuals, came the next day, his first in New York. Then in Philadelphia on 4 October, the day before the Chicago speech, he laid down the line about priesthood.

He told seminarians in Philadelphia of the importance of fidelity to the 'free and irrevocable commitment' they would make at ordination. (It was free beforehand, and could be decently withdrawn from – something that college heads and diocesan directors of training, anxious not to have money and effort wasted, had not always stressed; it was irrevocable afterwards.) It included celibacy:

> Human dignity requires that you maintain this commitment, that you keep your promise to Christ no matter what difficulties you may encounter, and no matter what temptations you may be exposed to . . . And so, during these years in the seminary, take time to reflect on the serious obligations and the difficulties which are part of the priest's life. Consider whether Christ is calling you to the celibate life. You can make a responsible decision for celibacy only after you have reached the firm conviction that Christ is indeed offering you this gift, which is intended for the good of the Church and for the service of others . . . Remember that in the final analysis perseverance in fidelity is a proof, not of human strength and courage, but of the efficacy of Christ's grace.

To an audience of priests, later in the day, he took the point further. The priesthood was not only permanent and celibate; it was also – and here the Pope leant on the account of the calling of the apostles at Mark 3.13 – male.

> Priesthood is forever – *tu es sacerdos in aeternum* – we do not return the gift once given. It cannot be that God who gave the impulse to say 'yes' now wishes to hear 'no'.
>
> Nor should it surprise the world that the call of God through the Church continues to offer us a celibate ministry of love and service after the example of our Lord Jesus Christ. God's call has indeed stirred us to the depths of our being. And after centuries of experience, the Church knows how deeply fitting it is that priests should give this concrete response in their lives to express the totality of the 'yes' they have spoken to the Lord who calls them by name to his service.
>
> The fact that there is a personal individual call to the priesthood given by the Lord to 'the men he himself had decided on' is in accord with the prophetic tradition. It should help us too to understand that the Church's traditional decision to call men to the priesthood, and not to call women, is not a statement about human rights, nor an exclusion of women from holiness and mission in the Church. Rather this decision expresses the conviction of the Church about this particular dimension of the gift of priesthood by which God has chosen to shepherd his flock.

The Church, in the person of the Pope, knew best.

In between these two speeches to priests, he paused to deliver a reproof to Philadelphia's Ukrainian-Americans. There had been murmuring among them at the Vatican's appointing as their archbishop a priest who was little known to them. The Pope reminded them, in their new and fearsomely ornate cathedral, that Paul VI had contributed a stone from the tomb of St Peter to be incorporated in the building; and 'this stone was meant to serve as a sign of the fidelity of the Ukrainian Church to the see of Peter'. Differing traditions might enrich the universal Church; but 'the ecclesial communities that follow these traditions are called to adhere with love and respect to certain particular forms of discipline which my predecessors and I, in fulfilling our pastoral responsibility to the universal Church, have judged necessary for the well-being of the whole Body of Christ'.

Late that afternoon, in the harvest-festival atmosphere of rural Iowa near Des Moines – 'Here in the heartland of America the valleys, the hills have been blanketed with grain . . .' – he laid aside reprobation for a while as he talked to the largest crowd the state had ever seen. The big Chicago speech came next day. After a second day there, he made three important utterances on Sunday 7 October in Washington, his last call.

At the Catholic University of America he spoke to the presidents of similar places of learning across the country about academic freedom. It was 'the deepest and noblest aspiration of the human person', he said (in the idiom he could by now be said to have personalized), 'to come to the knowledge of truth'. But the Christian academic, in his research and teaching, would 'let himself be enlightened by his faith'. The central point followed: 'An undiminished dedication to intellectual honesty and academic excellence are seen, in a Catholic university, in the perspective of the Church's mission of evangelization and service.' The power of the Gospel should permeate thought patterns.

That meant, in plain terms, toeing the bishops' line. 'If then your universities and colleges are institutionally committed to the Christian message, and if they are part of the Catholic community of evangelization, it follows that they have an essential relationship to the hierarchy of the Church.' The Church needed her theologians; 'but true theological scholarship, and by the same token theological teaching, cannot exist and be fruitful without seeking its inspiration and its source in the word of God as contained in sacred scripture and in the sacred tradition of the Church, as interpreted by the authentic magisterium throughout history.' So freedom did not exactly mean freedom after all. 'It behoves the theologian to be free, but with the freedom that is openness to the truth and the light that comes from faith and from fidelity to the Church.'

The word was essentially the same at a prayer service for nuns in the austere, mosque-like Shrine of the Immaculate Conception:

they must do what the Church wanted. 'Faithfulness to Christ, especially in religious life, can never be separated from faithfulness to the Church.' This 'ecclesial dimension', he went on, required 'on the part of individual members as well as entire institutes, a faithfulness to the original charisms which God has given to his Church, through your founders and foundresses'. In other words, the Church wanted jobs distributed as they had always been, and nuns with ambitions to be priests had no choice but to renounce them and submit. 'Your life must be characterized by a complete availability: a readiness to serve as the needs of the Church require'. Nor was that all. As a symbol of this submissiveness, 'it is not unimportant that your consecration to God should be manifested in the permanent exterior sign of a simple and suitable religious garb. This is not only my personal conviction, but also the desire of the Church, often expressed by so many of the faithful.'

In his last main speech in America, on the Mall in Washington (the long grassy space between the Capitol and the needle of the Washington Monument), he returned to his Chicago targets: sexual intercourse outside marriage, divorce, contraception, and in particular abortion. There was no escaping the conclusion that those were the things he had particularly come to denounce. Human life was precious, he said, because it was the gift of God and the fruit of love. 'This is why life should spring up within the setting of marriage and why marriage and the parents' love for one another should be marked by generosity in self-giving.' Sacramentally married couples had the help of Christ 'to develop their love in a faithful and indissoluble union, and to respond with generosity to the gift of parenthood'. That generosity included the acceptance of new life. 'Decisions about the number of children and the sacrifices to be made for them must not be taken only with a view to adding to comfort and preserving a peaceful existence. Reflecting upon this matter before God, with the graces drawn from the sacrament, and guided by the teaching of the Church, parents will remind themselves that it is certainly less serious to deny their children certain comforts or material advantages than to deprive them of the presence of brothers and sisters'. And from that implicit attack on contraception the Pope moved to an explicit attack on abortion. Because every person was unique as a creature of God, 'we will stand up every time that human life is threatened. When the sacredness of life before birth is attacked, we will stand up and proclaim that no one ever has the authority to destroy unborn life.'

Spelt out across America, it was a formidable litany of prohibitions; and the most formidable thing about it was its finality. No exceptions were admitted, no special cases, no scope for individual or pastoral judgement. The variousness of human weakness was not to be met with an equal variety of treatment. If a number of lives were spoiled as a result, it was in order that a greater number might be benefited.

At the time, disagreement was muted. It had no chance against the general fervour. Aside from one or two unsuccessful legal moves against receiving the Pope at public expense when Church and State were constitutionally distinct, the only overt protests while he was still in the country were from advocates of women's ordination. 'God is an equal-opportunity employer'; 'a woman's place is in the sanctuary'; 'equal rites for women' – they were the biggest banners in the crowd on Pennsylvania Avenue when the Pope arrived at the White House, and they pursued him round Washington. The most explicit challenge came from a leader among American nuns: Sister Mary Theresa Kane, president of the Leadership Conference of Women Religious and administrator of her own order, the Sisters of Mercy of the Union. (Her family was New York Irish: her mother was from County Galway.) She had been chosen to make a speech of greeting to the Pope, before he spoke himself, at the first stop of his Washington Sunday: it was the service for seven thousand nuns in the cavernous interior of the Immaculate Conception church. About half of them were not wearing 'suitable religious garb': Sister Kane's only concession to it was a jewelled cross in the lapel of her tailored brown suit.

Standing at a lectern at one end of the long platform – the Pope was in the middle – she told him that American women had been inspired by his spirit of courage, and were grateful to him for exemplifying it in reminding them of their responsibilities to the poor. These civilities over, she said in a soft but steady voice what she had resolved to say:

As I share this privileged moment with you, Your Holiness, I urge you to be mindful of the intense suffering and pain which is part of the life of many women in these United States.

I call upon you to listen with compassion and to hear the call of women, who comprise half of humankind.

As women, we have heard the powerful messages of our Church addressing the (need for) dignity and reverence of all persons.

As women, we have pondered upon these words. Our contemplation leads us to state that the Church in its struggle to be faithful to its call for reverence and dignity for all persons must respond by providing the possibility of women as persons being included in all ministries of our Church.

I urge you, Your Holiness, to be open to and to respond to the voices coming from the women of this country, whose desire is for serving in and through the Church as fully participating members.

At the end of her speech she knelt and kissed the Pope's ring, and he laid his hand on her head in blessing. Two bishops sitting with him on the platform both believed that he had not in fact heard what she said. They themselves were only able to make it out, given the acoustics of the shrine, from the nature of the applause. Even if the Pope had heard it, his command of English was not such as to allow him to respond to it off the cuff. He did the only thing in his power: he made a number of impromptu references to Mary, 'the handmaiden of the Lord', as the model for nuns, and then took up his own prepared speech – the one that urged 'a readiness to serve as the needs of the Church require'.

As he began to speak, about fifty nuns rose to their feet, wearing blue armbands. They remained standing throughout his speech, in silent protest against the line which he had taken elsewhere and now reiterated. At one point, when he called on his hearers to give 'greater public witness' to their beliefs, another nun took him at his word. She rose and joined the standing group.

Sister Kane said later: 'I didn't mean to be dramatic, and I had prayed a great deal about it. I said what I had to say respectfully. I believe in the dialogic approach.' But it was apparent that something approaching half the audience at the shrine was on the Pope's side and saw no need for dialogue. A nun from Middleburg, Virginia, said to a *Washington Post* reporter afterwards: 'It disturbs me that she says we have all this pain and agony because we can't be priests. I am perfectly happy. I don't want to be a priest, and I don't think women should be.' An Illinois sisterhood took space in the same paper for an advertisement headed 'Apology'. ('We, who most likely speak for the large majority of religious women in the United States, apologize to His Holiness, Pope John Paul II, for the public rudeness shown him . . .')

In general, it was difficult to tell how great the volume of disagreement was with the whole range of papal prohibitions. For the Mass on the Mall in Washington, after the burden of the papal message had had a week to become known, the throng was comparatively small. More than a million people were expected: the police, who had sectioned off the Mall and could count the crowd accurately from the air, reckoned it at 178,000. That may have partly followed from the weather: under an inky sky, a cold wind blew so hard that the Pope had trouble keeping the large Communion wafer on the shallow paten with which he had been provided. The crowd thinned fast, too, after the sermon. These occasions are commonly less numinous in total than television's proper concentration on the altar makes them appear; but on the Mall the numbers of people streaming away well before the end were proportionately much larger than elsewhere. Many of the comments collected by journalists indicated that a main reason for the drift was disappointment that the Pope should choose the discouragement of abortion as his crowning theme. The atmosphere was certainly unpropitious. Washington diocese contains a low proportion of Catholics; the District of Columbia has the highest abortion rate in the United States; and the campaign against abortion was not the most popular of themes there at the time, since ingenious action in Congress by anti-abortion lobbyists had contrived to threaten the supply of money for paying federal Government employees.

On the other hand, crowds elsewhere – except when rain held numbers down in Boston and New York – could stand comparison with turnouts in Ireland. John Paul II was more warmly received in Harlem than Catholicism's long ill-success with American blacks would seem to have warranted; at the other end of the scale senior politicians judged that with an election year approaching it was on the whole worthwhile to be seen with him, and he was the first of his line to visit the President in Washington. John Kennedy, a Catholic President, had said defensively in 1960 that there would be no Pope at the White House in his time; in 1965, when Paul VI came to the United Nations, Lyndon Johnson thought it prudent to meet him only at the Waldorf Astoria Hotel in New York, and with no photographers by. In the subsequent fourteen years the suspicions of Rome as a kind of rival to secular powers had eased. Yet John Paul II helped to create his own Washington welcome. Jimmy Carter, devout Baptist, decided in July that he and the Pope should meet at the White House, but 'in a private manner'. He was emboldened by advance public interest to modify the arrangements a little; and after the Pope's success in New York it was decided that the numbers to be invited to the White House lawns to witness his private call on the President should be raised from seven thousand to ten. A lot of the tickets went to friendly congressmen for their constituents; and at least four hundred names were put forward by the Carter-Mondale 1980 campaign committee – the body busily trying to secure Carter's renomination, with his vice-presidential colleague Walter Mondale, as the Democratic candidate.

It was repeatedly said that if the Pope had been running for president himself he would have won in a landslide. Certainly there were frequent parallels, in his American journey, with the progress of a presidential candidate. There was the throb of motor-cycle engines, the open car, the glad-handing till the hand swelled. In the same tradition, local politicians would sometimes do a bit of their own glad-handing before he arrived: the Governor of Illinois and the Mayor of Chicago were at the airport well ahead of his arrival for that purpose, and before a Mass in a Chicago car park two members of the city council were distributing pictures of the Pope from a satchel. There were the secret-service code words: the Pope was Shepherd. (His chartered Boeing 727 was

Shepherd 1, with Shepherd 2 and 3 for the press.)

There was the sheer expense. One altar alone, in Grant Park, with 27,000 pots of yellow and white chrysanthemums on it, cost 212,000 dollars. The expense fell not so much on the Vatican as on American Catholics, and bishops were put to the same shifts as political parties to gather in the money. In Philadelphia Cardinal Krol took a phone call from Walter Annenberg, local newspaper-owner and former American ambassador to Britain. Annenberg offered to contribute to the costs in Krol's diocese. 'I asked him', Krol recalls, 'what sum he had in mind. He said "Twenty-five or fifty thousand." I said, "Well, now, Mr Ambassador, you wouldn't expect me to settle for twenty-five if you have it in mind to make it fifty." He said "Fine. Fifty it is, then." '

There was the fatigue. The Pope was already tired when he began in Boston, despite having made use of his special Aer Lingus bed on the way over. By the end of his main New York day his face was ashen. The problem was partly of his own making. Cardinal John Carberry of St Louis said of the heavy schedule: 'The laity have all been blaming the bishops, but he himself is to blame, you know. He's very much his own man. He sees a pro-gramme and adds things to it at once.' In Philadelphia, a brief period at Krol's house set aside for rest was used for prayer instead. Krol went to call him for his next appointment and found him on his knees: 'The man wasn't in Philadelphia, he wasn't in my house, he was totally enveloped by prayer.' At Des Moines he was tired enough to fall asleep in a helicopter against the clatter of the blades. In Chicago, he said: 'There is a Polish saying – he who gets up early in the morning, God blesses them. But perhaps, sometimes, he who gets up early in the morning wants to sleep all day.' The programme had the same effect on his entourage. When he said goodbye in Washington to the American security men who had travelled round with him, one of them said to him: 'Come back again, but not before 1983: we're very tired'; and the Vatican men joined feelingly in the laughter. Yet the Pope, at any rate, could always be revived by the sight of an audience or of hands to shake. Both in Chicago and in Washington, having decided to go to bed, he suddenly insisted on bursting outside again into the ever-waiting crowd. On the Chicago occasion, he and his party were jostled in the throng. People at the back of the crowd started to climb over the shoulders of those in front. The Pope's Vatican guards began to lay about them very roughly. The Pope spoke to them with real anger – in Italian.

Operating in a variety of foreign tongues, and notably English, must also have been tiring. It was claimed that he had been practising his English throughout September on any of his Vatican staff who could understand him. Bishop Thomas Kelly, secretary of the Bishops' Conference, travelled everywhere with the Pope in the planes and helicopters, establishing a perceptible rapport. He said: 'I don't think the public realize how limited his English is, because he gets the emphasis and meaning very well when he says Mass and in his speeches. But you realize in conversation that it is limited.' Archbishop Jean Jadot, the well-born Belgian in the post of apostolic delegate in Washington, said English was the Pope's 'fifth or sixth language' in point of skill – after Polish, French, Italian, Spanish and possibly German. Latin and Russian would probably come in above English too. In impromptu speech at the United Nations the Pope was heard using correct though accented French, and it was the language he and Jadot used together. (Unobsequious, industrious, pastoral, Jadot had helped to humanize the American Church and its bishops. But his work needed time, and a sympathetic presence in the Vatican, to take effect.)

Other influences which might have tired the Pope were the rivalries which his coming set up. The Church vied with the secular power: American bishops had been furious with the Vatican when they discovered in July that the Pope planned to make the United Nations his first American call. While the argument raged, arrangements were delayed to the point where journalists occupied the clergy house at St Patrick's Cathedral in an attempt to force hard information out of New York diocese. The compromise reached in the end was that the Pope should pause first in Boston on a para-ecclesiastical occasion: a visit to the sickbed of Cardinal Wright – not a particular friend, but still a senior Vatican official. Wright then passed, in mid-August, beyond the reach even of papal visits; but dates were by then set, and Boston was first stop. (Its geographic and ethnic link with Ireland – 'the next parish after Galway' – made it in any case a logical landfall.) Further rivalries remained. Diocese vied with diocese in the splendour of the appointments and in claims about the size of crowds. Krol was delighted to have *Time* on his side for the claim that the crowd of a million at Logan Circle in Philadelphia was the largest of the American tour; but the claim was contested on behalf of the Grant Park congregation in Chicago. The figures in fact originated with Irish-American policemen in each city whose loyalty for the moment was to the local church rather than the truth. And Bishop Maurice Dingman of Des Moines – who had forwarded to the Vatican the farmer's letter which had resulted, after a Marcinkus inspection, in the surprise Iowa stop – capped the big-city boasts with one of his own: 'It was we who made the cover of *Time*.'

As against all that, the Pope had certain pleasures to cheer him. He was deluged with presents. In New York, not counting the flowers, they would have filled a fair-sized van. There was a good deal of sports gear: ski clothes, jogging outfits. 'Mostly by very good makers', a New York cleric reported with a tinge of envy. 'And there were an awful lot of socks.' Much of this the Pope never set eyes on: it was sorted in a Rome warehouse, and the Pope issued only with what was judged papally usable. Some he saw, though. Jadot's housekeeper, a French-Canadian nun, crocheted a pair of brown wool slippers with the initials JP in gold on the toes. One of his favourite presents was the picture he was given by the Austrian Secretary General of the United Nations, Kurt Waldheim: it was a bronze bas-relief of St Stephen's Cathedral in Vienna. John Paul II used to stay in Cardinal Koenig's palace opposite, breaking his journey between Krakow and Rome, in the days before he became Pope.

He had the consolations of music. In Chicago he was especially feasted. He heard the Chicago Symphony Orchestra play Bruckner's fifth symphony, and Luciano Pavarotti (the Italian operatic tenor) sing the Bach-Gounod 'Ave Maria'. ('That was a lucky accident', said Monsignor Richard Rosemeyer, organizer of the Chicago arrangements. 'The Chicago Lyric rang up and said they would like to perform for the Pope, but as they had done so in Rome earlier in the year we turned them down. We thought others should have a chance. Then as an afterthought they said they had Pavarotti rehearsing with them; he would like to sing for the Pope. That transformed everything. To get Pavarotti – we could scarcely believe it.') Chicago has more Poles in it than any city outside Warsaw; and he heard '*Sto lat*' there so often that he said 'People will think it is the Polish national anthem'. He himself returned the compliment to Chicago by crooning a good-night Alleluia to the mesmerized crowd. And outside St Matthew's Cathedral in Washington, as they had done at Madison Square Garden, the schoolchildren sang him their football rouser: 'Rack 'em up, stack 'em up, bust 'em in two – Holy Father, we're for you.'

He had a different satisfaction the following morning, when he landed at Andrews Air Force Base outside Washington. His aides had supposed that Andrews was in the District of Columbia; but they discovered in time that it was not. Along with Zbigniew Brzezinski, Carter's Polish-American adviser on national security, Vice-President Mondale was on the windy tarmac: in him, the Pope declared, 'I greet the whole American people and in a particular way all the citizens of' – and he leant on the first half of the name – 'MARYland'. There was lusty cheering from local loyalists, few of whom had previously spotted the fitness of the name. It was in fact derived from Henrietta Maria, queen of Charles I of England: a stout Catholic, but not the Queen of Heaven.

At a gathering for the Washington diplomatic corps the Pope met the Russian ambassador Anatoly Dobrynin, longest-serving ambassador in the city and hence the dean of the corps. The Pope asked him, in Russian, what he had to do as dean. Dobrynin explained that he had only been in the job a year and was still learning it. 'I am in just the same position', said the Pope.

If it was more than a civility of conversation, no one would have guessed it from his bearing in the United States. He marched straight into a complex and unfamiliar state of affairs and started laying about him. As a result, he brought the papacy and the American Church into opposition. It was not the first such encounter: more than a hundred years before, American bishops had been among the least happy at Pius IX's infallibility decree. This time the bishops ought to have been contented enough. The Pope had quoted their pastoral letter and put his own weight behind it. Their problem was the knowledge that American lay opinion had taken little notice of the letter when it was published and was taking less now. They had adjusted their expectations accordingly.

On the state of opinion, ordinary observation was supported by survey evidence. Of a sample of American Catholics questioned for a poll run by Associated Press and NBC News before the papal visit began, 50 per cent were prepared to tolerate abortion on demand; 53 per cent believed priests should be allowed to marry; 63 per cent thought divorce acceptable even when there were children in the case; and 66 per cent said they would like the Church to approve artificial birth control. On that last point in particular, practice and precept among American Catholics had permanently parted company. Catholic couples were known to be widely using contraceptives, and without any great feelings of guilt about it. A young bishop from the Midwest said his priests told him it was rare for people to confess contraception as a sin: they mentioned it only to ask for permission to go on practising it in their particular circumstances. They saw it as a matter for the individual conscience. Tracy Ellis said after the Pope's departure: 'I fear trying to get people to stop is like whistling for rain at a clear blue sky. They won't.'

Bishops could not so easily employ a historian's objectivity in describing things as they were; but they recognized them none the less. Many of them also had enough historical sense to perceive the virtues of tolerance: it had been the meat on which the Catholic Church in the United States had grown great. America was one of Catholicism's most impressive conquests: the proportion of Catholics in the population had been raised from less than one percent in the 1780s to almost a quarter in the 1980s; and that had not been achieved by insisting that only one course of conduct or belief was the right one. The origins and cultures of the growing population – Irish, Italian, central European, Hispanic – were far too diverse for that. In a famous incident in the 1880s, Cardinal James Gibbons of Baltimore saved the Knights of Labor, America's earliest trade union, from Vatican condemnation: the Holy Office was worried at the thought of Catholic working men associating with Communists and atheists. Gibbons successfully counselled 'masterly inactivity'. It became a guiding principle within the fold. American Catholicism needed the toleration of other Churches in the nation. It was true that liberty of conscience had been declared by Gregory XVI in an 1832 encyclical a false and absurd aberration. But if it was to be extended to Catholics in the United States by upholders of other faiths, as it largely was, then American Catholic leaders had very little choice but to proclaim it as a general right – which their own followers then exercised. If you were free to be a Catholic, you were free to be your own kind of Catholic. This tradition was extended, in matters of family morality, by the essentially Protestant doctrine of the informed individual conscience as it arose from the Second Vatican Council.

Vatican II created its own problems. Seminaries moved into the cities: rote learning and rigid discipline became impossible to maintain. (Among seminaries which had their share of student rebellion in the 1960s was St Charles Borromeo, where the Pope spoke in Philadelphia.) The effort to confront the secular and find in it something of merit produced understandable strains between traditionalists and comparative modernists. American bishops, who have earned in the main a reputation for being better organizers than thinkers, found it impossible to draw new lines to which orthodoxy could retreat. Yet none of this was out of the way. 'Those who have knowledge of the Church's history will not be unduly troubled by the post-Vatican II turmoil', says Tracy Ellis. 'That has been the normal aftermath of ecumenical councils since Nicaea in 325.' The spirit of tolerance and movement was in line with the history of American Catholicism, touched as it had been by the history of America itself.

So as the American Church entered the 1980s its bishops understood better than the Pope that the day of dogmatic morality was long gone. His list of things not to be thought of they were already thinking about every day. Divorce was identified by Archbishop Edward McCarthy of Miami as 'the main problem we face – no doubt about it'. Sample conversations suggest that the great majority of American bishops agree with him. But they are a long way beyond merely ruling divorce inadmissible and therefore divorced people unwelcome at church. They recognize that such a course would defeat their aims, both pastorally and in point of Catholic numerical advance. So they issue thirty thousand annulments a year – in essence, certificates that a broken marriage never really happened in the first place, which washes the divorce away as well. 'There's an element of legal acrobatics in it', a Chicago cleric specializing in this work acknowledged to a man from *Le Figaro*, 'but the sabbath was made for man, not man for the sabbath.' Beyond that, they go to some lengths to see that the divorced among their flock – who hugely outnumber the decently annulled – can stay within the fold. One bishop saw as the main problem 'developing a theology that will embrace those who are on their second, even third, marriage, but who continue to come to church and the sacraments'. By the traditional teaching, to be divorced is to be in mortal sin, and to take the sacraments when in mortal sin is to put one's name down for eternal damnation beyond the possibility of erasure. Yet here were American bishops devising ways of changing all that. After all, if they lost the divorced husband or wife they risked losing the next generation as well. Another bishop called it 'a difficult problem, but a happy one in a way. In the pre-conciliar period, when people moved to number two that was the last we saw of them. Now they want to continue coming to church – *and* we get the children.'

The other main area where American bishops knew they had trouble, even before the Pope's visit, was the priesthood. It was here that Vatican II had its chief effect. Krol, who chaired a bishop's committee on the problem, said: 'There is no denying that an impatient minority of priests have not been obedient to the Church in the years following the Second Vatican Council. There have been storms right through the history of the American Church, but I think the Church has never encountered so severe a storm as following Vatican II.' Archbishop John Quinn of San Francisco, president of the United States Bishops' Conference from November 1978, saw a significant gap here: 'Vatican II said a lot about service, but it had little to say about priesthood. When you go into it, that is so.' Finding themselves in a world where their old authority and functions were becoming blurred, thousands of priests applied for release from their orders. (One cardinal had a stroke when he learned that his priest secretary wanted to leave the priesthood to marry. Of two bishops who left the episcopate, one went for that same reason.) Although Paul VI was reasonably diligent in clearing these applications, granting over thirty thousand of them, some hundreds were left pending when he died. A good many of these were from Americans. There was some feeling that, under John Paul II's new immobilist regime, these cases at least should be settled. 'The priests whose papers had been submitted before John Paul II was elected should be given special consideration', said Father John Alesandro, President of the United States Canon Law Society. 'They should be judged under the old rules under which their papers were submitted.' But in the course of his American visit John Paul II said not a word about them.

By the end of the 1970s the proportion of priests to laity in America was low, and falling. Numbers of laypeople were increasing still, but the out-turn from the seminaries was not making up the gaps among priests. In the minds of bishops, this ranked with the new marriage habits as a pressing problem. One of them said: 'The first-class parish priest imbued with the spirit of the Council is a jewel beyond price – and I want an awful lot of 'em.'

As for the priesthood of women, it had become a far livelier issue than information reaching the Vatican can have shown. Women filled the theological colleges: once trained, they abounded in church posts. One bishop said: 'Good, honest, holy women want to serve the Church in the priesthood. We must move towards that – though at the moment only some of us bishops favour it.' Quinn acknowledged that there were such bishops and even archbishops, though they were not in a majority; and he said of the women applicants: 'They won't be put off. There is a sincere and genuine demand from American women – especially nuns – for ordination.' He went on: 'But I don't see them getting the priesthood in the foreseeable future; so giving them scope for service in other ways has got to be developed.' Another bishop took much the same line: 'Theology neither favours nor disagrees with the idea of women priests, but culturally it is a big step. The immediate task is to give women the widest possible responsibility in the Church while the discussion on women priests continues.'

That prescription for at least the essential minimum of change commanded general assent. Another bishop said: 'The woman with her rosary beads is no longer prepared to sit in the pew leaving involvement to others. She will soon be a figure of the past.' And indeed the point was widely accepted by the time of the

Pope's visit: women were more and more employed to read lessons, serve at the altar, distribute Communion, administer the chalice (when Communion was in both kinds). Yet the Pope's influence was effective against even that degree of change. The bishops thought it wise that at his services the distributors of Communion should have no laypeople – and *a fortiori* no women – among them.

It is safe to say that little changed in American Catholicism as a result of the Pope's visit; and it is a criticism of the Pope to say it, because he specifically asked for change. He set himself that test, and failed it. Among believing Catholics, married couples went on seeking divorce in much the same melancholy proportions. The sales of contraceptive devices did not diminish. Sex outside marriage remained a commonplace. Countless homosexual liaisons, casual and permanent, persisted. Abortion and euthanasia were still discussed and practised. Men continued to leave the priesthood, in fact if not by papal permission; women continued to seek to join it. And nuns could still be seen in plain clothes. These were not majority tendencies, but they were real.

Speaking of the Second Vatican Council, John Paul II sometimes employed the theology of 'signs of the times' which John XXIII had called in aid to explain it. It was always a difficult notion, since there was no reliable way of telling which signs represented a movement of the Spirit and which did not. But, certainly, John Paul II was not tempted to discern 'signs of the times' in those manifestations of a changing morality in America. He understood his function as pope very differently. Not for him to accept the present as given and to do what he could with it. He sought to make a jump back to the past; and not even the past as it was so much as the past as precept had tried to make it. He believed it was possible to replace a diversity of moral practice with a unity.

Unity from diversity: it was a theme he warmed to. It was also one which his American hearers well understood. His most apt and eloquent address in the United States was his sermon in Grant Park; and there, quoting both the song 'America the beautiful' and the Latin motto on the great seal of the United States, he made that his central point.

In the first two centuries of your history as a nation, you have travelled a long road, always in search of a better future, in search of stable employment, in search of a homestead. You have travelled 'From sea to shining sea' to find your identity, to discover each other along the way, and to find your own place in this immense country.

Your ancestors came from many different countries across the oceans to meet here with the people of different communities that were already established here. In every generation, the process has been repeated: new groups arrive, each one with a different history, to settle here and become part of something new. The same process still goes on when families move from the south to the north, from the east to the west. Each time they come with their own past to a new town or a new city, to become part of a new community. The pattern repeats itself over and over: *E pluribus unum* – the many form a new unity.

Yes, something new was created every time. You brought with you a different culture and you contributed your own distinctive richness to the whole; you had different skills and you put them to work, complementing each other, to create industry, agriculture and business; each group carried with it different human values and shared them with the others for the enrichment of your nation. *E pluribus unum*: you became a new entity, a new people, the true nature of which cannot be adequately explained as a mere putting together of various communities.

It was an accurate rendering of the extraordinary romance of America – the way in which those vast and heart-stirring expanses had absorbed the flotsam of every people under heaven and made them, in certain senses, one nation. Yet the diversity remained. That was the secret. He forgot that, when the service was over, his audience of close on a million people would disperse to the German and the Irish and the Polish and the Swedish and the Czech and the Italian and the Yiddish sections of the city, each of them living its own kind of life and as often as not talking its own language. (Chicago was long known as a city where forty languages were spoken.) Diversity was not outlawed. Unity supervened only because it was not pressed too hard. America was culturally pluralist.

In the same way, and partly for that reason, it was morally pluralist too; and the Pope had not digested that. It was not a condition he thought appropriate within Catholicism. Poland, where if a monolithic atheist State was to be faced at all it must be faced by an equally monolithic Church, had prepared him differently. There, his moral admonitions were dutifully received by the faithful. Plurality of moral practice could be rebuked from above with no expectation of causing surprise and some of meeting success. In America, on the other hand, the attempt merely drew attention to the public impotence of religion.

There was a parallel in the United Nations speech. Finding a just settlement of the Palestinian question, reducing expenditure on arms, securing human rights internationally – it was unexceptionable stuff, carefully keeping its distance from the extremes both of right and left; and it made absolutely no difference. These were fields for the exercise of diplomacy, not theology. Indeed, it set for the whole tour the image of a man stumping the country handing out precepts which his office had lost the ability to enforce.

Because he was much admired as a human being, John Paul II doubtless touched many hearts in secret – the appropriate place for religious activity. Each witness could derive something of what he needed. High principle and self-control could be seen to confer wholeness. But when the words were spoken the effect was lessened. A girl to whom he wordlessly gave a flower outside St Patrick's Cathedral in New York said: 'It was like it was just him and me.' When he spoke, raining down an equal depth of unargued and largely negative precept on the infinite variety and sensitivity of humankind, the outcome was not so happy.

9

Opening to the East

By the end of 1979 John Paul II had been Pope for fourteen months. But he still puzzled commentators in search of a coherent strategy. They were bewildered by the range and diversity of the problems tackled in so short a time. 'He has said enough, and written enough,' wrote Henri Fesquet in *Le Monde*, 'to occupy an entire pontificate.' And he was only just starting. The prodigious output had not made the line of the pontificate much clearer. The Pope was like a conjurer who deftly managed to keep a large number of plates spinning through the air: the eye followed the plates, wondering if one would fall to the ground, rather than the hands. Or, to change the metaphor, he had opened up front after front: much had been started, nothing had been concluded.

One thing, however, was perfectly clear. There was a dramatic contrast between the last years of Paul VI and the beginning of the pontificate of John Paul II. As he neared the age of 80, Paul VI, though he never lost his lucidity, tired easily and could not contemplate long journeys: he left Italy for the last time in 1970. John Paul II was fit, in his prime, reluctant to stay put. Apart from his spectacular globe-trotting, he travelled extensively within Italy – to Assisi, to Monte Cassino, to Loreto and Ancona, to Pompei and Naples, to a shrine of Our Lady in the Dolomites (where he became, according to an excited Vatican Radio commentator, 'the first pope to recite the Angelus above the height of 10,000 feet').

But the contrast was not merely between the weakness of old age and relatively youthful fitness. There was a perceptible change of mood. Paul VI's many gifts did not include a vivid public presence. His voice was high-pitched and cracked easily, his sentences were long and often impenetrable. Though he spoke frequently of Christian joy, he did not manage to communicate it to dutiful and respectful crowds. John Paul II was the master of crowds. He could relax them and put them at their ease. He could switch from the grave to the humorous apparently at will. In Polish and Italian, at least, his impromptu asides created an atmosphere of cheerfulness and good will. When the aeronautics team of the Italian air force produced three supersonic bangs during his sermon outside the cathedral at Loreto (Our Lady of Loreto being the patroness of airmen, since the holy house of Nazareth was reputedly transported to Loreto by celestial means), he surveyed the sky and announced: 'I am always happy to be interrupted by young people.' At Castelgandolfo one Sunday a stentorian voice suddenly bellowed out '*Viva il Papa*!' 'I wish I had a voice like yours', said the Pope; 'I could use it in my job.'

The success with crowds and the immense popularity were not in doubt. But especially after the razzmatazz of the United States trip the first critical voices began to be heard. Triumphalism – an attitude of self-sufficiency which has nothing to learn from anyone – was the main charge. Was there not a danger of the Pope becoming a performer? John Paul II showed that he was not unaware of these accusations by replying to them, discreetly, in a sermon at Pompei on 21 October. He had prepared for his American journey, he explained, 'on his knees'. The essence of his ministry was the Eucharist, and his main task was 'to open the ways of the Spirit'. He did not doubt that this had happened in the United States. 'The rest', he added, 'is a display that in human terms could be judged superficial.' It was as well to have this warning early on in the pontificate. The Pope was not duped by the vast crowds, and did not behave demagogically towards them.

Another contrast with Paul VI was John Paul II's complete disregard for protocol. While Paul VI was always hampered by protocol – he did not want to 'commit his successors' – John Paul II refused to be so constrained. He plunged into crowds and seized babies with evident relish (not always shared by the astonished babies). He discovered a way of slipping out of the Vatican unnoticed, without the motor-cycle escort that was supposed to accompany him when he went to the foreign State of Italy. In October 1979 he spent an evening at the Polish College on the Aventine Hill, where he was entertained with national dances and songs. The same discreet exit (possibly the gate off the Piazza di Sant'Uffizio) was also used for introducing important guests in secret. Thus a few days later Sandro Pertini, the diminutive President of Italy, had lunch with the Pope, spent three hours at the Vatican, and was in and out again before anyone suspected where he was.

Moreover, John Paul II made the papacy personal to an extent never before attempted. He did not exploit the prestige of remoteness. He baptized a baby, presided over a marriage, wrote personally to small boys who lost a parent. Private audiences multiplied, and often ended with an invitation to lunch. The Polish Sisters of the Sacred Heart, in charge of the domestic arrangements, learned to be prepared for anything. 'The-day-I-had-my-audience-with-the-Pope' became a new conversational gambit. Leszek Kolakowski told John Paul II that he didn't want to burden him with his own problems, since the Pope had to bear on his shoulders all the problems of the world. 'Don't we all?' asked the Pope. 'Don't you? Isn't that the human condition? I'm not special in that regard.'

Roman parish priests, accustomed to seeing the Pope only as a distant figure on a balcony, were invited to meet him. Of course, his attempt to be the parish priest of the whole world was subject to ordinary human limitations: he could not meet everyone who wanted to see him. But as far as possible he was accessible. Even those not granted an audience sometimes reported that when he addressed a crowd he seemed to be speaking to them personally. That may have been an illusion, but it was a common one. The general reponse to his personalizing of the papacy could be summed up by adapting a phrase of Pascal: one expected to meet a pontiff, and one met a brother.

Popularity, disregard for protocol, rhetorical skills, the common touch: this heady combination permitted John Paul II to act effectively on the Church as a whole, on the Roman Curia (which was at his service) and on the world at large. Of those three interrelated spheres of activity, it was the first which most engaged his attention. How did he use his popularity to act on the Church as a whole?

After a year of the pontificate the alarm bells began to ring among liberal churchmen. They were troubled at the thought that while the Pope defended human rights with admirable vigour when he was addressing the nations, he repressed them within the

Church. The barque of Peter, they feared, was about to go astern. What had gone wrong was that there had been a misunderstanding of the real convictions of John Paul II. On the day after his election he committed himself to the implementation of Vatican II, and he never wavered in that commitment. It was, he told the special meeting of cardinals which gathered in Rome from 5 to 8 November 1979, 'the main task of the pontificate'. But being 'for the Council' meant one thing in the West and quite another in Poland. In the West it meant a readiness to admit mistakes and to learn from other Christians and the world; it meant an openness to radically new questions; it meant that the Church, aware of its pilgrim status here below, was 'constantly in need of purification'. The Council meant, in other words, liberation and reform. But at the meeting of cardinals John Paul II made it clear that his interpretation of the Council was very different. He criticized false notions of 'liberty' and 'renewal'. For him Vatican II was an end and not a starting point; it settled questions rather than opening them up. It had led to a dangerous crisis in which the most fundamental doctrines were called into question; it had caused a crisis in priestly and religious life. It was time, therefore, to press hard on the brakes. Yet because John Paul II continued to speak, with total sincerity, of his desire to implement the Council, the change was not immediately noticed.

The evidence that the papacy of John Paul II would be one of restoration began to pile up. On 16 October, the first anniversary of his election, he published an apostolic exhortation, *Catechesi Tradendae*. Although this document was the official response of the papacy to the submission of the 1977 Synod, and although Paul VI and John Paul I had already worked it over, it remained a very personal statement. John Paul II was in the unusual position of both taking advice and giving it. Catechesis had always been one of his major concerns.

He understood it in a broad sense as the initiation into and the maturing of Christian faith. His own preaching illustrated what he meant by catechesis. It was a constant recall to fundamentals. He described its purpose as follows:

> We live in a difficult world in which the anguish of see-
> ing the best creations of man slip away from him and

turn against him creates a climate of uncertainty. In this
world catechesis should help Christians to be, for their
own joy and the service of all, 'light' and 'salt'.
Undoubtedly this demands that catechesis should
strengthen them in their identity and that it should continually separate them from the surrounding atmosphere
of hesitation, uncertainty and insipidity (56).

This section of the apostolic constitution was headed 'The joy of
faith in an uncertain world'. It was the clearest statement to that
time of a programme for the pontificate.

As it worked out in practice it involved a strong reassertion of
Catholic identity, a rejection of fuzziness and blurred edges, the
confident proclamation of faith to a drifting and disturbed world.
But each of those positive characteristics of faith, very properly
commended by John Paul II, had its shadow side. The reassertion
of Catholic identity took pleasure in stressing the differences
between Catholics and their fellow Christians – and so proved
damaging to ecumenism. The rejection of vagueness could also
put an end to necessary theological questioning. And the confident proclamation of faith might seem to rule out those whose
faith was groping or searching – and so to bring them distress
rather than consolation. John Paul would not have appreciated
the Peter Ustinov maxim: 'We are divided by our certainties and
united by our doubts.'

That those three dangers were not just remote possibilities was
proved by an inspection of the record. John Paul II's comments
on ecumenism were uniformly friendly and courteous, but he
usually contrived to add warnings about various dangers. Thus
the apostolic constitution on catechesis, after reminding Catholics
that ecumenism was a duty imposed on them by Vatican II and
cautiously commending an ecumenical approach to catechesis,
contained this cold-waterish passage:

But the communion of faith between Catholics and
other Christians is not complete and perfect; in certain
cases there are even profound divergences. Consequently
this ecumenical collaboration is by its very nature
limited: it must never mean a 'reduction' to a common
minimum (33).

Significantly, John Paul II reserved his strictures on the perils of ecumenism for the Churches of the West, for those which issued from the Reformation. He spoke differently of Eastern Orthodoxy. Yet the dialogue which had made most progress, at least on the theoretical plane, was that between Catholicism and Anglicanism. The work of the Anglican/Roman Catholic International Commission, concluded in 1977, was entirely based on the conviction that the search for what was held in common would not be a reduction of the Gospel but on the contrary a mutual enrichment. It seemed that, as far as the West went, John Paul II had an alas-alack view of the ecumenical task: he lamented disunity, but had no very clear idea of how it was to be overcome.

The mariology that was such a notable feature of the pontificate was another way in which one kind of Catholic identity was asserted while many Protestants were dismayed and antagonized. A member of the Secretariat for Christian Unity argued that 'the Pope, like anyone else, has the right to his private devotions'. No doubt that was true. But a pope's private devotions have a way of becoming public. For John Paul II, no Marian shrine was too insignificant, none too dubious for notice: if not a visit, then at least a mention. The point was again illustrated at the Angelus of 11 November. He spoke, as was his custom, of the country whose bishops had visited him the previous week. He contrived to a make a brief geographical and statistical survey of Paraguay and Uruguay without mentioning that they were both military dictatorships. In both countries, he reported, the Church seemed to be doing very well, thanks to the shrine of Florída in Paraguay and the national shrine of Caacupé in Uruguay, where Our Lady was honoured as 'Virgen de los Milagros'. Nor was that all. In the same week, Bolivia had undergone its 212th military coup. The Pope expressed the hope that fratricidal strife would cease there, and entrusted a peaceful solution of the problem to the intercession of 'the Virgin of Copacabana' (the local shrine). There was apparently no trace of irony here. John Paul II simply had his own map of the world.

If ecumenists in the West were given food for thought, theologians reeled under a series of blows. The only advice John Paul II had for them was that they should hew close to the magisterium or teaching authority of the Church and not deviate from it by an iota. A brief paragraph of his address at Maynooth in Ireland had been devoted to the task of theologians. It said:

> Only when the teaching of theologians is in conformity with the teaching of the College of Bishops, united with the Pope, can the people of God know with certitude that that teaching is the faith which has been once and for all entrusted to the saints (Jude 3). This is not a limitation for theologians, but a liberation; for it preserves them from subservience to changing fashions and binds them more securely to the unchanging truth of Christ, the truth which makes us free (John 8.32).

It is difficult to escape the suspicion that these warnings were based on the notion that all the troubles of the Church in the post-conciliar period were to be blamed on unruly theologians. They were made the scapegoat for the crisis. That had been the theme of an address given by Cardinal Wojtyla to the Congress of Polish theologians in 1971. Theologians, he said, had 'a purely consultative function', and some of them had been sowing seeds of doubt by questioning such basic doctrines as the Trinity, the nature of Christ, the real presence of Christ in the Eucharist and the indissolubility of marriage. The same tone, nine years later, crept into the apostolic exhortation of October 1979. It contained a warning for catechists:

> Catechists . . . must have the wisdom to pick from the field of theological research those points that can provide light for their own reflection and their teaching, drawing, like the theologians, from the true sources, in the light of the magisterium. They must refuse to trouble the minds of children and young people, at this stage of their catechesis, with outlandish theories, useless questions and unproductive discussions, things that St Paul often condemned in his pastoral letters (61).

The suggestion was that theologians were rocking the barque – though why they should wish to do so remained unexplained. The three dismissive adjectives – 'outlandish', 'useless' and 'unproductive' – revealed a certain animus against theologians and a curious view of theological activity. One of the submissions of post-conciliar theologians was that they did not invent the questions they discussed but found them in ordinary pastoral work: they derived their questions from the people of God.

Theologians must stick close to the magisterium. They must not be allowed to become an alternative magisterium. That was the constant theme of John Paul II. He said it at the Catholic University of America in Washington. He said it again when he addressed the International Theological Commission in Rome on 26 October. The ITC had been founded in response to requests made at the 1969 Synod, when many bishops felt that the theological advice available to the Pope from the Roman universities was too narrow. It was set up to make permanently available in Rome the expertise of the theologians who had shaped the Council. It had thirty members from all over the world. But its reports had been increasingly ignored. Karl Rahner, the German Jesuit scholar, had resigned from it on the grounds that it was 'stewing in its own juice'. He said in an interview: 'It sets itself problems, and speaks about them in a more or less praiseworthy way, but nothing else happens.' John Paul II's speech completed its domestication. Though the theologians participated in the magisterium to some extent, he wished to stress the words 'to some extent'. They should never be confused with 'the authentic magisterium itself', which was endowed with 'the charism of truth, which cannot be communicated to anyone else, and which cannot be substituted for by anyone else'. It seemed, then, that there was very little for theologians to do other than support and comment favourably on what the magisterium had to say. Theology became precisely what it had tended to be before the Council: a branch of apologetics.

These exhortations to theologians were backed up by deeds. The Sacred Congregation for the Doctrine of the Faith, formerly known as the Holy Office and before that as the Inquisition, came back into business. It had been relatively somnolent during the pontificate of Paul VI and issued no condemnations. The first post-conciliar condemnation was of a French Dominican, Jaques Pohier, whose book *Quand je dis Dieu* was said to contain 'a number of errors and dangerous affirmations'. The judgement passed on him meant that he was forbidden to say Mass in public or to teach in public. He accepted the conditions. That was in April 1979. Later in the year, the Congregation was hunting bigger game.

First Edward Schillebeeckx – a Flemish Dominican teaching theology at the Catholic University of Nijmegan in the Netherlands, and among the best known of Catholic theologians – came under fire for a book originally published in Dutch in 1974. Its English title was *Jesus, an Experiment in Christology*, and despite its arduousness it was, like most of his other books, a best-seller. He was summoned to Rome for December 1979 in order to defend himself, though as late as October he did not know precisely what the charges against him were, nor who his two judges would be, nor who would act as his defence lawyer. (All three were to be appointed by the Congregation.) Schillebeeckx braced himself to go to Rome, but was pessimistic about his chances of being understood by Roman theologians formed in a different tradition. He explained that his book was an attempt to help people grasp how Jesus was experienced by his contemporaries. 'Jesus shows us what God will be for us and also what man must be for God. I do not deny that Jesus is God, but want to assert that he is also man, something that has been overlooked. It is precisely as man that he is important for us. But when you say that, you are suspect.' The case aroused a good deal of protest among northern European theologians, Catholic as well as Protestant. Emerging on 15 December from his Rome hearing, Schillebeeckx described it as friendly – 'perhaps too friendly'. He added that his views were shared by theologians of the Orthodox Churches; and this showed a certain cunning, given John Paul II's demonstrated interest in a rapprochement with them. There nevertheless seemed little doubt that when the papers in the case passed to the Pope his judgement would be adverse.

Four days later it was disclosed that proceedings had gone even further against a theologian yet better known: Hans Küng, the Swiss scholar teaching at Tübingen in West Germany who had been a star of the international lecture circuit since the early 1960s. In this case, too, part of the trouble was the handling of the Jesus story. 'Demythologizing is inescapable', Küng wrote in his widely read and translated book *On being a Christian*. His understanding of the divine sonship was by no means literal. But the issue on which he had been in intermittent trouble with Rome for years was papal infallibility. Küng sat noticeably loose both to the doctrine itself and to Vatican requests that he should explain his cool view of it. The burden of a book he published in 1970 (*Infallibility? An Enquiry*) was that infallibility resided in the Church, not the pope, and consisted in the Church's general persistence in 'the truth of Jesus Christ', notwithstanding all errors that might be committed by theologians, bishops and even the pope himself. Despite a number of Vatican declarations and exhortations, Küng repeated the offence in sharper form in the spring of 1979, apropos a work by another Swiss academic, August Hasler. Hasler's book provided scholarly evidence for believing that Pius IX was of unsound mind by the time of the 1870 Council, that he bullied the bishops into approving his infallibility dogma, and that it was in consequence invalid. Küng supplied an approving preface.

In October 1979 Küng made his attack more personal. In *Le Monde* of Paris and in *The New York Times* he published a review of John Paul II's first year in office. The article cast doubt on the Pope's qualities as a man open to the world, a spiritual leader, a pastor, a believer in collegiality, an ecumenist and even a Christian; and in a climactic paragraph it opposed almost every position he had taken on his American journey:

> Is the commitment in the Church to human rights in the world honest, when in the Church itself, at the same time, human rights are not fully guaranteed – for example, the right of priests to marry, as is guaranteed in the Gospel itself and in the old Catholic tradition; the right to leave the priesthood with official dispensation after a thorough examination of conscience (rather than the inhumane practice reintroduced by this Pope of forbidding bureaucratically this dispensation); the right of theologians to freedom in their research and expression of opinion; the right of nuns to choose their own clothing; the ordination of women, as can certainly be justified by the Gospel for our contemporary situation; the personal responsibility of married couples for the conception and the number of their children?

When the Congregation concluded from all this, two months later, that Küng could 'no longer be considered a Catholic theologian nor function as such in a teaching role', the Pope's concurrence was not in doubt. Küng, for his part, gave notice that he would not submit quietly.

Hasler's case was known to be passing through similar processes; and Congregation officials were reading other suspect christologists besides Schillebeeckx: Piet Schoonenberg of Holland, David Tracy and Monika Hellwig of the United States. Even Leonardo Boff was being examined – not precisely for being a liberationist, but for having published a book in 1972 called *Jesus Christ Liberator.*

In all these cases, the Vatican had in its own terms little choice. It was operating a closed system in which truth was held to be what the Church said it was. To acknowledge that truth might reside anywhere else would have been to lay the system open with potentially disastrous consequences. Yet virtually all other modern intellectual pursuits except Roman Catholic theology were used to a different and less authoritarian approach. The Roman line, therefore, risked perpetuating what Küng called 'ignorance and obscurantism among the ordinary people and widespread de-Christianization and lack of faith among the educated classes'. It was also a powerful obstruction to any serious reunion between Roman Catholicism and all those Protestant denominations which permitted freer play to the enquiring intellect. But there John Paul II had already demonstrated his coolness.

There were other signs of the times in Rome. The fate of the Society of Jesus, some 27,000 strong, is always a good indication of the way the ecclesiastical breeze is blowing. Jesuits have the reputation of thinking for the Church as well as with the Church. They provided many of the *periti* or experts whose work made the Second Vatican Council possible. On 21 September 1979 the General, Pedro Arrupe, together with his top advisers, had an audience with John Paul II. The third paragraph of the Pope's speech read:

> From reports I receive from every part of the world, I am well aware of the great good which so many Jesuits are accomplishing through their exemplary life, their

apostolic zeal, their sincere and unconditioned fidelity
to the Roman Pontiff.

Connoisseurs of pontifical style knew that this praise boded
trouble to come. It did. The Pope went on:

At the same time I am not unaware – drawing on a few
other sources of information – that the crisis which in
recent times has troubled religious life and is still troub-
ling it has not spared your Society, causing confusion
among Christian people and concern to the Church, to
the hierarchy, and personally to the pope who is speaking to you.

It was tough, but it was vague. Jesuits had been criticized before,
and could take it on the chin. Paul VI had uttered dire warnings in
his time, and John Paul I had prepared a similar address which
death alone had prevented him from delivering.

But this time there could be no eluding the seriousness of the
charges. Arrupe wrote a letter to his men in which he said that 'a
call from three popes leaves little room for doubt that it is the
Lord himself who, surely with love, but also with insistence,
expects something better of us. We cannot wait any longer.' That
was dated 19 October, feast of the North American martyrs.
Some suspected that there would be more North American martyrs before long, for the Pope had drawn attention to four needs
which seemed to fit the United States scene: resistance to secular-
izing tendencies, 'austerity and discipline in religious and
community life, fidelity to the magisterium of the Church, and
the priestly character of our apostolic work'. It was difficult to
know precisely what was being hinted at in this language. It
created a mood of uneasiness and guilt in which any charge could
be made to stick. It is no doubt invidious to name names, but it
was unlikely that John J. McNeill, whose sympathetic book on
homosexuality had just appeared (without his permission) in
Italian, would feel greatly encouraged. And those who like
William Callahan of Washington had been advocating the cause
of women's ordination were given pause. Neither topic was on the
agenda of this pontificate. To add to the general gloom there were
distinct signs that Opus Dei, a secretive and right-wing Catholic
group founded in Spain in 1928, had the favour and the ear of the

Pope. There was even talk that Opus Dei might take over Vatican Radio from the Jesuits – a prospect which made some Jesuits, at any rate, heave a sigh of relief.

John Paul II also turned his attention to the problems of the troubled Dutch Church (or the Netherlands Province of the Roman Catholic Church, as it preferred to be called). Nothing could more clearly illustrate the contrast of style with Paul VI. Where he had been hesitant, John Paul II was decisive. Paul VI took a diplomatic approach, being reluctant to provoke a schism. To curb modernism he made two conservative bishops – Adrianus Simonis at Rotterdam, Johannes Gijsen at Roermond. The unfortunate result was that by January 1979 there was hardly any serious issue on which the seven Dutch bishops could agree, and their President, Cardinal Jan Willebrands, reported this sad fact to the Pope. He acted swiftly, summoned them to Rome and met them individually in March, telling them to patch up their quarrels. This intervention having failed, they were again summoned to the Vatican in January 1980 for an unprecedented special synod which bound the Dutch hierarchy to apply traditional teaching in matters of Church order.

But the mass of the faithful were neither ecumenists nor professional theologians; they were neither erring Jesuits nor quarrelsome Dutchmen. What messages were they picking up from this exciting new pope? The difficulty in answering the question lay in the vast diversity of situations – a shanty-town dweller in South America would have a different perception from a European in the leafy suburbs, and a Pole would see things differently from an African. There was another difficulty: the medium seemed to obfuscate the message, so that in the popular enthusiasm aroused by the journeys of John Paul II people simply forgot or omitted to attend to what he was actually saying. He got a good press where Paul VI, having said exactly the same thing, got a bad press. The reason he was able to get away with almost anything was that the novelty of his pontificate and the charism of his presence provided a distraction from what he actually said.

Nowhere was this truer than in the United States. Despite the fact that the majority of American Catholics no longer had any objection to birth control, John Paul made his clearest declaration against it when he addressed the American bishops in

Chicago on 5 October. And lest there should be any mistake or ambiguity, on 3 November he showed that he had no sympathy whatsoever with those who had been advocating change. He was addressing a body called the Liaison Centre for Research (CLER is the acronym in French) – a group of doctors, psychiatrists, marriage guidance counsellors and others who had been working on the search for a reliable 'natural' alternative to artificial contraception. He told them that so-called pastoral solutions which bent the rules were not to be allowed. The claims of conscience were not even mentioned. The widespread disregard for official teaching was sternly met in a passage about married couples:

> It is good that they should grasp how this natural ethic corresponds to a properly understood anthropology, and in this way they will escape the snares of public opinion and permissive legislation and even, as far as possible, contribute to the correction of public opinion.

He deliberately challenged the conventional secular wisdom and met it head-on. But instead of arguing the case, he asked a series of questions based on ecological considerations (the superiority of the natural to the artificial), on self-mastery as the key to human dignity, on the natural desire to have children, and on the selfish consequences of refusing to have children. He was, on this occasion, addressing the converted. CLER would give the answer he expected. The search for a reliable, easy, non-artificial method of spacing births would be intensified. Science, so the theory ran, would eventually confirm what the Church had been saying all along and what Paul VI, risking unpopularity, prophetically announced in 1968. It also went without saying that any bishop who saw the topic for the 1980 Synod, 'The role of the Christian family', as an invitation to discuss birth control would have to think again. The ground had been pre-empted.

The same could be said of the other controverted questions in the field of sexual morality. At Chicago on 5 October abortion, pre-marital sex, euthanasia and divorce were also rejected. Homosexuality, male and female, was included in the same list. It was not surprising that the Pope should reassert traditional Catholic moral teaching in these matters. But there were, all the same, at least two worrying features about the way it was presented. The first was that John Paul II appeared to be building up an identikit picture of a dissident in the Church who proposed a whole package of reforms in sexual matters. But this was to attack a straw man. Each question needed to be distinguished from the others. Those who had found, often with the help of their priests, a 'pastoral' solution to birth control, did not for that reason advocate a loose approach to abortion. Indeed, their opposition to abortion might be strengthened. It was misleading and harmful to lump all the questions together. The second cause for distress was that the reaffirmation of a principle did nothing to change a given situation. The indissolubility of marriage was upheld even by those who drew attention to the obvious fact that many hundreds of thousands of Catholics were separated or divorced. The problem concerned not indissolubility as such, but rather how such people should be dealt with pastorally, how they should think of themselves, whether they were to be banned from what they had come to hope was a compassionate Church. The mere reiteration of indissolubility did not make their problem go away.

One by one the hatches had been battened down. There seemed little prospect of development in any direction. One by one the leading ideas of the Council had been re-interpreted and rendered harmless. The charisms of all the priestly people of God? But they were not, John Paul II told the American bishops in Chicago, 'independent of the magisterium', and were only fully operative when the faithful had been 'nourished by the word of God, faithfully transmitted in its purity and integrity'. The signs-of-the-times theology, by which the Holy Spirit could be detected at work in the movements and trends of our own age? But the signs of the times, John Paul II told the nuns in Washington, must first be discerned by the magisterium. Collegiality, which made the bishops of the world co-responsible with the pope for the government of the Church? But for John Paul II, collegiality meant that the bishops backed up and sustained the pope. It was difficult to see how change of any kind could ever edge its way into a Church conceived on this model.

There was one role left for laypeople. They were appealed to from time to time on controverted questions. The Pope addressed them, in populist fashion, over the heads of the band of dissidents who were leading them astray. At Maynooth he spoke of 'silent anguish among the people of God' about priests who sought to leave the priesthood. In Washington he quoted the desire 'often expressed by so many of the faithful' that nuns should not wear plain clothes. Such evidence as existed in the West did not support the notion that either body of opinion was substantial. It did seem that a reading of public opinion in Poland was being made the norm for the universal Church.

All these trends were noted, if nowhere else, in the Roman Curia, the papal bureaucracy. The word 'curia' simply means court, and in a court everything depends on the favour, or the presumed favour, of the prince. So the three thousand members of the Roman Curia pay more attention than others to the words of the pope, since he is their employer and they are at his service. They are also accustomed to reading documents carefully and appreciating the nuances which indicate a change of direction. By November 1979 it was clear to them that John Paul II was engaged upon a work of reaction and restoration. One of them drew attention to the words used in addressing nuns in Maynooth and pointed out their wider application: 'The sisters too have known years of searching, sometimes perhaps of uncertainty and unrest. These have also been years of purification. I pray that we are now entering a period of consolidation and construction.' In other words it was high time that a stop was put to the post-conciliar crisis.

Most members of the Curia had every reason to be content with the new regime. The first pope from outside Italy for 455 years did not appear to be on the point of turning the administration upside down. He made no spectacular appointments from outside the Curia. The job vacated by Cardinal Wright's death (Prefect of the Sacred Congregation for the Clergy) went to a 69-year-old Italian ex-diplomat of conservative inclinations, Cardinal Silvio Oddi. Promotion continued to be orderly and to respect the career structure. It followed the ecclesiastical equivalent of Buggins's turn: Monsignor Buggins had been around long enough, made no notable mistakes, and was due for a move upwards. Substitute, say, Bugnini for Buggins, and it will no longer seem so facetious. Indeed, Cardinal Agostino Casaroli, the Secretary of State, once said of his career that 'promotion to the rank of under-secretary came by the natural process of growing older'.

In fact, however, Casaroli's own appointment as Secretary of State was the most significant of the pontificate. It showed that in the re-shaping of the Curia, and especially of the key department of the Secretariat of State, the Pope was concerned to play down the Italian factor and give increased attention to Eastern Europe. Casaroli had been associated with the *Ostpolitik* since John XXIII dispatched him to Vienna for a United Nations meeting on consular relations in 1961. As his *sostituto* or number two he was given Archbishop Eduardo Martinez Somalo, a Spaniard. This was unheard of: the *sostituto* had traditionally been an Italian and the principal link with the Italian Republic. He could be expected to have many friends in the Christian Democratic Party. Martinez did not have such contacts. Meanwhile, Casaroli was replaced as the head of the Council for the Public Business of the Church – in effect the foreign ministry – by Achille Silvestrini, previously his number two; and the new deputy was Monsignor Andryas Backis. Silvestrini had been involved in the Helsinki Conference, and Backis was a Lithuanian whose father had been the last ambassador of independent Lithuania to the United States. All of which meant that still more attention would be paid to Eastern Europe. (Cardinal Koenig thought Backis the Pope's most significant appointment.) In addition to these moves, a Polish desk was set up in the Secretariat of State – necessary for translation if nothing else.

No one could complain of a Polish mafia invading the Roman Curia. John Paul was scrupulously careful about not bringing in more Poles; but those who were already there, along with other Slavs, were rapidly promoted. No doubt he knew that it was said of Pius X, formerly Patriarch of Venice, that he had 'turned Peter's barque into a gondola'. Canoeing is a more solitary occupation. But there is informal as well as formal access to the pope; and here Poles, especially Cardinal Wladislaw Rubin, came into their own. As one curialist put in, 'Bishop Jacques Martin, Prefect of the Pontifical Household, is the ordinary means of communication with the Pope: he is the lift – but there is also a back staircase.'

What did the Curia think about the Pope? A particularly difficult question, since it is traditional in the Curia not to let one's feelings be known – to maintain what is known as *una figura di bronzo*, a poker face. A rough distinction may be made between the 'old curia', made up of the congregations or departments which existed before the Second Vatican Council (e.g. the Congregation for the Doctrine of Faith, the Congregations for Bishops, Clergy, Evangelization, etc.), and the 'new curia', consisting of conciliar or post-conciliar bodies in which the possibility of learning from others is not dismissed in advance (e.g. the Secretariats for Christian Unity, Non-Christian Religions and Non-Believers). To label the old curia conservative and the new curia progressive would be too simplistic. But the distinction provides at least a starting point for understanding the reactions of a complex institution.

We have already seen that the Congregation for the Doctrine of the Faith was revitalized. Though Paul VI had sometimes reminded it that it had also the positive task of encouraging or promoting theological research, it was evidently much happier in its traditional role of denouncing theological errors. It could not do this without the approval of the pope. At the Secretariat for Christian Unity, on the other hand, the prevailing mood was of apprehension. One of its quarrels with the Congregation for the Doctrine of the Faith was precisely the question of literal adherence to conciliar formulas. The Congregation insisted on it. The Secretariat was prepared to envisage the possibility that dogmatic statements of the Church might be time-bound, that they set out to answer some questions and not others and that what counted, therefore, was the actual faith of the Church today. Secretariat officials could point out, ironically enough, that these principles were not the wild invention of some eccentric theologian but were contained in a document published, in happier days, by the Congregation itself (*Mysterium Ecclesiae*, 5 July 1973). They were the basis of ecumenism. Both Catholics and Protestants might have moved on from their credal statements. The word 'transubstantiation', for instance, was not the only possible way of expressing the Catholic faith on the Eucharist. Even the Council of Trent stated only that it was 'an apt expression', which left the door open for other, equally apt, expressions. The Anglican/Roman Catholic agreement on the Eucharist relegated the term to a footnote, while emphasizing strongly the common faith of both Churches that Christ was 'really' present in the sacrament. In this crucial debate, it began to be clear that John Paul II favoured the views of the Congregation.

When he visited the Secretariat for Christian Unity at 1 Via dell'Erba he noted that it was pressed for space. 'But then,' he added mysteriously, 'one senses that you are a young organization.' No one knew quite what that meant. It could be innocuous. It could be sinister. For the time being the Secretariat put a brave front on things, drawing attention to the numerous positive statements on ecumenism made by the Pope, and insisting that one should not foreclose issues but should rather maintain for as long as possible the ambivalence of the pontificate. Tactically, it was the best that could be done.

Taken as a whole, though, the Curia was still uncertain about the Pope's attitude to it. He paid surprisingly little attention to its problems. Though he systematically visited all the offices and talked in the friendliest possible way to nearly all the staff, it seemed to take him a long time to decide what he wanted the Curia to do. 'He says little', was one comment, 'and asks a lot of questions.' Some members of the Curia began to feel neglected. The immense popular success of the Pope further widened the gap. 'The Pope blesses crowds and prays', said another disgruntled curialist, 'but he doesn't govern.' What he probably meant was that the Pope had not yet read a document the official had prepared for him months ago. It was not that the Pope did not work hard: on the contrary, he was up at five in the morning – an hour earlier than Paul VI; but the time at his desk was devoted to his own projects and the preparation of his journeys. That left little time to examine the papers submitted by the Curia.

In short, the Curia felt bypassed. The Pope appealed over its head either to the masses, on whom he had a hold it could not possibly compete with, or to the local bishops of particular countries, whom he seemed to regard as the proper interlocutors for a pope in the administration of the Church. The visits to Ireland and the United States made it clear that he was going to trust the local episcopal conferences in the planning of his visits and the content of his sermons. The principle worked in the other direction too. Every five years bishops pay their *ad limina* visit to

Rome, grouped by country. These visits are not new: they are one of the oldest expressions of lived collegiality. But John Paul II referred to them almost every Sunday morning and emphasized them in such a way that, once again, the Roman Curia seemed circumvented. His preferred source of information was the local episcopate rather than the reports which his diplomats sent back through the appointed channels.

The most dramatic illustration of this trend was the meeting of cardinals (it was not done to call it a consistory) held in Rome from 5 to 9 November. Nothing like it had happened for four centuries. Though cardinals were nominally the chief advisers of the Pope, they never met as a body except on his death. The two conclaves of 1978 had given a rare chance to know each other better. Despite intrigues, of which the Anglo-Saxons had professed to be largely unaware, they had forged a unity among themselves which could be of use in the future. True, the Synod was the body which was supposed to express collegiality: but it met only every three years, its topics were fixed well in advance, and it had no flexibility of response to new questions. The very fact that the meeting of cardinals was called at all was a setback for the Curia; and a worse blow was that one of the three topics for discussion was curial reform.

Paul VI had asked the Curia to reform itself. John Paul II asked the cardinals how to reform the Curia. No very precise suggestions emerged from the meeting. There was much talk of 'restructuring' and cutting out over-lapping competences or wasteful duplication. Since, moreover, the reshaping of the Curia was linked with the need to economize (also strongly stressed at the meeting), it seemed that an axe was poised. But where might it fall? Some rationalization seemed obvious and necessary. The Committee on the Family could be integrated into the Council for the Laity without great loss. The likelihood of such a move was greatly strengthened when Archbishop Moreira Neves, the Council for the Laity's Brazilian Vice-President, was shifted to become the number two at the Congregation of Bishops, and when the President of the Committee on the Family, Archbishop Edouard Gagnon, went unaccountably missing from Rome. A much more alarming suggestion was that the three Secretariats – for Christian Unity, Non-Christian Religions and Non-Believers – should be fused into one. But apparently this suggestion, which would have spelt the death of ecumenism, was resisted. The official statement at the end of the meeting referred vaguely to 'the substantial validity of the present structures of the Curia'; but that did not prevent its adding that proposals had been made 'with a view to introducing some desired improvements into the structure and functioning of some curial bodies'. The axe was still in position. Changes in the system were not excluded. Monsignor Buggins might have to look out.

The meeting of cardinals was remarkable in another way. It discussed the finances of the Church – or at least of its central administration. The Pope spoke of the 'fables and myths' concerning the vast wealth of the Vatican, and said that the only way to dissipate them was 'to consider the matter objectively'. Previous attempts to do just that had not always been well received. It was obvious that St Peter's could not be razed to the ground and replaced by apartment-blocks. And the treasures of the Vatican museums were mostly inalienable and could not help with cash-flow problems. But now, for the first time ever, a statistic was given: the deficit forecast for the year 1979 was over twenty million dollars, and worse was expected for 1980. It was also said that the deficit was covered 'thanks to voluntary offerings coming from the Catholic world, and particularly through Peter's Pence'. No details were provided about that collection, but the best sources indicated that it had doubled since John Paul II became Pope. At the same time, though, the papal journeys had greatly added to outgoings.

Apart from helping to dissipate 'fables and myths', what was the point of revealing this single statistic? It could hardly be said that the veil of mystery had been torn asunder. And in any case a deficit of twenty million dollars, although worrying as a trend, was not in itself catastrophic. Dioceses like Chicago and Munich had much bigger turnovers than that. To the cardinals and their people from all over the world the message was: 'We need help.' But it was not simply that the Vatican was bringing out the begging bowl on its own behalf. John Paul II himself spoke of the urgent need for Churches that were 'rich and free' to help those that were 'neither rich nor free'. Cardinal François Marty of Paris pointed out that nearly half the dioceses of the world were unable to support themselves. Collegiality meant mutual help.

But the disclosure of that statistic also contained a message for the Roman Curia. It was a declaration, first of all, that the tradition of secrecy, which had always been jealously protected, could not be relied upon in future. Its second effect was to warn the Curia that there would have to be cuts. One prelate admitted gloomily: 'It doesn't mean that Peter's barque is going to sink beneath the waves, but it does mean that half our jobs are at risk.'

There was a third topic on the cardinals' agenda which at first blush seemed less arresting than finance and the reform of the Curia: they were invited to consider the theme of 'the Church and culture'. They may well have been a little nonplussed by this, but the vague phrase hinted at a concern very close to the heart of John Paul II and one likely to characterize his pontificate. It was in fact a grandiose project. The Pope aspired to do something to close the gap between reason and revelation, between science and faith. His experience of living in Communist Poland had made him particularly sensitive to the propaganda charge that 'modern scientifically-minded man' could regard faith only as a nostalgic survival, doomed to disappear. On one level, his study of phenomenology had been an attempt to rebut that claim.

But what could an individual, even a pope, do to reverse and roll back what many consider to be a twentieth-century trend? He could begin, as John Paul II did in a speech to the Pontifical Academy of Sciences, by rehabilitating Galileo (whom in 1633 the Holy Office had forced to recant, under threat of torture, his belief that the earth went round the sun). In many ways, it was a most curious event. In the Sala Regale of the Vatican were gathered most of the seventy academicians, chosen not for their faith but for their scientific eminence, ostensibly to commemorate the hundredth anniversary of the birth of Albert Einstein. Yet Einstein was hardly mentioned in the Pope's speech. Instead John Paul II devoted most of his time to Galileo. 'The greatness of Galileo is recognized by all', he said, speaking in French, 'but we cannot deny that he suffered greatly at the hands of churchmen and church bodies.' He called for an inter-disciplinary study by historians, scientists and theologians which would honestly recognize the wrongs that had been committed but, by the same token, would help to banish the mistrust between science and religion which continued to exist in some minds. John Paul II then asserted the freedom of scientific research and, again reflecting his Polish experience, linked it with religious liberty: 'Just as religion needs religious liberty, so science legitimately claims freedom of research.' Blandly assuming that liberty of thought and enquiry were assured under his own system, he turned the reproach against his old adversaries. Every people had the right to research 'in complete freedom from any kind of international servitude or intellectual colonialism': that was code language for saying that science could not be made to serve the purposes of the Communist Party.

There had been a misunderstanding, he went on. Galileo was right to claim that the two sources of truth – revelation and science – could not, in the end, contradict each other. In Galileo's time the problem was exacerbated by the way theologians adhered to a literal interpretation of scripture. John Paul II quoted a letter of Galileo's to Christine of Lorraine: 'Scripture can never lie, provided one understands its real meaning, which is often hidden and very different from what the plain meaning of the words might suggest.' On this he commented: 'Galileo introduces a way of interpreting the scriptures which goes beyond the literal sense, but which attends to the intentions of the author and the literary form in which they are couched.' And the Pope's commentaries on the 'anthropology of the Book of Genesis', with which he regaled his Wednesday audiences at the end of 1979, made some use of this principle. Old Testament fundamentalism had had its day.

In his inaugural address to the cardinals he suggested a new institution which would 'seek a proper expression of the relationship between the Church and the wide field of anthropology and the human sciences'. Pius XI had set up the Pontifical Academy of Sciences in 1922 when the threat to faith appeared to come from the physical sciences; John Paul II was feeling after an analogous body which would hold dialogue with psychology and sociology. The cardinals had the excuse of the financial crisis for suggesting that the idea should not be implemented immediately. Marty pointed out that the work was already being done – by the Jesuits in Paris and no doubt elsewhere. Not everyone saw the advantages of more centralization. But it seemed likely that more would be heard of the idea later.

A writer in *Unità*, the Italian Communist daily, grasped the deeper implications of the Pope's strategy. Under the heading 'Galileo is no longer wrong', the paper explained that John Paul II, having won over the masses, was now addressing himself to the intellectuals – knowing that without intellectual support his popular success could prove a bubble.

Gradually, then, the pontificate of John Paul II took a definite shape. It was to be a highly personal pontificate with a hyper-active, interventionist pope who passionately wanted to communicate the values of the Gospel as he understood them. The emphasis was to be on order and discipline rather than on freedom and experiment. In the opening period of the pontificate the masses were mobilized, allegedly dissident theologians quelled, wayward Jesuits brought to heel, the Dutch nettle grasped, the Roman Curia tamed and finally intellectuals wooed (if not, like the young people in Madison Square Garden, 'wowed'). The trouble – or perhaps the saving grace – was that none of those things could be brought about by metaphysical proclamation. The recalcitrant human material might refuse to be pushed around. The Pope's authoritative words could contribute to a new situation; but they could not create it. Still, no one could doubt that John Paul II had tried to take a firm grip on the Church. And no one could any longer complain of a lack of leadership.

There remained the question of what this vigorous, unHamlet-like leadership meant for the world community. For a pope is also, to use the jargon of students of international affairs, a 'transnational actor'. To some extent the answer lay in the journeys. Despite the emphasis on their spiritual or pastoral nature, each journey involved tackling a political issue. Mexico posed the problem of liberation theology and 'the national security state'. Poland was the obvious place to confront the Communist world. Ireland provided an opportunity to denounce violence as a means of solving problems. The visit to the United States was the first brush with a pluralist society. Immense trouble was taken over the preparation of these journeys. John Paul II took his duties as Bishop of Rome seriously, and involved himself more directly in the life of the diocese than any of his predecessors in this century. But he reserved most of his major pronouncements for his journeys, when he was assured of maximum media coverage. The pope in Rome becomes, after a while, a familiar figure to whom less and less attention is paid. A travelling pope arouses much more interest. John Paul II grasped this point. 'It is as though', said one of his aides, 'he is always travelling in spirit: even when he is here in Rome, he is thinking of his next journey.' By the end of 1979 twenty-three invitations had been received and not rejected outright.

Even apart from the spectacular journeys, the international scene was not neglected. Messages and envoys were dispatched to the world's trouble spots. The Pope appealed for the boat-people of Vietnam, the refugees of Kampuchea, the hostages held in the United States Embassy in Teheran. He did not appear to make much of a dent in any of these intractable situations – though he could claim that his intervention in the Beagle channel dispute had averted a war between Chile and Argentina.

But the most obvious way in which John Paul II made an impact on the international scene was through the development of a vigorous *Ostpolitik* – the whole complex web of relations between the Church and those Governments of Eastern Europe which between them control the lives of some sixty million Catholics. This was where John Paul II felt at home. This was the area in which he had long experience and specialist knowledge. This was where people in the West, who thought themselves the centre of the universe, might have most difficulty in following him. During the pontificate of Paul VI, the complaint of the Eastern Europeans was that the Vatican did not understand their problems, tended to act above their heads, showed insufficient resolution in dealing with Communist powers. It was also alleged that the Vatican was so anxious to come to terms with the Russian Orthodox Church that it was prepared to sacrifice the Catholics of Lithuania and accept the humiliation of the Catholic Church in the Ukraine. The embrace of the Vatican and the Kremlin was – in the blunt language of Cardinal Josef Slipyi, Metropolitan of the Ukrainians – an obscene insult to the blood of the martyrs of the Gulag Archipelago. These complaints suddenly ceased with the election of John Paul II. He was a Slav, after all. Moreover, he acted swiftly on all levels.

First he patched up the quarrel with the Ukrainian Catholic Church and Slipyi. Slipyi had seen his Church in the Ukraine destroyed – legally it does not even exist any more – and spent eighteen years in a Siberian labour camp. He was freed in 1963 through the personal intervention of John XXIII with Nikita Khrushchev, but on condition that he did not attack the Soviet Government. After a few years of silence Slipyi began to do little else, living in Rome and always prepared to show his Siberian prison clothes to interested visitors. John Paul II wrote him a soothing letter on 19 March 1979 to say that the Ukrainians, too, had the right to religious liberty. Whether or not as a result, the Catholic-Orthodox meeting fixed for Odessa at the end of April was cancelled at the last moment because, said Moscow, 'of organizational difficulties'. The Ukrainians, like other Uniates – Eastern Churches in communion with Rome but keeping their own language and rites – have always been a source of friction between Rome and Moscow.

Elsewhere he seized the initiative. In January 1979 Vatican Radio began broadcasting a Mass in Polish. It had never happened before: the Secretariat of State had been reluctant to upset the Polish Government. The Secretariat was over-ruled, and the Pope celebrated the first Mass himself. Vatican Radio started broadcasting its commentaries on papal events in Italian and Polish. But the most striking initiative was the visit to Poland. From a Soviet point of view, the worrying thing was not that the Pope was Polish and that he was going home to a Communist country: it was that he was a Slav who spoke as a Slav and in Gniezno presented a vision of a wider Europe, culturally and spiritually united, which would include all the Slav peoples.

It was a much more aggressive *Ostpolitik* than Paul VI's. Paul VI found himself engaged in delicate diplomatic minuets in which, on the whole, Governments led and the Vatican followed. The theory was that the Vatican would inch forward from concession to concession. Under John Paul II, it was the Vatican which acted, and Governments had to respond as best they could. John Paul II's *Ostpolitik* was brisk and potentially destabilizing, in that he consistently echoed the language used by dissident

groups. It was a risky business, and the stakes were high. Where
Paul VI had played diplomatic chess, John Paul II appeared to be
playing poker.

The effects of all this were not clear. In Poland, in particular,
there were certain signs of the 'great awakening' which the Polish
bishops had claimed after the Pope's visit. Church congregations,
marriages in church, baptisms, confessions, candidacies for the
priesthood – they all increased markedly. On the other hand, it
had to be acknowledged that by the end of 1979 there was no sign
in Poland – or anywhere else beyond the Iron Curtain – of
specific concessions by the regime to the familiar litany of Church
demands: permission to build more churches, an end to censorship of independent Catholic publications, the regular broadcasting of a Mass for the housebound sick and elderly, the
granting of legal status to the Church as an organization. Even in
Poland the most that could be said was that, while no changes had
occurred, people's expectation of eventual change had been
heightened; and that itself represented a new danger for the
authorities.

The outline of what might be called the *Fernostpolitik*, which
concerned China, was harder to descry. Something was afoot; but
its nature was a closely-guarded secret. There were said to be 532
Jesuits – the report came from Spain – with a knowledge of
Chinese prepared to go to China at the drop of a biretta. Certainly
the China of Chairman Hua was not the China of Chairman Mao,
whose memory was being discreetly neutralized. There was,
however, not much evidence that Hua's openness to Western
technology included an openness to Western religion; and he did
not call on the Vatican during his 1979 journey to Europe. But at
Castelgandolfo on Sunday 19 August John Paul II told the crowd
that he prayed daily for the great Chinese people, the most
numerous in the world. He gave detailed statistics which showed
that, though Christianity had never made a profound impact on
Chinese society, nevertheless the investment of missionary man-
power had been considerable. In the most significant part of the
speech (which Casaroli had no doubt pondered carefully before it
was delivered) he said: 'After thirty years, the news we have of
these brothers of ours is scant and uncertain. We continue,
however, to entertain the hope that we will be able to renew that

direct contact with them which spiritually has never been broken.'
It was a signal to the 'patriotic priests' who had survived by
faithfully toeing the party line. Were they in schism or not? The
Pope's language recognized their very real difficulties and posited
an enduring spiritual link which could be the key to the resolution
of the problem. But public response to his feelers was a long time
coming.

This Pope of surprises sprang another surprise when he announced, only ten days in advance, that he would visit Turkey
from 28 to 30 November. Vatican spokesmen had been busily
denying that such a visit was contemplated. They did not blush.
They did not resign. But they looked sheepish. And indeed their
denials had made sense. For Turkey was in an unstable political
condition, with a new Government that had just taken office and
an average of three political murders a day. Moreover, with 50
American hostages being held in Teheran, it hardly seemed the
most propitious moment to be going to next-door Turkey and
speaking of opening a friendly dialogue with Islam. But that
was not the main point of the visit. Its purpose was to go to
Istanbul and celebrate the feast of St Andrew (patron of the
Church of Constantinople) with Dimitrios I, honorary primate of
the Orthodox Churches as Ecumenical Patriarch. Andrew had
introduced his younger brother Peter to Jesus. It was therefore to
be a symbolic encounter – the embrace of Peter and Andrew; the
reconciliation of the Roman Catholic Church with the Orthodox
Churches.

It was certainly the most bizarre of John Paul's international
journeys till that date. Not only were there no motorcades, cheering crowds, ticker-tape parades, or babies to be kissed, but during
the first day there was not a single word uttered in public. The
Turkish Government, anxious and apprehensive, managed the
remarkable feat of reducing John Paul II to silence. It surrounded
him with armed guards and tanks. It arrested potential assassins.
It gave him a welcome as cold as the winds blowing down from
the Anatolian mountains. On his arrival at Esenboga, the Ankara
airport, he was not even allowed to address the troops with his
carefully prepared Turkish phrase, 'Greetings, soldiers'. He put
the note sadly away in his pocket. He managed to kiss the ground:
it was the only departure from protocol.

The reasons for this coolness were obvious. The 45 million Turks are predominantly Moslem, though they are regarded as heretical by other Moslems because of the process of secularization they underwent in the 1920s under Ataturk. There are only a few thousand Orthodox Christians, the last survivors of the Greek empire, and a handful of Catholics. So it was made very plain that the Pope was regarded as a head of State rather than a religious leader – an honoured guest from a State with which Turkey had diplomatic relations. He had described his previous journeys as pastoral or apostolic. Asked on the plane to Ankara to define this one, he said it was 'a fraternal visit'.

The truth of that became clear when John Paul II escaped from the Turkish Government and finally reached the Phanar in Constantinople, seat of the Ecumenical Patriarch. The importance of the visit was generally underestimated, journalistic interest had declined, the points at issue were subtle. Yet it had great ecumenical significance. It marked a new stage in the Catholic dialogue with the Orthodox Churches; at the same time it revealed something vital about the underlying strategy of the new pontificate, and provided at last the elusive key to it. The emphasis of the pontificate was to be on the East, with the West expected to tag obediently along. The Church's centre of gravity had shifted eastwards.

There is no understanding the Orthodox without a sense of symbolic events and symbolic gifts. They can be more important than laborious verbal explanations. John Paul II attended Dimitrios I's Eucharist in the Orthodox Cathedral of St George; the next day Dimitrios attended the Latin Eucharist in the Catholic Cathedral of Constantinople. There was no intercommunion ('a reminder of the pain of division which we still feel', explained the Pope). But the mere presence at each other's liturgy was significant: it had never happened before. The 'kiss of peace', exchanged in both liturgies, was also highly significant. Here were two brother patriarchs – of the East and the West – declaring publicly that their Churches were 'sister Churches'. Moreover, Dimitrios presented John Paul with a stole as a gift: that meant that he was recognizing him as a priest ('*axios*', 'he is worthy', as the Greeks cry at an ordination). In return, John Paul gave Dimitrios a copy of the picture of Our Lady of Czestochowa from his native Poland. It was a reminder that there were links, buried deep in history, between Poland and Constantinople. John Paul thought in centuries. During his visit he several times alluded to the fact that the mission of St Cyril and St Methodius, who set out from Constantinople in the ninth century to convert the Slav peoples, reached and baptized the Vislani tribe of southern Poland. He concluded from this that Poland had a special role to play as intermediary in the dialogue between East and West, between the first Rome and the 'second Rome' – Constantinople.

That explained why the dialogue between the Catholic Church and the Orthodox Churches meant so much more to him than the dialogue with the Churches which issued from the Protestant Reformation. He was careful, however, not to oppose the two dialogues, while clearly stating which had the priority for him. The goal was nothing less than the restoration of full communion between the Catholic Church and all the Orthodox Churches. Such unity, he said, 'would be a fundamental and decisive step in the progress of the *entire* ecumenical movement. Our division has perhaps not been without some influence on later divisions.'

That cryptic remark harked back to a theory advanced by the French Dominican, Yves Congar, as long ago as the 1950s. He argued that if the schism between East and West had not occurred – it is usually dated 1054 – then perhaps the Reformation would not have happened either. The Western Church would not have been able to impose its juridical style as the norm for the whole Church; and there would have been an acceptance of differences, whether theological or disciplinary, as complementary rather than divisive. The way back was the way forward.

Even apart from historical destiny, there were many reasons why John Paul II should find an opening to the East more congenial than an opening to the Protestants of the West. The Catholic Church shared with Orthodoxy vast areas of agreement on doctrinal matters, notably christology and the sacraments. Both were equally firm in their devotion to Mary; and by going on 30 November to Ephesus, the site of the Council which declared Mary to be the *theotokos*, the Mother of God, John Paul II reminded all Christians that mariology was no recent invention but part of their most ancient tradition. Orthodoxy, moreover, knew the importance of monasticism, and was resolutely opposed to the ordination of women. Even where there were differences in disciplinary practice, as on married priests and the admissibility of divorce, the differences pre-dated the separation and were not, therefore, insurmountable barriers to reunion.

The papacy itself remained the principal obstacle. It was likely to be one of the most important points at issue in the ensuing theological dialogue (prepared by the 'dialogue of charity' inaugurated by Paul VI and Athenagoras, Dimitrios's predecessor). The Orthodox could not accept the idea of primacy of jurisdiction. Consequently, John Paul II's own account of how he understood the primacy was listened to with close attention in the Orthodox Cathedral of St George in Constantinople. If he had put a foot wrong, he could have wrecked the forthcoming dialogue in advance. In fact, he contrived to speak of his own office in 'Greek' and wholly non-juridical terms. He described Peter as the 'chorus-leader of the apostles', a phrase used in the Orthodox liturgical texts (where Peter is usually linked with Paul). That was acceptable. He said that Peter, 'as a brother among brothers, was entrusted with the task of confirming them in faith'. No trouble there. The only slightly perilous remark was that Peter was also charged with the mission of 'ensuring the harmony of apostolic preaching'. But 'harmony' is a Greek term, and the statement did not immediately indicate that the Congregation for the Doctrine of the Faith would soon be operating in the Orthodox Churches. If that had been the case, the Joint Catholic/Orthodox Commission need not have bothered to meet.

But meet it would, though it was an unwieldy body, with thirty members on each side. The Catholic team included five cardinals (including William Baum of Washington and Basil Hume of Westminster). On the Orthodox side, the remarkable thing was that the thirteen Churches were able to agree on the membership of the Commission at all. It was also interesting that their side included six lay theologians, compared with none at all in the Catholic team. Women were nowhere in sight. But was it to be just another talking-shop? All the signs were that this late-twentieth-century attempt at reunion with the Orthodox was determined to avoid the mistakes made by the Council of Florence in 1439, which produced an agreement but could not make it stick. There were important differences of method. First,

Church leaders were now to be involved from the start – and would themselves gradually be committed to the dialogue. It was not to be the preserve of experts. Secondly, no one was in any hurry: there would be time for the psychological preparation of the people on both sides. Finally, and most crucial of all, the dialogue was to start from points of agreement – the sacraments and the Trinity – rather than of divergence.

John Paul II talked vaguely of the year 2000 as a possible date of reunion. No doubt most of the members of the Commission would be dead or in retirement by then. This long time-scale, however, did not mean that reunion was postponed to the never-never: it would allow time for the work of the Joint Commission – which could be completed within a few years – to be accepted by all the individual Orthodox Churches involved. Asked about his Turkish visit during the air journey home, the Pope said: 'We are in another dimension. But we are serving the great cause of the coming of the Lord'.

'We are in another dimension.' That was true, and made it difficult for Westerners to follow him. For what he seemed to have in mind was a realignment of the Christian forces in Europe. Behind the Ecumenical Patriarch in Constantinople there loomed the shadow of the Patriarch of Moscow. That was the ultimate goal. Moscow had sometimes claimed to be 'the third Rome'; and, as Dostoevsky foresaw, the title would be carried on in the twentieth century in a secularized form. John Paul II thought in pan-Slav terms. He distinguished between frontiers on the map and the frontiers of the mind. Thus for him the easternmost boundary of Europe was not a traceable line but rather 'the frontier of the penetration of the Gospel and secondly the frontier of the invasions coming from Asia'. Though it could not be pinned down, John Paul had two criteria for determining where it might run. He asked of the peoples of this frontier region: 'To what extent is their sense of humanity and the dignity of man derived from the Gospel? Where does servile passivity, derived from centuries of slavery, begin?' Thus his campaign for human rights in Eastern Europe had a different significance from President Carter's. It was an appeal to, and an evocation of, Christian values in the Soviet Union and elsewhere; they might have been overlaid, but they had not yet been extirpated. Like Alexander

Solzhenitsyn, John Paul II appeared to believe that Soviet society corresponded less and less to what its people wanted and needed, and that there would be a disintegration of Communist regimes, not through any pressure from outside, but because their hollowness would become clear. Only a Slav could conceive such a vision; perhaps only a Pole could think it realizable.

In this vast perspective, comprehending past, present and future, American and European agonizing over birth control and the ordination of women seemed merely an irrelevant distraction. The Church in the West was to be brought rapidly under control so that the grand design might be steadfastly pursued. False interpretations of the Second Vatican Council, leading to a perpetual and anarchic re-examination of all questions, were to cease. The time of experiment was over. Nuns were to return to prayer and their habits. An ecumenism which led to doctrinal uncertainty and moral laxity was reproved. The clergy were to stay at their posts and preach the Gospel. In this process a few bones might be broken: that was sad, but not finally tragic. The beauty of John Paul II's grand design was that the West would eventually be forced to fall in behind him. As the strategy unfolded and registered its first successes, Western Christians, Catholic and Protestant, would applaud – for they too were for human rights, and believed in the power of the Gospel to crack open the most recalcitrant structures. Even Latin America – where turmoil and wretchedness had not been much lessened in the months after the papal visit to Mexico – would be taught a lesson about authentic liberation theology and delivered from its obsession with Marxist utopias.

There was a message, too, for oil-rich Islam. Despite the twentieth-century trends described by gloomy sociologists, Christianity was not going to curl up and lie down before the process of secularization. On the contrary, it would be revitalized by those who had known persecution at first hand. Christianity would reaffirm its central religious core, and at the same time illustrate the power of an idea. Then it could stretch out a hand to Islam. Preaching in the chapel of the Italian Embassy in Ankara on 29 November, John Paul II said: 'I wonder if it is not urgent to recognize and develop the spiritual bonds which unite Christians and Moslems, precisely at this moment when we are entering together upon a new period of history.' He went on to speak of the 'spiritual patrimony of Islam, its value for man and society, its ability to offer to young people a sense of direction and to fill the void left by materialism . . .' That was the basis for a dialogue in quest of shared moral values: those who believed in monotheism could stand together against atheism and materialism. There, was the little matter of the Ayatollah Khomeini, with his habit of consigning people to what he picturesquely called 'the dustbin of death'. But he was old, could be isolated, and was not truly representative of an Islam which knew the Allah of mercy as well as of justice.

It is fair to say that the cardinals did not really know what they were doing when they elected Karol Wojtyla pope on 16 October 1978. Or rather, they knew that they were electing a Polish pope and breaking with a 455-year tradition; but they did not know what the implications would be. They liked the man, felt a need for change, and could not risk another premature death. Yet it would have been possible to get to know Wojtyla better: the data were all there, unread and neglected, in his numerous writings and in the history of Poland. The most important fact about him was always that he was Polish. Not merely did he find it difficult, but it was no part of his plan, to leave Krakow behind. That did not mean that he was incapable of universal leadership; only that he would be universal in a Polish style. The West had either to understand that style or be condemned to misunderstand him. His historical perspective and overall strategy were not an ordinary part of Western mental equipment. He would quote, with the utmost seriousness, a book published by R. L. Buell shortly after the outbreak of the 1939 war. It was called *Poland, Key to Europe.*

There were two snags about this grandiose strategy. The first was that it might simply fail, that the forces of inertia would prove too great, that not enough people would share the vision which could make it work. The troops in the West might be prepared to applaud, but not to move. Yet even if it failed, it would be a magnificent, very Polish failure. John Paul II would have given hope to many who had forgotten what the word meant. That aim was best put in the streets of Harlem in New York when he said: 'If we are silent about the love of Jesus, the

very stones will cry out. For we are an Easter people, and Alleluia
is our song.' Whatever happened, that would remain a summary
of his message at its best.

But the second snag was that John Paul II might not have the
time to realize his vision. He had set himself an impossible
schedule. He pushed himself, deliberately, to the limits of
physical endurance (and beyond the limits of most of his camp-
followers). That was evident in Ireland and the United States. But
it was part of his habitual way of life in Rome. It raised a question
or two. Why should he behave in this unreasonable way? Why
should he not pace himself as he moved towards the year 2000
which so fascinated him?

The Roman rumour-mill, never at a loss to explain such
mysteries, had a story to account for the frantic pace of the pontificate. It alleged that some time in the 1960s Cardinal Karol
Wojtyla went to see Padre Pio, the celebrated Franciscan whose
hands bled with the wounds of Christ. Padre Pio was also reputed
to be gifted with second sight. (Graham Greene once waited for
three days to go to confession to him, and then fled as his turn
came.) According to the story, Padre Pio said: 'One day you will
be pope. But your pontificate will be short and it will end in
bloodshed.' So there it was. The Pope kept up such a daunting
pace because he felt that he did not have much time left.

With Padre Pio dead, the story could only be checked with
John Paul II himself. And he was not talking. But he was certainly
aware that he drove himself hard. He offered a quasi-justification
at the Angelus of 4 November 1979, feast of his patron, St
Charles Borromeo. He said that just as St Charles, Archbishop of
Milan, had made his life's work the implementation of the Council of Trent, even so his own main task was the implementation of
Vatican II. Then he referred to St Charles 'as an example of
pastoral love and episcopal service, combined with a dedication
which disregarded fatigue and even mortal danger'. That suggested that he knew the risks he ran. He had thought the matter
over, and decided that they were worth taking.

A Note on Origins

Readers curious about the mechanics of co-authorship may care to know that chapters 1, 7 and 8 of this book were written by John Whale (*The Sunday Times*'s religious affairs correspondent), with additional reporting, particularly from the United States, by Muriel Bowen (a *Sunday Times* specialist writer, who also interviewed bishops in Europe and America and provided new matter on the October 1978 conclave); chapters 2, 3, 5 and 9 are by Peter Hebblethwaite (author of *The Runaway Church* and *The Year of Three Popes* – Collins, London, 1975 and 1978 – and Rome correspondent of the American *National Catholic Reporter* as well as occasional contributor from there to *The Sunday Times*); chapter 4 is by Tana de Zulueta (another Rome-based contributor to the paper), and chapter 6 is by Nicholas Carroll (*The Sunday Times*'s long-serving diplomatic correspondent, who had the help of his Polish-born wife Bisia). The whole has been edited by John Whale.

Works which the authors have made use of, besides the two Hebblethwaite books, are these:

Roger Aubert and others, *The Christian Centuries, vol. 5: The Church in a Secularized Society* (Paulist Press, New York, and Darton, Longman and Todd, London, 1978).

Mary Craig, *Man from a Far Country: a portrait of Pope John Paul II* (Hodder and Stoughton, London, William Morrow, New York, 1979).

George Blazynski, *Pope John Paul II, a biography* (Weidenfeld & Nicolson, and Sphere, London, Delacourt Press, New York, 1979).

Mieczyslaw Malinski, *Pope John Paul II: the life of my friend Karol Wojtyla* (Burns & Oates, London, Seabury Press, New York, 1979).

Giuseppe Propati, 'L'affermazione dei valori umani negli studi di Karol Wojtyla', *Rassegna di Teologia*, Jan. – Feb. 1979, pp.6-18 (on Wojtyla's Scheler thesis).

Ulrich Simon, *A Theology of Auschwitz* (SPCK, London, 1978).

Justice, Love & Peace: Pastoral letters of the Irish bishops, 1969-1979 (Veritas, Dublin, 1979).

Catherine Rynne, *Knock 1879-1979* (Veritas, Dublin, 1979).

Edward Schillebeeckx, *Jesus, an experiment in Christology*, translated from the Dutch by Hubert Hoskins (Collins, London, Seabury Press, New York, 1979).

Hans Küng, *Infallible? an enquiry*, translated from the German by Eric Mosbacher (Fount Paperbacks, London, Doubleday, New York, 1977).

Hans Küng, *On being a Christian*, translated from the German by Edward Quinn (Collins, London, 1976 and Fount Paperbacks, London, 1978, Doubleday, New York, 1976).

Hermann Häring and Karl-Josef Kuschel, *Hans Küng, his work and his way*, translated from the German by Robert Nowell (Fount Paperbacks, London, Doubleday, New York, 1979).

Karol Wojtyla, *The Acting Person*, translated from the Polish by Andrzej Potocki (Reidel, Dordrecht and New York, 1979).

Karol Wojtyla, *Easter Vigil and other poems*, translated from the Polish by Jerzy Peterkiewicz (Hutchinson, London, Random House, New York, 1979; quoted by permission).

John Paul II: Message for World Peace Day; *Redemptor Hominis*; Letter to all the priests of the Church (all Catholic Truth Society, London, 1979).

Scriptural quotations are as far as possible from the Revised Standard Version Common Bible (Collins, London and Cleveland, 1973).

Index